PROPHETIC WORDS FROM THE HEART OF THE FATHER FOR A NATION & A PEOPLE:

IN GOD WE TRUST

2012

Kerrie E. Bradshaw, R.N., B.S.N.

PROPHETIC WORDS FROM THE HEART OF THE FATHER FOR A NATION & A PEOPLE:

IN GOD WE TRUST – 2012

Kerrie E. Bradshaw

Cover Art: Don Robertson
Editor: Christie Roe Pride and Brenda Grelock
Photo: Shuttershock

ISBN: 978-0-9896120-1-2

Acknowledgement

To Ruach HaKodesh (Holy Spirit):

For his faithfulness to teach me to hear
His voice and the heart of the Father

TABLE OF CONTENTS

FOREWORD

This book will go forth for My glory into the land. It is speaking to My people; a voice in the dark night calling those who are Mine to wake up. These words bear witness to believers and non-believers alike; the day of salvation is *now*. You are not guaranteed tomorrow. Why tempt the Lord your God? Fall at My feet and surrender all ~ every plan, purpose, and dream; even your will and desires. Watch Me transform your life. Many are in a danger that is growing greater every day. *Today* is the day of salvation. Do not tempt the Lord your God, for no one knows the day nor the hour of redemption. I come as a thief in the night to gather the elect from the four corners; they will worship Me as one voice, in Spirit and in truth. What a glorious day it will be when you see Me face to face! I AM speaking to a people and a nation. Are you listening? This is a call to repentance.

Ezekiel 33:1-9 *¹Again the word of the LORD came to me, saying, ² "Son of man, speak to the children of your people, and say to them: 'When I bring the sword upon a land, and the people of the land take a man from their territory and make him their watchman, ³ when he sees the sword coming upon the land, if he blows the trumpet and warns the people, ⁴ then whoever hears the sound of the trumpet and does not take warning, if the sword comes and takes him away, his blood shall be on his own head. ⁵ He heard the sound of the trumpet, but did not take warning; his blood shall be upon himself. But he who takes warning will save his life. ⁶ But if the watchman sees the sword coming and does not blow the trumpet, and the people are not warned, and the sword comes and takes any person from among them, he is taken away in his iniquity; but his blood I will require at the watchman's hand.'*

⁷ "So you, son of man: I have made you a watchman for the house of Israel; therefore you shall hear a word from My mouth and warn them for Me. ⁸ When I say to the wicked, 'O wicked man, you shall surely die!' and you do not speak to warn the wicked from his way, that wicked man shall die in his iniquity; but his blood I will require at your hand. ⁹ Nevertheless if you warn the wicked to turn from his way, and he does not turn from his way, he shall die in his iniquity; but you have delivered your soul.

INTRODUCTION

On August 21st just three weeks before 9/11, I felt this overwhelming need to send an email out over an email group called God-Seekers. In this email, which went out all over the world, I felt led by the Lord to send a challenge. This challenge was for the sleeping giant called the church to awaken, rise up, and speak the true word of God; to stop the apathy. We needed to declare what is right and what is wrong; we needed to stop being bullied into silence by a very vocal minority and to confront the overwhelming evil that was descending upon the nation. We needed to stop letting our rights as believers be stripped away. The email was pretty long, but that sums up the gist of it. At that time, little did we know, what the near future held. The events of 911 shocked the nation. More than that, the pervasive evil increased, which we have seen multiplying and assaulting our very way of life, as the Hordes of Hell were subsequently released against everything this nation held dear.

The enemy made great inroads in our Country; not just into the minds of the people who were embolden in a demonic degree to push their evil, godless agenda, but Muslim's bent on our destruction have infiltrated the highest offices in the land. A Jezebel Spirit/Malignant Narcissism with an Anti-Christ agenda invaded, using its witchcraft to hypnotize the masses ~ even the media ~ into promoting and propagating its agenda. We have seen shocking lies and deceit of the highest order while people make excuses and turned a blind eye.

I didn't know then what I know now, but the responses to the God-Seekers email were horrifying to me. I can sum them up by quoting the response of one person; "Oh honey, don't worry about it; we don't have to do anything, God will take care of everything. I was shocked and angry; I broke down and cried, "God forgive us."

That's the attitude that moved us into this position in the first place; self-proclaimed Christians being deceived by the enemy and believing they do not have a role in the kingdom. They didn't have to do anything because God would take care of everything. God chose people to accomplish His purposes and to spread the Gospel. He could have chosen angels, but He didn't. He chose us! Jesus said in **Matthew 10: 7-8** *7 "And as you go, preach, saying, the Kingdom of Heaven is at hand. 8 Heal the sick, cleanse the lepers, raise the dead, cast out demons. Freely you have received, freely give."* In **Mark 16:15** He said to them, *"Go into all the world and preach the gospel to every creature."* **Mark 16:17-18,** *"And these signs will follow those who believe: In My name they will cast out demons; they will speak with new tongues; 18 they will take up serpents; and if they drink anything deadly, it will by no means hurt them; they will lay hands on the sick, and they will recover."* So it's clear that we have something to do...We are to continue what Jesus began.

I believe the attitude that we don't have to do anything began with two primary teachings; The first is the church as a whole sees no need for Baptism of Holy Spirit. The failure to follow the biblical example of baptism in water and the Holy Spirit has led to a belief that the gifts of the Spirit are not for today. As a result, those who claim to be God's people do not walk in the fire and power, and rivers of living water as God intended. The church is impotent, looking very much like the world. Jesus *COMMANDED* the people to tarry in Jerusalem for the Baptism of Holy Spirit. We read in the word that not all who heard the command obeyed, and many left. The same is true today.

Acts 1:4-5, *And being assembled together with* them, *He commanded them not to depart from Jerusalem, but to wait for the Promise of the Father, "which," He said, "you have heard from Me; 5 for John truly baptized with water, but you shall be baptized with the Holy Spirit not many days from now."*

The second teaching of concern so prevalent in this nation is the pre-tribulation rapture. The excuse for doing nothing is, "Well, Jesus is coming for me soon and I'm outta here." There is this attitude that says I have read the end of the book and I know how it turns out, so I can care less what happens. Apathy prevails. The problem with this attitude is that God gave each of us an assignment. We are a seed planted in His kingdom. The parable of the talents still applies and souls hang in the balance. The cost is high to not obey the Lord, especially when claiming to serve Him. This teaching is discussed further detail at the end of this book.

During the stunning wake-up call as a nation on 9/11, people searching for answers flooded churches. Instead of getting a glimpse of the God of the Bible, they found church impotent and just like the world. The answers they sought; the God of miracles who parted the Red Sea, healed the sick, raised the dead and cast out demons, was nowhere to be found. New Age, the occult, and the wisdom of man invaded and the church was wholly unprepared for this influx of people looking for answers and truth...looking for God's Word and His power. They were praying to see and know the heart of Jesus.

John Hagge once stated, "The thing that makes you the angriest, is the problem God is going to give you to solve" and that is how It worked with me. God doesn't choose the one whom we expect, or the most qualified in the natural, but HE ALWAYS EQUIPS THOSE HE CALLS. "

In 2007, the Lord told me to sponsor a Yucaipa, California satellite for a national event called ReignDown, USA. The churches and the people were, for the most part, not interested in joining us to pray for the people, the nation, and the church.

A handful of Pastors agreed to participate. There were two from our city and two from the surrounding cities. We agreed to meet every week for prayer at the park which hosted the event. I found myself standing at the foot of the cross with another pastor, waiting for the others. He turned to me and started naming one by one the majority of the churches in the town and what denomination of Baptist they were. I listened, but had no idea why he was telling me this. I said I had no idea all those were Baptist churches, let alone there were that many different types of Baptist. He said nothing further.

Two days before the event, I received a call from the park telling me we could not use the park they had given us permission to use a month prior. We needed to change parks. Though the majority of the churches in town refused to participate in ReignDown USA, they did participate in Relay For Life® to raise money for the cancer research, which was scheduled on the same day, at the same time, in the same park.

In spite of 22,000 website hits and people who drove hours to participate. We only had 150 of the remnant join us for prayer and raised $80 dollars, which was donated by one of the pastors. It did not even cover the cost of the water we brought for the event. One Pastor got up to speak and broke down in tears at the lack of participation.

Relay For Life®, on the other hand, had many of the local churches involved. The participants came to the ReginDown information booth in error, all wearing T-shirts with the name of the person they were walking in honor of. According to the local newspaper report, 495 people attended and walked for those dead, raising $95,000 dollars. This is a bible belt town; it had more churches than stores at that time. It was heartbreaking that 495 people could show up and walk in the name of the dead, but only 150 people could be bothered to come out for the nation and the church to pray, praise, and worship the living God.

Although I was heartbroken, it didn't hit me until the next day while in church. During worship, the Lord began to speak to me. I grabbed tithe envelope after tithe envelope to write the words, and the tears began to flow. I cried, grieved, mourned, and interceded for the city, the church, and the nation for the next 30 days. God was showing me the hard hearts of the people, the pastors, the churches, and the nation. I begged God to remove the burden. The pain was too much. I was literally mourning the death of the church and the nation. It was as if I was seeing and feeling God's heart and it was breaking. I kept begging God to take it away, and He kept saying, "No, I am giving you a glimpse."

I responded, "I don't like what I see."

He replied, "Neither do I."

That was not the only time He gave me a glimpse. It happens a couple times per year, and I cry and mourn the death of all we hold dear while interceding and begging God for mercy.

I ran into the pastor who had named all the Baptist denominations that day at the foot of the cross. He asked me, "Are you frustrated yet?"

I responded, "A little, but it is not going to stop me from doing what God tells me to do."

To which he replied, "Good." He then asked me if I knew why he had told me about all of the Baptist churches in town. When I responded that I did not, he stated, "I wanted you to understand what you were up against in this town. They will never accept you as a woman, as a preacher, and as one who is spirit filled. They also have no idea what you are talking about. They have no idea what you mean when you say 'God spoke to me' or 'God told me.' They don't know what to do with you." Years later, after God started Praising in the Park, this belief structure is a major stronghold in my town and it continues to be a battle.

Fast forward to December 13, 2009; it was a morning like any other. I woke up, spent time in prayer and worshipping the Lord. Suddenly, He stopped me in my tracks and gave me a vision of a flag. Visions are not unusual for me, as that is one way God speaks to me.

God showed me this flag and told me to make a *In God We Trust* flag. He gave me the vision and the meaning of the symbolism. He showed me a map of the United States and flag poles popping up with *In God We Trust* flags waving. God said He would be coming back soon, but not quite yet. He has something for us to do first and desires we take a public stand for Him. To have the remnant raise a banner in honor of the God of this nation...To show a visible/tangible sign to those who have sought to remove Him from the public arena that God is still God, and He still rules this nation. He's still on the throne. He hasn't been forgotten by His people and THAT fact will not change no matter how loud the anti-God crowd gets nor how many lawsuits they file. God will honor the remnant that honors him.

Martin Luther King said, "The ultimate measure of a man is not where he stands in moments of comfort and convenience, but where he stands at times of challenge and controversy. There is no doubt we are living in times of great challenge and controversy."

Martin Luther King also stated;

"I say to you, this morning, that if you have never found something so dear and precious to you that you will die for it, then you aren't fit to live. You may be 38 years old, as I happen to be, and one day, some great opportunity stands before you and calls upon you to stand for some great principle, some great issue, some great cause, and you refuse to do it because you are afraid. You refuse to do it because you want to live longer. You're afraid that you will lose your job, or you are afraid that you will be criticized or that you will lose your popularity, or you're afraid that somebody will stab, or shoot you, or bomb your house. So you refuse to take a stand. Well, you may go on and live until you are ninety, but you are just as dead at 38 as you would be at ninety. And the cessation of breathing in your life is but the belated announcement of an earlier death of the spirit. You died when you refused to stand up for right. You died when you refused to stand up for truth. You died when you refused to stand up for justice." Dr. Martin Luther King, Jr. From the sermon, "But, If Not," November 5, 1967.

We are here to stand for the Lord. We are to be His heart where He has planted us. In retrospect, this God-Seekers word was a prophetic word; a call to action for the people who claim to be children of God to wake up, repent and prove that they were...but I didn't know it at the time. The church is in danger, invaded by the occult, Eastern religions and New Age teachings, which has led to a false hyper-grace, emergent church mentality where tolerance is mistaken for love.

More than that, the Lord was calling me; giving me a glimpse of my calling as He said to wake the dead in the pews and speak to His remnant, to challenge them to stir up the gifts of the Spirit. It was a call back to truth, spiritual power, and the basics of the Word of God, so the church will become the body of Christ, as God intended. They will have the mind of Christ. They will be the hands, feet, eyes, ears, and the very will, breath and heart of God in this land. Holy Spirit wants to come to church and return it to purity, power, and authority in the name of Jesus. The church of this nation has strayed far from the very God they claim to serve.

The Lord has shown me many times, and I have often preached, that this watered down version of the Gospel has people sitting in pews, but they're serving another Jesus. When confronted with the words of Jesus, those words in red in the Bible, many have accused me of being harsh and judging them. They throw the scripture in my face; "*Judge not lest you be judged*" (**Matthew 7:1**). When I point out those are not my words, but the Words of Jesus, they have accused me of not walking in love and assure me that their Jesus would never say that.

I'm sure "their" Jesus would not, but they are in danger serving another Jesus and another Gospel. I'm convinced that if Jesus or any of the Apostles came into the churches of today, saying the very same things recorded in the Word of God, they would not be recognized. They, too, would be accused of judging and not being in love. Tolerance and condoning sin is not love; it's not God's love, which is based upon truth. Jesus showed mercy for sin, but He never condoned sin. There is much preaching and talk about God's grace and His love, but no one wants to talk about that side of God. No one wants to talk about the fact God hates wickedness, or if they do they agree God hates sin and wickedness, he hates all but theirs. God is a two edged sword. Praise the Lord He is love, grace and mercy, but He is also Holy, justice and judgment.

God is asking each of us...Who do you say I am? Are you embarrassed of Me? Will you take a public stand?

There's too much apathy and silence in the body of Christ. Remnant America is a reflection of our hearts. REAL CHANGE starts with humbling ourselves before the One True God and then He will heal our land and hearts. Souls hang in the balance. We do know that the Word of God clearly states that evil will continue to take hold and progress, and it will be as in the days of Noah. I believe the Lord showed me it will also be as it was in the days of Jesus. Believers will be persecuted and martyred; we can see this agenda progressing rapidly, but that did not stop the early disciples and it cannot stop us today. We must fulfill the plans and assignment we are given as followers of Christ, whether it turns out to be a pre-tribulation or a post-tribulation rapture.

This series of books are the words from Our Father's heart to a nation and a people. He is calling us back to Him, the One True God; back to His truth.

2012

A CALL TO REPENTANCE

values and the exhorting a hyper-grace message which has run truth out of the church.

The problem with that is God is not interested in your self-esteem or worldly values; He is interested in your character, and your character being molded and conformed to Christ. Separate from the world, God does not do things the way the world believes is right. The churches are catering to pleasing men, not God. In **1 Thessalonians 2:3-6**, we read;

3 So you can see we were not preaching with any deceit or impure motives or trickery. 4 For we speak as messengers approved by God to be entrusted with the Good News. Our purpose is to please God, not people. He alone examines the motives of our hearts. 5 Never once did we try to win you with flattery, as you well know. And God is our witness that we were not pretending to be your friends just to get your money! 6 As for human praise, we have never sought it from you or anyone else.

That is backwards in church today. Preachers are failing to preach the hard truth of God's Word, opting for psychobabble, love of money, and the praise of man to fill pews. They speak of self-love and self-esteem while Christ speaks of self-sacrifice and serving others. Under Jesus, the one who is the greatest is the least of these.

Many who preach are not messengers approved by God. Their purpose is not to please God, but to please men. God examines the motives of the hearts, and they will have to answer to Him. I wish I could remember where I read this or who said it so I can give proper credit; as close as I can remember, I read, "While evangelizing those searching for Christ, these pastors at the same time evangelize those who know Christ back into the world; preaching more secular and psychological rather than calling them out of the world."

Preaching the message of Christ crucified and resurrected, and all that it entails, has been silenced in many churches. The cross is offensive. Remember when Peter rebuked Jesus after He talked about His approaching death on the cross? Jesus said, "Get behind me Satan, for you are not mindful of the things of God, but the things of men. Whoever desires to come after me let him deny himself." One version says "forget about yourself," another version exhorts us "to give up ourselves and our own desires," while yet another says "let him disown himself and pick up his cross and follow me." *For whoever desires to save his life will lose it, but whoever loses his life for my sake and the gospels will find it* (**Mark 8:34**).

True grace is a powerful truth. There is a mix of truth and dangerous error that is now the commonly preached grace message. This is a dangerous thing and gives many a false sense of security. It leads to and promotes compromise and sin, all in the name of Jesus; the very God people claim to serve. There is no longer teaching that people have to lay down their lives and be transformed by Holy Spirit into the likeness of Christ; they just have to feel good enough about themselves, motivated enough to come forward and say a sinner's prayer, which is not capable of saving them.

Sadly, many Pastors do not understand true salvation. Successful preaching has become all about numbers; judged solely on how many attend, are baptized and say the sinner's prayer. No more is success judged by change in character, integrity, honor, faithfulness to the gospel and the spiritual health and well-being of their congregation.

The Lord wants our trust and faith to be in Him alone, not in the scheming, cunning, conniving plans of men. Do you remember in **2 Samuel** when the anger of the Lord was aroused against Israel and He moved David to number/count Israel and Judah?

10 And David's heart condemned him after he had numbered the people. So David said to the LORD, "I have sinned greatly in what I *have done; but now, I pray, O' L*ORD, *take away the iniquity of Your servant, for I have done very foolishly."*

*11 Now when David arose in the morning, the word of the L*ORD *came to the prophet Gad, David's seer, saying, 12 "Go and tell David, 'Thus says the L*ORD: *"I offer you three things; choose one of them for yourself, that I may do it to you." 13 So Gad came to David and told him; and he said to him, "Shall seven years of famine come to you in your land? Or shall you flee three months before your enemies, while they pursue you? Or shall there be three days' plague in your land? Now consider and see what answer I should take back to Him who sent me."*

*14 And David said to Gad, "I am in great distress. Please let us fall into the hand of the L*ORD, *for His mercies are great; but do not let me fall into the hand of man."*

*15 So the L*ORD *sent a plague upon Israel from the morning till the appointed time. From Dan to Beersheba seventy thousand men of the people died. 16 And when the angel stretched out His hand over Jerusalem to destroy it, the L*ORD *relented from the destruction, and said to the angel who was destroying the people, "It is enough; now restrain your hand." And the angel of the L*ORD *was by the threshing floor of Araunah the Jebusite.*

*17 Then David spoke to the L*ORD *when he saw the angel who was striking the people, and said, "Surely I have sinned, and I have done wickedly; but these sheep, what have they done? Let Your hand, I pray, be against me and against my father's house."*

Remember how the Lord pared down Gideon's army to only 300 men? God is more interested in faithfulness than numbers. God does not need numbers to achieve victory. We should be falling on our face repenting for making it all about numbers. Numbers are not a reliable gauge of true salvation or hearts transformed by the power of God. One person who walks in obedience can move mountains. The churches are full of people who think they are following Christ, they believe they are Christians, but the

Lord told me they were the dead in the pews; they have never come to know the true Jesus.

We are going to discuss some of the more predominant teachings of the false grace movement. Some teachers may teach all of these, or a few of these, or make one or another more prominent.

Michael Brown, in an article entitled, "Confronting the Error of Hyper-Grace," said;

"One of the foundational doctrines of the hyper-grace message is that God does not see the sins of his children, since we have already been made righteous by the blood of Jesus and since all of our sins, past, present and future, have already been forgiven. That means that the Holy Spirit never convicts believers of sin, that believers never need to confess their sins to God, and that believers never need to repent of their sins, since God sees them as perfect in his sight."

If this assertion were true, then why did God say He chastens those He loves? **Hebrews 12:6** *For the LORD disciplines those he loves, and he punishes each one he accepts as his child."* **Proverbs 3:11-12** *¹¹My son, do not reject the discipline of the LORD Or loathe His reproof, ¹²For whom the LORD loves He reproves, Even as a father corrects the son in whom he delights.*

If this were true, why did James state; **James 4:1-5** (NKJV)

Pride Promotes Strife

⁴ Where do wars and fights come from among you? Do they not come from your desires for pleasure that war in your members? ² You lust and do not have. You murder and covet and cannot obtain. You fight and war. Yet you do not have because you do not ask. ³ You ask and do not receive, because you ask amiss, that you may spend it on your pleasures. ⁴ Adulterers and adulteresses! Do you not know that friendship with the world is enmity with God? Whoever therefore wants to be a friend of the world makes himself an enemy of God. ⁵ Or do you think that the Scripture says in vain,

"The Spirit who dwells in us yearns jealously"? He rebuked them for being "friends of the world" and "adulterers and adulteresses" and being those things they were an enemy of God. Why did Paul warn the Galatians that they were no longer living in grace, but in bondage to legalism?

Why did Jesus rebuke 5 of the 7 churches in Asia Minor in the book of Revelation? Why did He attest that He would spew the lukewarm out of His mouth? If God does not see our sins, why did James say that if a believer who sinned was sick, God would forgive him when He healed him **(James 5:14-15)**? Why did the Lord discipline the believers in Corinth for their sins, and in **1 Corinthians 11:32**, state, *When we are judged by the Lord, we are being disciplined so that we will not be condemned with the world?*

Revelation 3:19 reads, "*in those whom I love, I reprove and discipline; therefore be zealous and repent.*" Why did Jesus say about Holy Spirit, "*And when He has come, He will convict the world of sin, and of righteousness, and of judgment.*"? Why would this be necessary if hyper-grace were truth?

The reason is because it's not truth and God loves us enough to tell us the truth! He does not want us to live a life of sin, which only brings destruction. His desire is for us is to live life more abundant. What does light have in common with darkness? His grace is not a license or excuse to sin; to the contrary, it is sufficient for us to overcome everything that comes our way. In **Titus 2:11-12**, we read, *¹¹ For the grace of God that brings salvation has appeared to all men,¹² teaching us that, denying ungodliness and worldly lusts, we should live soberly, righteously, and godly in the present age.*

We need to learn to discern the voice of God from the voice of the accuser. All too often, people lack discernment and mistake the voice of Holy Spirit and His conviction and correction for the voice of the accuser, whose goal is to bring condemnation. They ignore Holy Spirit's voice within, or they attack the one God uses to bring correction and conviction. As has been said, hyper-grace takes it even further. People who believe hyper-grace believe they are perfect and Holy in the eyes of God. They believe there is no need for correction, confession, repentance, conviction of sin, or transformation, because God may see the sin of others, but he surely does not see "MY" sin.

False grace teaches us to belittle, mock, or vilify anyone who differs from their position. Their favorite attacks include pointing a finger at you, demanding you stop judging them, calling you legalistic, labeling you a Pharisee, a manipulator, a wolf, a false teacher, or accusing you as the one who is preaching a counterfeit gospel. Some of the popular teachers of this doctrine have even asserted that those who do not believe in the hyper-grace movement are living under the law; manipulating and "managing" sin, walking in fear and not love, and even doing so for" the money."

Their goal, even their doctrine, is to exalt false grace above obedience. We have all heard statements which are shocking attempts to convince believers that they are not responsible for their sins; that because they are perfect in the God's eyes, sin is a nonissue. We have heard the accusations that focusing on sin makes one sin-conscious, rather than God-conscious, and as a result people take no responsibility for their actions. Many claim, and actually believe, the words of God apply to everyone but them. Some even argue that the words of Jesus were for the people of Jesus' day and not us.

I remember a worship leader telling me he was a homosexual. He viciously accused me of not having the love of Christ because I expressed belief that the Word of God was truth. He even became angry at me when I quoted Romans 1. He told me it was terrible thing to say, and he believed that those other things might be sins, but he believed that his "issue" was not lumped into the sin category. I let him know that he could believe what he wanted, but those were the words of God, not mine. He did not recognize the whole Word of God as truth, just the parts that he liked. One of the Pastors at his church even informed me that "Romans 1 can be interpreted in many different ways, but not the way I interpreted it."

This is scary stuff, folks. People are not recognizing the authority in the words of Jesus. Some even go so far as to deny the very words of the God they claim to serve. If you listen to anyone, or any teaching, that denies, ignores, or picks and choses from the Word of God, this should be labeled as suspect and raise red flags.

Mark 8:38: *Don't be ashamed of me and my message among these unfaithful and sinful people! If you are, the Son of Man will be ashamed of you when he comes in the glory of his Father with the holy angels.*

We choose to sin, and we will sin, but we do not *have* to sin. If it is true that we have no control over sin, why did Peter tell us that we are to be holy as God is holy? Why did Paul express in **Romans 6:15-16**, *"Well then, since God's grace has set us free from the law, does that mean we can go on sinning? Of course not!* [16] *Don't you realize that you become the slave of whatever you choose to obey? You can be a slave to sin, which leads to death, or you can choose to obey God, which leads to righteous living."*

If it were true we had no power to stop, then why did Jesus repeatedly exhort sinners to, go and sin no more? **2 Timothy 2:19**; *"Nevertheless the solid foundation of God stands, having this seal: 'The Lord knows those who are His,' and, 'Let everyone who names the name of Christ DEPART FROM INIQUITY."*

In **2 Peter 1:5-11** [5] *But also for this very reason, giving all diligence, add to your faith virtue, to virtue knowledge,* [6] *to knowledge self-control, to self-control perseverance, to perseverance godliness,* [7] *to godliness, brotherly kindness, and to brotherly kindness, love.* [8] *For if these things are yours, and abound, you will be neither barren nor unfruitful in the knowledge of our Lord Jesus Christ.* [9] *For he who lacks these things is shortsighted, even to blindness, and has forgotten that he was cleansed from his old sins.* [10] *Therefore, brethren, be even more diligent to make your call and election sure, for if you do these things you will never* stumble; *11 for so an entrance will be supplied to you abundantly into the everlasting kingdom of our Lord and Savior Jesus Christ.*

In **2 Peter: 1-3,** we also read the warning: *1But there were also false prophets among the people, even as there will be false teachers among you, who will secretly bring in destructive heresies, even denying the Lord who bought them, and bring on themselves swift destruction. 2 And many will follow their destructive ways, because of whom the way of truth will be blasphemed. 3 By covetousness they will exploit you with deceptive words; for a long time their judgment has not been idle, and their destruction does not slumber.*

Continuing on through **2 Peter**, we hear,

12 But these, like natural brute beasts made to be caught and destroyed, speak evil of the things they do not understand, and will utterly perish in their own corruption, 13 and will receive the wages of unrighteousness, as those who count it pleasure to carouse in the daytime. They are spots and blemishes, carousing in their own deceptions while they feast with you, 14 having eyes full of adultery and that cannot cease from sin, enticing unstable souls. They have a heart trained in covetous practices, and are accursed children. 15 They have forsaken the right way and gone astray, following the way of Balaam the son of Beor, who loved the wages of unrighteousness; 16 but he was rebuked for his iniquity: a dumb donkey speaking with a man's voice restrained the madness of the prophet. 17 These are wells without water, clouds carried by a tempest, for whom is reserved the blackness of darkness forever.

18 For when they speak great swelling words of emptiness, they allure through the lusts of the flesh, through lewdness, the ones who have actually escaped from those who live in error. 19 While they promise them liberty, they themselves are slaves of corruption; for by whom a person is overcome, by him also he is brought into bondage. 20 For if, after they have escaped the pollutions of the world through the knowledge of the Lord and Savior Jesus Christ, they are again entangled in them and overcome, the latter end is worse for them than the beginning.

21 For it would have been better for them not to have known the way of righteousness, than having known it, to turn from the holy commandment delivered to them. 22 But it has happened to them according to the true proverb: "A dog returns to his own vomit," and, "a sow, having washed, to her wallowing in the mire."

How do teachers deny and blaspheme the Lord? They do it through disobedience, outright rebellion, half-truths, and a desire to please men rather than God. All the while they are proffering, and promoting their own teachings, encouraging disobedience and rebellion to the Word of God. This is particularly dangerous for people listening from the pews who will not take the time to read the Word of God for themselves, instead swallowing everything they are taught. Many leaders who live a life filled with sin tell us they cannot cease from sin, and that grace allows for sin, all the while contradicting the Word of God by creating a god in their own image that is not as powerful as our true God who says we can do all things through Christ including victory over sin. They are repeatedly caught in grave sin, yet continue to preach and their minions follow along condoning the sin. Jesus repeatedly spoke to people that they were to go and sin no more. Would He have said that if it were impossible? Jesus came as a human and entered into every aspect of human life, showing us we, too, can have victory.

2 John 1:7 (MSG), *There are a lot of smooth-talking charlatans loose in the world who refuse to believe that Jesus Christ was truly human, a flesh-and-blood human being. Give them their true title: Deceiver! Antichrist!*

Jesus came to our earth and walked as a human, under the power of Holy Spirit, to demonstrate to us that we can overcome every challenge by relying on Holy Spirit, just like He did. We can face EVERY situation, trial, sin, and temptation just like He did. We can heal the sick, raise the dead, cleanse the lepers and cast out demons just like He did. The same Holy Spirit that lived inside of Jesus while on the earth is the same Holy Spirit that raised Him from the dead, created the heavens and the earth, AND lives inside of *us*.

1 Peter 2 tells us that this is the kind of life Christ lived...He suffered everything that came His way in order for us to know it is possible, and to know how to appropriate the power of God in all circumstances.

Jesus said He gives us the victory over sin when we chose to abide in Him and the apostles taught the same thing. Repeatedly they taught that we were to cease from sin and obey Jesus, yet we read there will be teachers among us who cannot cease from sin in their own lives, AND teach others it is okay to be a sinner, even sin boldly, because in their mind we have no control over ourselves or sin.

So let's take a look at some of what this false grace message claims; of course, it would not be revealed by these teachers quite as bluntly as I am sharing here, because that would expose the lie...

False grace believes grace is a license to sin.

It teaches that God forgives our sins, past, present and future and therefore does not look upon our sin.

False grace does not believe, nor teach, that true repentance is necessary.

False grace says, we are allowed to sin, and others say we only need to say we are sorry but then may continue in our iniquity.

False grace is basically a play on the *get out of jail free* card from the game Monopoly®...only it is a *get out of hell free* card.

It presents like the Las Vegas commercial, "What happens in Vegas, stays in Vegas," or in some church circles, not...God sees it all.

False grace believes that I can live any way I want.

It also presents that I can do whatever I want.

False grace believes that I am saved, but I still sin because God did not make me capable of sin-free living. It is God's fault, not mine, that I am not walking obediently.

False grace supposes that once we repeat the sinner's prayer, we are saved.

Once we say the sinner's prayer and are "saved," Holy Spirit does not convict us of sin, instead He convicts us of our righteousness. We read the scripture earlier that the reason Holy Spirit came was to convict the world of sin; false grace teachers state that this is only in order to draw us to salvation.

False grace believes God is a good God who is only overtly loving and kind; He does not prune, punish, discipline, rebuke or convict us of sin.

It teaches that if I *say* I believe in Christ, God will not send me to hell. Unfortunately, salvation is more than just believing; the Word tells us that even the demons believe and tremble.

On those same lines, some teach that because God is a good God, loving and kind, there is a purgatory or a holding place. They deem that for a fee you can buy, or even pray, a person out of purgatory and into Heaven.

False grace believes in the *once saved always saved* doctrine. **John 8:34** teaches us that, *Jesus answered them, "Most assuredly, I say to you, whoever commits sin is a slave of sin."*

Matthew 7 21-23: *2 "Not everyone who says to Me, 'Lord, Lord,' shall enter the kingdom of heaven, but he who does the will of My Father in heaven. 22 Many will say to Me in that day, 'Lord, Lord, have we not prophesied in Your name, cast out demons in Your name, and done many wonders in Your name?' 23 And then I will declare to them, 'I never knew you; depart from Me, you who practice lawlessness!'"*

John 14:15, *"If you love Me, keep My commandments."*

John 14: 23-24, [23] *Jesus answered and said to him, "If anyone loves Me, he will keep My word; and My Father will love him, and We will come to him and make Our home with him.* [24] *He who does not love Me does not keep My words; and the word which you hear is not Mine but the Fathers who sent Me."*

Matthew 28:20, *"...teaching them to observe all things that I have commanded you; and lo, I am with you always, even to the end of the age."*

False grace believes we do not have to do anything in our relationship with God; God does everything. God chose to use people to do His work on earth. He commanded us to heal the sick, raise the dead, cleanse the lepers, cast out demons, and spread the gospel to reach the nations.

False grace seeks to please man, not God, and tickles ears preaching what people want to hear.

False grace believes I can do whatever I want as long as I slap the Name of Jesus on what sounds good to me to make it legitimate..

False grace accepts that Jesus is my Lord and Savior, but I do not have to obey his Word. I can choose to agree with some parts, but it is just a guide, not truth to live by.

False grace teaches that I do not have to go in through the narrow gate.

False grace doubts that I have to stay on the narrow road.

False grace believes that you only talk about the positive things in God's Word; His love, grace and mercy, never about His justice, judgment and hating wickedness. Reaping what we have sown is only discussed in the context of blessing, not the consequence.

False grace considers it finger pointing and judging when we quote scripture, or point out the absence of fruit in lives that walk in overt sin.

False grace believes it is okay to vilify anyone who points to the truth of God's word or disagrees with their position.

False grace believes Holy Spirit is unnecessary. It also subscribes to the notion that spiritual gifts and the fruit of the Spirit are unnecessary.

It is accepted as truth that God's transforming power is not for all to receive...And that the renewing of our minds in Christ is unnecessary.

False grace believes that God does not chasten, prune, or discipline those whom He loves.

False grace preachers focus on making money, and are often more concerned about numbers than changed lives.

This system preaches a different gospel, abuses people and puts them in bondage to man, often faking spirituality and the supernatural.

False grace is wholly untrue! It teaches very perilous doctrines that have misled, and are continuing to deceive, millions of professed Christians.

There is also a doctrine of universalism which believes that *all people* will be, saved, regardless of who they are, what they have done, whom they call "god" and what they believe...Universalism believes God is a good God, therefore He will keep all whom He created. The Lordship of Christ, the propitiation for our sins...this is all left behind as "unnecessary" to a God who created us for His pleasure and glory ~ He loves us and will keep us, regardless, they believe.

The word grace in Greek is *Charis,* which is defined as a manner or act, the divine influence upon a heart and its reflection in lives. I like the way that is written; the divine influence upon a heart and its reflection in our lives. Grace means getting what we do not deserve. Contrary to most people's definition, God gives us the desire, ability, and power to overcome sin through His grace. Our ability comes through help of Holy Spirit and the authority of God. He daily works in us to enable us to make the correct decisions, to be obedient, and to follow the voice of the Shepherd. This is all done through HIS power and authority, which is the grace of God. Grace is our teacher through Holy Spirit and His grace is sufficient to overcome anything that comes our way, including sin. Grace is not and never has been an excuse for sin, and it not, nor has it ever been instantaneous forgiveness for our willful sins.

Salvation is by grace, and grace is Jesus, the bridge joining our imperfections with God's perfect law.

1 John 2:1, *My little children, these things I write to you, so that you may not sin. And if anyone sins, we have an Advocate with the Father, Jesus Christ the righteous.*

Titus 2:11-14: *For the grace of God that brings salvation has appeared to all men, teaching us that, denying ungodliness and worldly lusts, we should live soberly, righteously, and godly in the present age, looking for the blessed hope and glorious appearing of our great God and Savior Jesus Christ, who gave Himself for us, that He might redeem us from every lawless deed and purify for Himself His own special people, zealous for good works.*

Ephesians 2:8-9 *For by grace you have been saved through faith, and that not of yourselves; it is the gift of God, ⁹ not of works, lest anyone should boast.*

The scriptures teach us that we are saved by grace through faith, and if we walk in the Spirit and abide in the Lord, we will go and sin no more, just as Jesus instructed. This will not be in our own strength, but in His strength, as His grace is sufficient for us to overcome. **Galatians 5:16** tells us if we *"walk in the Spirit, and you shall not fulfill the lust of the flesh."*

Romans 6:5-14, *For if we have been united together in the likeness of His death, certainly we also shall be in the likeness of His resurrection, knowing this, that our old man was crucified with Him, that the body of sin might be done away with, that we should no longer be slaves of sin. For he who has died, has been freed from sin. Now if we died with Christ, we believe that we shall also live with Him, knowing that Christ, having been raised from the dead, dies no more. Death no longer has dominion over Him. For the death that He died, He died to sin once for all; but the life that He lives, He lives to God. Likewise, you also, reckon yourselves to be <u>dead, indeed to sin</u>, but alive to God in Christ Jesus our Lord. Therefore, <u>do not let sin reign in your mortal body, that you should obey it in its lusts. And do not present your members as instruments of unrighteousness to sin</u>, but present yourselves to God as being alive from the dead, and your members as instruments of righteousness to God. For sin shall not have dominion over you, for you are not under law but under grace.*

Death no longer has dominion over Jesus or us, "for death where is your sting?" **(1 Corinthians 15:55)** Some have falsely concluded from the scripture that we are "not under law but under grace" and that law and grace are mutually exclusive. "Law" or "legalism" has come to be an insult and accusation thrown around by the hyper-grace crowd, however, our being under grace does not mean we are immune to law. Nor does it mean that law does not apply to us in Christ. It is not essential or necessary for a Christian to keep God's divine law by their own power; law has a stigma attached to it, it has come to mean a bad thing. Although the Torah has become synonymous with the law, because it contains the law, the word law and Torah actually means teaching, direction, instruction, or doctrine. Not one of us would argue we are exempt from God's teachings, direction or instructions.

Grace does not free us from being subject to God's teachings, instructions and directions. Rather, it means that we have forgiveness when we defy them, provided we meet God's conditions. The Apostle Paul taught in **Romans 6:14–15** *For sin shall not have dominion over you, for you are not under law but under grace.* We are not justified by the law alone; we are, praise the Lord, justified by His grace through our faith. We learned that grace is a teacher, therefore we must be humble and have a teachable spirit. Scripture has instructed that we are to deny ungodliness and worldly lusts, living soberly, righteously and godly; sin should never reign in us.

We learned that true grace is not a covering for the sin of a person who continues to sin. True grace is not merely "undeserved favor," as so many of us have been taught. Grace is a teacher; to those who receive it, it is a change agent ~ transforming us by Holy Spirit. When a person refuses to see the Word of God as absolute truth, he or she is unteachable and lacks humility. People who ignore God's Word, refuse sound counsel and choose not to deny ungodliness and worldly lusts are not receiving the grace of God that leads to salvation.

David wrote, "*Show me Your ways, O LORD; teach me Your paths. Lead me in Your truth and teach me, for You are the God of my salvation.*" **Psalm 25:4-5**.

James 4:6, *God resists the proud, but gives grace to the humble; therefore submit to God.*

The scary part of this false grace message which people fail to understand, is that if they do not receive the true grace of God that leads to salvation, then they are in fact *unsaved*. This false grace message does not lead to salvation. The purpose of grace is to transform our lives, change our behavior, and give us the mind of Christ right here and now ~ not in our future life in Heaven.

Grace, as we have stressed, is not an excuse for sin. It is not God's stamp of approval, justification or righteousness in Christ over our willful sin and wicked lives. **I John 3:7-8** spells it out clearly, *"Little children, let no one deceive you. He who practices righteousness is righteous, just as He is righteous. He who sins is of the devil, for the devil has sinned from the beginning."*

We must do as James instructed, rather than make excuses we need to *Submit to God, resist the devil, and he will flee from us.* **James 4:7**.

We cannot be using the excuse that we are human. As I said earlier, Jesus came as a human to show us how it can be done. Additionally, the Bible is full of examples of people just like us who lived obedient, faithful lives. Paul reminded us **2 Corinthians. 5:10**, *"For we must all appear before the judgment seat of Christ, that each one may receive the things done in the body, according to what he has done, whether good or bad."*

This will be difficult for many to hear in this day and age of contaminated bible teaching. The meaning of God's grace has been perverted, and the twisted teaching is prevalent today. God's grace is not unconditional, it is conditional to our obedience in faith.

Ephesians 2:8–9, *8 For by grace you have been saved through faith, and that not of yourselves; it is the gift of God, 9 not of works, lest anyone should boast.*

Romans: 5:1–2; *Therefore, having been justified by faith, we have peace with God through our Lord Jesus Christ, 2 through whom also we have access by faith into this grace in which we stand, and rejoice in hope of the glory of God.*

James. 2:17–26; *17 Thus also faith by itself, if it does not have works, is dead. 18 But someone will say, "You have faith, and I have works." Show me your faith without your works, and I will show you my faith by my works. 19 You believe that there is one God. You do well. Even the demons believe—and tremble! 20 But do you* want to know, O foolish man, that faith without works is dead? *21 Was not Abraham our father justified by works when he offered Isaac his son on the altar? 22 Do you see that faith was working together with his works, and by works faith was made perfect? 23 And the Scripture was fulfilled which says, "Abraham believed God, and it was accounted to him for righteousness." And he was called the friend of God. 24 You see then that a man is justified by works, and not by faith only. 25 Likewise, was not Rahab the harlot also justified by works when she received the messengers and sent them out another way? 26 For as the body without the spirit is dead, so faith without works is dead also.*

Matthew 7:21, *The obedient works upon which salvation is conditioned do not nullify grace for they do not earn salvation.*

Matthew: 1:21, *You shall call His name Jesus, for He will save His people from their sins.*

Jesus humbled himself and came to earth to live, eat, laugh, teach, love and die for His creation. He resurrected to life and is our advocate before the Father. He justified us by His blood. We are His sons and daughters because of His love, grace and mercy. He has set us apart as a holy nation; kings and priests unto Himself. There is only one way to the Father, and that is through the son. There is only one way to receive true grace, and that is through faith in Jesus and His finished work on the cross and His resurrection, for Jesus is grace. This is the only gospel that forgives our sins and leads us to salvation. God is a God of restoration. He is always about restoration of severed relationships to Himself, as well as restoring His children with one another. Grace comes from God, solely through Jesus Christ and Jesus Christ alone and His grace gives us victory.

Philippians 3:9, Paul tells us of the righteousness we have received "*through faith in Christ, the righteousness which is of God by faith.*"

Paul wrote in **2 Corinthians 7:1**, "*Since we have these promises, dear friends, let us purify ourselves from everything that* *contaminates body and spirit, perfecting holiness out of reverence for God."*

1 Corinthians 15:3-4: *"For I delivered to you first of all that which I also received: that Christ died for our sins according to the Scriptures, and that He was buried, and that He rose again the third day according to the Scriptures."*

In **Romans 6:6**; Paul reports, *Our old man was crucified with Him, that the body of sin might be done away with, that we should no longer be slaves of sin.*

And in **Romans 6:15-22**, Paul stated, *15 Well then, since God's grace has set us free from the law, does that mean we can go on sinning? Of course not! 16 Don't you realize that you become the slave of whatever you choose to obey? You can be a slave to sin, which leads to death, or you can choose to obey God, which leads to righteous living. 17 Thank God! Once you were slaves of sin, but now you wholeheartedly obey this teaching we have given you. 18 Now you are free from your slavery to sin, and you have become slaves to righteous living. 19 Because of the weakness of your human nature, I am using the illustration of slavery to help you understand all this. Previously, you let yourselves be slaves to impurity and lawlessness, which led ever deeper into sin. Now you must give yourselves to be slaves to righteous living so that you will become holy. 20 When you were slaves to sin, you were free from the obligation to do right. 21 And what was the result? You are now ashamed of the things you used to do, things that end in eternal doom. 22 But now you are free from the power of sin and have become slaves of God. Now you do those things that lead to holiness and result in eternal life.*

Over and over the scriptures exhort us to stop sinning. We hear the same thing from Paul who defended the Gospel of grace in his letter to the Galatians.

So, we have looked at what grace is and what it is not; let's sum it up...

Grace is not an excuse or license to sin. Sin always leads to death. God hates wickedness and the wicked.

Disobedience is sin.

We need to be obedient in our faith to receive grace.

In Christ we are no longer slaves to sin. Jesus set us free; we are now a slave of God.

Grace is a teacher. It is God's power, and is sufficient to help us overcome anything that comes our way.

True grace always leads to everlasting life.

Christ was not born to die a brutal death, then be resurrected for you, and I to live the same way we did before He drew us to himself! We were born for such a time as this, to display His glory to the world, to be the light in the darkness, to be His voice and heart. We are called to be a voice that speaks truth in the face of lies.

Thank you to the following:

http://israeliteindeed.wordpress.com/calvinism/sin-boldly-the-false-grace-message

Michael Brown, "Confronting the Error of Hyper-Grace

Repentance

There is no salvation without repentance. Just like there is true grace and false grace, there is true repentance and false repentance. Satan ALWAYS has a counterfeit.

Today, we are told that when we came to Christ, all our sins, past, present and future were forgiven. The false grace message so popular today will tell you repentance is not necessary. At a minimum, if we would apologize to a loved one or friend when we do wrong, why would we think it is not necessary to apologize to the Lord when we grieve Him?

Repentance is more than we are taught today' it is not just saying we are sorry to the Lord and then continuing on in our sin...Repentance has to be more than lip service; it is heart change. We come to the realization that our sin IS sin. Much like the example of the homosexual worship leader who could see all the sins listed in Romans 1 as sin, but he did not lump his own "issue" into that category. He could not call his choice of behavior "sin," he said it was an "issue," though clearly written in scripture with all the others which he knew were sin. When we recognize, admit, and confess our sin by coming into agreement with the Lord, we are on the path to true repentance. When we get to this point and confess our sin to the Lord, scripture tells us **1 John 1:9** *If we confess our sins, He is faithful and just to forgive us our sins and to cleanse us from all unrighteousness.*

Matthew 3:8-10 (NLT), says, confession and repentance is more than lip service. We are to *"prove by the way you live that you have repented of your sins and turned to God. Don't just say to each other, 'We're safe, for we are descendants of Abraham.' That means nothing, for I tell you, God can create children of Abraham from these very stones. Even now the ax of God's judgment is poised, ready to sever the roots of the trees. Yes, every tree that does not produce good fruit will be chopped down and thrown into the fire."*

False repentance realizes our behavior is out of line, or out of the norm. Maybe we are upset we were caught in our sins. We do not like the effects our sin has on us or others, so we decide we will not do it again. We are looking to change ourselves in our own strength. We may come to the Lord and give lip service, or even cry out and apologize, but we are more concerned with ourselves and mediating the pain we have caused and our conscience rather than focusing on how our behaviors are grieving the Lord, and how we need to make things right with a Holy God.

It is those unconfessed sins that build up between us and the Lord which make Him feel far from us. We must confess our sins. By doing so we are not telling the Lord anything He does not already know. We are coming into agreement with the Lord and His Word. More than that, true repentance is not just admitting and turning from our sins, but a breaking of our hearts into true sorrow for our sins. We know deep in our spirit, not just with superficiality, that we have sinned against the Lord and deserve judgment. This leads us to humble ourselves before the Lord, seeking His mercy. We ask the Lord for His guidance, strength and help to overcome. We come to understand we have grieved the heart of God and then seek to change, desiring to obey His Word, depending upon His strength and Holy Spirit from here on out.

There is a lasting change. Sometimes it is dramatic and other times it is progressive. We must be convinced there is no other way but God's way of thinking and acting. His word is absolute truth, and our heart needs be hungry for more of Him in order to live for Him. That is what leads us to true salvation and comprehension of our need for a Savior.

We need to be blood bought, sanctified, and justified. We are either all in or we are all out with God. There is no middle ground. We cannot be double-minded, swayed by every whim. When we are completely surrendered, Holy Spirit, the true grace of God, will make the changes in us and He will move us from glory to glory. This is the grace that leads to repentance, that leads to salvation.

True Prosperity, Blessing, and Favor
Sermon

http://www.youtube.com/watch?v=ubjX7o_pKkw

In the Old Testament, we have example after example of faithful men who prospered in a financial sense with crops and livestock, gold, etc. These men were abundantly blessed. There was Abraham, Joshua, Isaac, Joseph, Uzziah, Hezekiah, Job, David, and Solomon - to name a few. The material blessings on the lives of these men were a witness to everyone; Jews and Gentiles alike, of their blessed relationship with the Lord.

We have not been able to turn on a Christian television program over the past few years without receiving a prosperity message. We are told to give so we can get. If we want to be rich monetarily, we give money to get more money from God. Yes, it takes money to participate in some aspects of spreading the gospel, but it has become ALL about money in many circles. The bible does say to give and it will be given, pressed down, shaken together and running over. We will reap what we sow – but this applies to every aspect of life, not just finances. I do believe God wants His people to prosper, and I do believe in seed faith. I have planted many a monetary seed and watched the Lord move in a tremendous way.

I believe in tithing, in spite of those who tell me it's not for New Testament believers. I believe that is what God me to do and I obey. I believe that is the reason God protected my home and cars through this recession, - as I can see no reason in the natural why we still have our house and cars. I believe in giving offerings, and when the Lord speaks an amount to a ministry I give it. Sometimes the Spirit of the Lord says to sow into an anointed word of God that speaks to me and my situation and in obedience I give as I am told.

HOWEVER, it is not about money as much as it is about God looking for obedience and a step of faith. The truth is, God does not need our money, but money is a HUGE stumbling block to us because the society we live in revolves around it. The world's definition of prosperity is very different from God's. He asks us to sow into the kingdom at times to show us the condition of our heart. The kingdom view of money and prosperity is very different then the world's view.

God also asks us to give of ourselves and our gifts; not because He needs it, but because He chose and equipped you. He made you uniquely for such a time as this. He gave you gifts and He gave you choice to use everything for selfish purposes or for His glory.

Money is not the prime indicator of prosperity, as this world and some of the church would have us believe; there is so much more that we are missing when we focus on wealth rather than the Lord's definition of prosperity, blessing, and favor.

Dictionary.com defines favor as "*something done or granted out of goodwill, rather than from justice or for remuneration. The state of being approved, or held in regard, to prefer or treat with partiality.*"

Prosperity is defined as "*a successful, flourishing, or thriving condition, especially in financial respects; good fortune.*"

Blessing is defined as *special favor, mercy, or benefit. A favor or gift bestowed by God, thereby bringing happiness.*"

One day, the Lord spoke to me about favor, blessing, and prosperity from a kingdom perspective. He told me to look at the life of Mary, the mother of Jesus; to look at her life through the eyes of a woman, a wife, a mother, and a grandmother. To say the least, my definition of blessing, favor & prosperity radically changed.

So let's look at the life of Mary. How many of you think she was truly blessed to be the mother of Jesus, the Messiah? She was! How many through the centuries, or maybe even some of you, would have loved to have been the one God chose to be the mother of His Son? Mary was chosen to be the only woman in history to have this honor and privilege.

Her name was Mary – which comes from the word Mara – which means bitter. We do not know if her name reflected her condition, but we do know *the angel said "YOU are highly favored". The Lord is with you, blessed are you among woman* **(Luke 1:28).**

The angel said she was not just favored; she was HIGHLY favored. She was blessed and chosen as the one out of all women, past, present and future, entrusted to birth and raise God in the flesh - the Savior of the world. It's hard to wrap our brain around that.

As awesome as that must have been, let's consider for a moment the life she endured. She was a woman living in a time where woman were chattel; they were viewed as property, having no rights. She was pregnant, unmarried, accused of fornication – a sin punishable by being stoned to death. No one believed she was a virgin, and this baby was born of the Holy Spirit, not her parents, nor her fiancé, Joseph, and certainly not the religious leaders and town people. This was scandalous; shocking in her day. Just imagine what it would be like to tell the world that this was a virgin birth – either then or now. I was an obstetric nurse for several years; I heard that one all the time. Trust me when I tell you that there are thousands of claimed virgin births out there, and no one believes that.

I can't believe some of the things my family and church people have said to ME over the years, so I can only imagine the pain and the persecution she endured at the hands of her own family, friends and people. There was laughing, ridicule, accusation, finger pointing; they were likely merciless towards Mary. She probably endured these personal attacks her entire life. Mary had to birth the King of Kings in a manger, as if she, too, were an animal. She had to flee to Egypt to save the life of her son, and she had to live with the pain that all the babies in a city were killed because Herod wanted her child dead.

Let's imagine what was spoken about Jesus, as He was growing up...and even the things that were said to His siblings? Or, after Jesus began His public ministries...contemplate with me for a minute the terrible things they must have said about Him to His face, let alone behind His back. Talk about bullying! Mary witnessed this; it HAD to grieve her mother's heart! We know in the scriptures Jesus could do very little ministry and healing in Nazareth due to unbelief of the people. I am sure there was mocking too.

Three years later, Mary would watch a nightmare unfold. She could not protect her son - the boy she had raised into a man - the one whom she loved more than life itself.

The angel said she was blessed, and HIGHLY FAVORED, but this did not feel much like a life of blessing and high favor! She must have doubted and questioned, wondering why NOTHING in the natural looked like she was blessed and highly favored? I can only imagine the tears that flowed with her cries out to God - WHY? WHY IS THIS HAPPENING? WHAT DID I DO TO DESERVE THIS? WHAT DID HE DO TO DESERVE THIS? GOD WHERE ARE YOU IN THIS? WHY ARE YOU PUNISHING ME?

As a mother, I can only imagine what she went through. I consider the times I was on my face praying for my children, or one of the 9 kids we took in off the street. I reflect on times when my heart was breaking so badly that all I could do was either cry out in groaning sounds or beg the Lord to take me home because I could not handle the emotional pain and apparent senselessness any longer. I know many of you have gone through these same things.

We have the benefit of the Word of God, and we can look at the things Mary endured as a mother with hindsight. We read the words on a page, and we have read the life of Jesus hundreds of times, but the words seem to be in a documentary style ~ void of emotion. Yet to Mary, these were not just words - it was her LIFE. She did not have the benefit of the whole picture. She knew just a part. Just like we only see a part in our lives. She did not understand why all this was happening. Every crack of the whip and every pound of the hammer flew in the face of the words of the angel...that she was "blessed and highly favored."

He was Messiah, the Savior, after all! The promised one that all of Israel should have been expecting. He was salvation for the entire world; past, present and future. One day He was welcomed as a king, with people waving palm branches and shouting; *Hosanna! Hosanna! Blessed is he who comes in the name of the Lord.*

The next day, rejected and beaten to a pulp, then crucified on a cross as a common criminal. As a mother, I can't fathom the pain, heartache, and emotional turmoil she suffered. There was nothing she could do to protect, help, or comfort Him. Her hopes, and dreams; all she thought might be the life of her son, the Messiah, Son of God, died that day on the cross.

How could Mary reconcile the words of the angel 33 years prior; *"you are blessed among woman and highly favored of God"* with the gruesome death Jesus suffered? The enemy came in like a flood as she replayed the events in her head. She must have begun to doubt and question just like the others. She was grieving, yet she did not run away. She stuck it out with the disciples.

She was there in the upper room to receive the outpouring of Holy Spirit. She saw the dream she thought had died resurrect and change the world. The Catholic Church takes Mary, worship of Mary and the eternal virgin myth to an extreme, but I am afraid the rest of us do not give Mary enough credit. Either way we are still talking about her today. She was a faithful, blessed and a highly favored woman of God, although I am sure her faith wobbled at times, as our does when things in the natural do not look like the things God has promised.

As I contemplated the life of Mary, it caused me to realize how much the definition of *prosperity, blessing, and the favor of God*, so commonly used today, is off track. So many think of blessing, and favor, and prosperity as only money, when it is so much more than that! God gives us *every* good thing. God gave Mary, Jesus. God blesses us to sow into HIS agenda. Are we willing to make the desire of God's heart the desire of our heart? Are we willing to give up everything we love? Are we willing to give God back the people and the things we love for His will to be done?

Paul, Peter, Mary Magdalene, and others were also blessed and highly favored of God. How many of you wish you were them? They were hand selected by Jesus himself to do powerful works. What an honor; talk about favor! They were not poor, but they were not exceedingly wealthy financially that we are aware of, yet all their needs were met. They were servants, just like the Master. They carried on with the work Jesus started on the earth and in their lives.

They were different; they stood out...Not by their material wealth as the Old Testament men of faith, but by their faithfulness and surrender to the Lord. They carried the presence of God with them.

God performed great miracles, and signs and wonders through them. They were persecuted terribly, just as their Master had been. They refused to compromise, and they were used by the Lord in a powerful way, preferring to store up their treasures in Heaven rather than on earth, where moths and rust destroy. We, too, will suffer for the kingdom of God ~ just as the disciples of old suffered, and just as our brothers and sisters around the world suffer. Being a disciple of Jesus was never promised to be a cake walk.

As I have said before, being a true follower of Jesus; being used by Him, ALWAYS comes with a cost. When the going gets tough, many people walk away. Our perspective changes in view of eternity; I am sure the disciples had no idea when they suffered and were martyred that their sacrifice would mean life to so many through the centuries. I am sure, though the eyes of retrospection, all of their suffering, which was not fully understood at that time, was worth it; even if it was just for one life to be saved.

The truth is, as children of the Most High God, we prosper. We are blessed by serving God and others. Each of us is highly favored by Him. Each has been given gifts and talents to serve. When we seek first the kingdom of God, then everything is added to us. That tells me we need to become wealthy with the presence of God; it is that overflow, the revelation that it is God in us that makes us prosper in all we put our hand to, which is truly life changing for us, as well as those to whom we minister.

We do need money to further the gospel, but we should not be serving the Lord to be rich monetarily or for what we can gain. We should not be giving money just to get money. Money is only a small part of the picture that has been blown out of proportion. I can guarantee you that if your prime motivator for serving and giving to the Lord is to get more money, you will not see the blessings of God. God is looking for a people who will not just seek His hand (what He can give them). He is not even looking for a people who will seek His face. He is looking for a people who will seek and BE His heart in this world.

We store up our treasures in Heaven, *not* on earth. Money cannot be more important in our life than God.

As I have said many times these past few years, that is what this shaking has been about and what we have been enduring as a nation, and as what we like to call the church; it is intended to remove all that is in our lives that is not of God. To remove everything that takes our focus off Him and makes us unstable in all our ways, so, we will focus on the Lord and not on man or material things.

The evidence of blessing, favor and prosperity; even the degree of hardship and persecution we face as God entrusts, is directly proportional to the assignment we are given to further the kingdom. That also includes our faith, our gifts of the Spirit, our money, our time and our talents. To whom much is given much is expected.

There are seven laws of prosperity that run throughout the Old and the New Testament according to the Dake Bible®:

1. **God must be with you**. In **Genesis 39**: *The LORD was with Joseph so that he prospered. The warden paid no attention to anything under Joseph's care, because the LORD was with Joseph and gave him success in whatever he did.* In **Jeremiah 20:11** - *But the LORD is with me like a mighty warrior; so my persecutors will stumble and not prevail. They will fail and be thoroughly disgraced; their dishonor will never be forgotten.*

2. **Obedience**. We must be obedient to all the Lord has asked us to do. **Deuteronomy 28:1-14** outlines the blessings for Obedience; Verses 1 and 2 read; *If you fully obey the LORD your God and carefully follow all his commands I give you today, the LORD your God will set you high above all the nations*

on earth. All these blessings will come on you and accompany you if you obey the LORD your God. **John 14:23** *Jesus replied, "Anyone who loves me will obey my teaching. My Father will love them, and we will come to them and make our home with them.*

3. Goodness to Israel. **Genesis 12:1-3,** *¹The LORD said ³ I will bless those who bless you, and whoever curses you I will curse; and all peoples on earth will be blessed through you."* **Psalm 122:6,** *Pray for the peace of Jerusalem: "May those who love you be secure.*

4. Meditation. Means to mutter to ourselves on the Word of God. In the **Psalms** we read that we are to meditate on God's Words day and night; His unfailing love. We are to meditate on God in our songs, in our hearts, and when considering all God's works, His mighty deeds, His precepts and His ways. Then we will be like a tree planted by streams of water, which yields its fruit in due season and whose leaf does not wither...whatever we do prospers.

Joshua 1:8 *Keep this Book of the Law always on your lips; meditate on it day and night, so that you may be careful to do everything written in it. Then you will be prosperous and successful.*

5. Faith. **2 Chronicles 20:20** *Early in the morning they left for the Desert of Tekoa. As they set out, Jehoshaphat stood and said, "Listen to me, Judah and people of Jerusalem! Have faith in the LORD your God and you will be upheld; have faith in his prophets and you will be successful."*

6. Seek God. **2 Chronicles 26:5**, *He sought God during the days of Zechariah, who instructed him in the fear of God. As long as he sought the LORD, God gave him success.*

Jeremiah 10:2, *The shepherds are senseless and do not inquire of the LORD; so they do not prosper and all their flock is scattered.*

7. Hospitality. Is the gracious reception and treatment of guests or strangers in a warm, friendly, generous wayAccording to the Dake Bible® there are three reasons some do not prosper:

1. **Rebellion.** Against God; resistance, defiance or an improper view of God and those whom the Lord places in our lives as authority. Failing to honor those who God said we should honor; a spouse, a parent, pastor, prophet.

   We talked about honor the second week of Praising In The Park in summer 2013; it can be viewed on the YouTube channel, bearwitnessmin.

2. **Hiding or covering over sins. Proverbs 28:23** *Whoever rebukes a person will in the end gain favor rather than one who has a flattering tongue.*

3. **Fighting God.** Similar to rebellion; we fight God by not obeying what He asks us to do, by not seeing those God placed in our lives to speak to us, by not receiving and using the gifts that God gives us, by not sowing our gifts, talents and money into the kingdom of God, and by rejecting the fullness of His Spirit.

El Shaddei means *all bountiful* and the All Bountiful One has promised His followers four things (believe me folks, we get the better end of the deal)...source: Dake Bible®:

1. Salvation

2. Prosperity

3. Healing and Health

4. He would take care of all our wants and needs – yes He even said wants. I was always told it was needs, but scripture is clear; God does take our wants into consideration. **Psalms 23:1** *I shall not want.*

Psalm 34:9-10, *Fear the LORD, you his holy people, for those who fear him lack nothing. 10 The lions may grow weak and hungry, but those who seek the LORD lack no good thing.*

Psalm 84:11, *For the LORD God is a sun and shield; the LORD bestows favor and honor; no good thing does he withhold from those whose walk is blameless.*

Matthew 21:22, *If you believe, you will receive whatever you ask for in prayer.*

Mark 9:23, *Everything is possible for one who believes.*

John 14:14, *You may ask me for anything in my name, and I will do it.*

John 15:7, *If you remain in me and my words remain in you, ask whatever you wish, and it will be done for you.*

John 15:16, *You did not choose me, but I chose you and appointed you so that you might go and bear fruit—fruit that will last—and so that whatever you ask in my name the Father will give you.*

Prosperity, blessing, and favor ~ in reality is becoming wealthy in God's divine presence; **Ephesians 3:19** (Amplified Bible) *[That you may really come] to know [practically, through experience for yourselves] the love of Christ, which far surpasses mere knowledge [without experience]; that you may be filled [through all your being] unto all the fullness of God [may have the richest measure of the divine Presence, and become a body wholly filled and flooded with God Himself]!*

When we consider prosperity, blessing and favor in our lives, we must realize God is not confined by time. He looks across the generations, while we see only what is in front of us. This is why the lives of Mary and the disciples, and the things they endured, seem at odds with our definition of blessing, favor and prosperity.

We need to be rich in God's divine presence; filled with God himself. Let me ask you, what will have to leave your life to allow you to be rich in the fullness of God's divine presence? What stands between you and the Lord today? Prosperity, blessing, and favor are not materialism. God is love, and everything we do must be motivated by love. Love is the anointing for prosperity, blessing, and favor and these are proportionate to the amount of God's presence in one's life. If we don't walk in the love of God, God's presence on our life will not increase. **1 Corinthians 13: 1-8**, Though I speak with the tongues of men and of angels, but have not love, I have become sounding brass or a clanging cymbal. 2 and though I have *the gift of* prophecy, and understand all mysteries and all knowledge, and though I have all faith, so that I could remove mountains, but have not love, I am nothing. 3 And though I bestow all my goods to feed *the poor,* and though I give my body to be burned, but have not love, it profits me nothing.

Prosperity is wholeness. His divine presence is the prerequisite for everything the Lord wants to do in our lives. If we get filled up on God's divine presence, we look to God to be our provider. We worry less about those distractions of self and our circumstances which cause us to compromise, such as thinking we need to work overtime, stepping out in our flesh to do things our way, or compromising who we are in some misguided mindset to "HELP GOD" answer our prayers or give us money and material things. When we do that, we are telling the Lord we do not trust Him to provide, rather than growing in faith and relationship with Him, His presence, and love.

When we choose to seek God's presence we will see the manifestation of the anointing. When we seek first the kingdom of God, everything else will be added to us. When we seek the fullness of God, spending time and resting in His presence, praise and worship, answers come. We receive wisdom to handle our situations; we work smarter using His wisdom and anointing, not harder

In His presence is fullness of joy. Everything we need is waiting in the presence of God. There is wisdom, favor, keys to the kingdom to open doors, breakthrough, divine appointments, and instruction. Why are so many of us content to talk about Jesus, or wear a Christian t-shirt, hang a cross around our neck, or place a sticker on our car but see none of the blessings of God?

The presence of God is real. It is tangible and lives inside you. The question is, are you running on empty, or are you filled to overflowing with the Spirit...the presence, love and anointing...of our Holy God? We need to abide in His presence. God is speaking to His children, yet most of the time we cannot hear through the distractions going on around us. We are stressed out and worn out; God is giving us the answers and instructions to prosper us, but we need to be still, and settle our spirits so we can hear. **Deuteronomy 8:18** says *God gives us power to get wealth."* **Isaiah 48:17** *"God teaches us to profit."* **Psalms 1-3;** *God gave us instructions on how to be prosperous and have good success.*

Not only are we promised abundant riches in the kingdom, we are given explicit instructions on how to go about getting it. The key is, it is not always about money. It never looks like we think it will look.

Each one of us is where we are right now because of an instruction we followed or an instruction we ignored. We need to rest and abide in His presence. Rest is a place where we do not doubt; a place where there is no struggle. We are called to cast our cares; cares we were never meant to carry in the first place. So often we allow our cares and worries to isolate and keep us out of the presence of God and keep us away from God's people. We need to be in that place with the Lord where we can clearly see and hear His instructions to receive the blessing, favor, and prosperity.

Simply put, prosperity is the harvest of blessing and favor we receive when we choose to abide in the presence of God; when we choose to trust Him no matter what it looks like, no matter what we are going though. He sees the big picture and He promises to work everything out for His glory. The purpose of prosperity, blessing and favor is to further the agenda of God, not our selfish agenda. We need to change our understanding of prosperity and put it into a proper perspective.

Maybe you're reading this and can relate to this message. What you have been taught about blessing, favor, and prosperity has only been about money, and you want the fullness of God's divine presence in your life. Maybe you have not understood the things that you have been going through as they fly in the face of the blessing, favor, and prosperity of God you have been taught.

I would like to pray with you; maybe you are reading and you don't know the Lord, or you need a fresh start. Will you receive His gift right now? It's no accident you are reading these words. This moment is the time of your salvation. Will you allow the Lord to open the door to the fullness of His divine love; the door to prosperity, blessing and favor? He imparts wisdom and healing, and longs to give you the desires of your heart. Will you pray now? Lord, hear my prayer ~ take me into Your kingdom, allow me to know You. Give me a fresh start in life, seeking You first above all things and trusting You with my life, in Jesus Name, Amen.

January 3, 2012

Warn My People

Warn My people! Warn them loudly that I am coming swiftly, like a thief in the night. Without warning, in the blink of an eye, your future is set. Your future is a decision of the heart. Take captive those thoughts of your old life, those things that are not of Me. Put on the mind of Christ with a future and a hope to ride out the coming crises in the protection of My arms. There is no safer place to be than *in* Me.

Stop relying on yourself and your own strength. You do so even when you do not think you are doing it. Abide in Me. I am the door in your present. I am the door to your future. Do not trust in chariots, horses, or kings; trust in the One whose name makes the oceans roar. I make the deaf hear and the mute speak.

Many will rise up to deceive you. They will sweet-talk you and lure you into putting your trust in them. Man is cunning and sly; not worthy of your trust for eternal salvation. Too many are serving man and not God; their relationship with the shepherd (Pastor) is more important than their relationship with the SHEPHERD (Jesus). Do not place your trust in the kingdom of men. Men have built ivory towers to exalt their kingdom, intending to keep My children subservient to them and not to the Kingdom. Many are being deceived into helping man build his kingdom. It is erected in the name of bigger buildings and mammon, often under the guise of Christianity. People are giving and giving into buildings yet not sowing into lives. Cold and unforgiving, these buildings of stone and brick; crumbling foundations laid on sand, teetering and tottering on the winds of time.

Their kingdoms will crumble. Their kingdoms will fall. Will you remain standing? Will you be in shock and dismay at what you helped create under the false pretense of My kingdom name? Cry out, "God have mercy!" You might be sincere, but sincerely wrong. No one has the whole story and no one knows the whole truth except My Father, Who sent Me to die for Our Creation.

Seek Me. Stop where you are and evaluate yourself. Evaluate your life in the light of My presence. Examine yourselves under the light of My Word. Look into the mirror of your soul and see who is reflected back at you. Who is your god?

I am coming swiftly. Time is dwindling down. The moment is now. The day of your salvation stands before you; arms wide open, desiring to bring you into My kingdom rest. Do not be deceived; clearly examine yourself while there is still time.

You have been taught that "acceptance" is the key. You have been taught that believing in Me is also a key. There are many who accepted Me and believed in Me but were never My children. It is a matter of the heart. Is it is a matter of childlike faith. It is a matter of willingness to trust and step off the precipice of life into My hand.

Allow Me to translate your life into the kingdom. Your thoughts become My thoughts, your words become My words, your heart becomes My heart. In this way, the kingdom perpetuates.

When people see you, do they see Me? Are you living like the world and doing your own thing, or are you living for Me? If they do not see Me in you, perhaps you are living a life far removed, with a token Jesus here, and a token gospel there. Return to Me, all you who are heavy laden, and I will give you rest. You have carried the load too long. You have entertained burdens you were never meant to carry. Lay it all down at the foot of the cross and move beyond the burden into life in My presence. In My presence your life can be ruled by My Spirit. Release the control you have sought so hard to hang onto. Release it to Me, your God. You can trust Me to do right. I love you.

January 5, 2012

THE DAWN OF A NEW DAY

The Lord expressed that parts of this word were for all persons, and the last part was only for some. Your spirit will bear witness.

It is the dawn of a new day. The temperature is rising. The stakes are higher and the train has left the station. It is on the track. There is a switchman, who can change the direction of the train. *If My people, who are called by My name, will humble themselves, and pray, and seek My face, and turn from their wicked ways; then I will hear from Heaven, and I will forgive their sins, and will restore their land* **(2 Chronicles 7:14).**

My people are living in these last days, yet many are blind leading the blind; others are skipping and singing, "la, la, la, la, la," totally oblivious to the changes about to befall them. Still others give way to fear and remain focused on circumstances. *If My people, who are called by My name, will humble themselves, and pray, and seek My face, and turn from their wicked ways, I will hear from Heaven, and I will forgive their sins, and will restore their land.*

Repent, for the kingdom of God is at hand. *If My people, who are called by My name, will humble themselves, and pray, and seek My face, and turn from their wicked ways, I will hear from Heaven, and I will forgive their sins, and will restore their land.* I will heal their land, the land I gave them. I will heal your own individual lands; the fields that I gave you to till, to sow, and to harvest.

If My people will forgive, I mean *really* forgive, renouncing their bitterness and anger at people and circumstances, even at Me, I will heal their land, their hearts and their minds. *If My people who are called by My name, will humble themselves, and pray, and seek My face, and turn from their wicked ways, I will hear from Heaven. I will forgive their sins and restore their land.* This is the land of their forefathers.

I am speaking to the generations of promise that went unfulfilled by disobedient generations. I plan to restore family blessings, lands, anointing and mantles that went unfulfilled in past generations. There are many blessings, spoken by faithful fathers over their children, which were lost in generations past. Those words were spoken out into the atmosphere, however, and those words, based upon My promises, will not be forsaken. They will be restored to My people who are called by My name.

Break off the curses of generations gone by. You live like you are under a curse, but you are blessed. The curse was taken upon My flesh and nailed to a tree to set you free. Ask for restoration of your familial blessing; call forth a double portion of the blessings, anointing, callings, and mantles that went unused and unclaimed in the past. They have been waiting for a worthy, obedient vessel to understand that the time is now. The time is now to arise. The time is now to claim your destiny.

The depression and oppression of past seasons are to be broken off. Like a baby bird coming out of his shell, you must struggle to break free of the mindsets of your past seasons. You are not who they say you are. You are not a failure. You are not unworthy of My love and blessing. They told you that I was not with you, but I was, holding you in My arms of love. I set you aside ~ to speak to you, to teach you, to love you. You are in a season of change. I took you aside to break things off your life that needed to go in order that you could handle My calling upon your life. You were not ready to walk in what I have for you, so I took you aside for a time of preparation. Just as Esther bathed in perfumes for a time, you required a lesson of faith and trust to get to know Me better.

Many have used this time wisely, but many have not. It is not too late to reclaim your destiny. It starts with a heart completely Mine; mere lip service will not do. We have moved past that point in the separation of souls; those who are truly Mine, and those who are merely deceiving themselves will become increasingly evident. You must decide. You know of them whom I am speaking. Do you desire a hope and a future in Me or in the world? The past is erased and the future is now. The train on the track is about to change directions. *If My people, who are called by My name, will humble themselves, and pray, and seek My face, and turn from their wicked ways, I will hear from Heaven, and I will forgive their sins, and will restore their land.*

The time is here. The time is now. Freedom awaits you. Break out of that shell; let Me clothe you with My grace and fill you with My mercy. Let Me impart to you My compassion, that you may see the people of this world the way I see them, with eyes and hearts of love.

For you, My child, I plan a double portion for your troubles. The pain and suffering you endured at the hands of others brings with it a double portion of anointing. Golden oil will flow down your lips when you speak, and the glory of the Lord will rest upon you. You will be hated by the world, for they hated Me first. But all the world will know you are My child. Your words will pierce the darkest of hearts and minds. As it was with Jeremiah, it will be with you. Truth costs; there is a price to be paid to proclaim it. There is also a price to be paid to ignore it.

God blesses you this day and puts His crown upon your head. He places a robe worn by your King around your shoulders. I, not your enemy, will lead you through the streets on horseback, shouting, *"Thus shall it be done to the man/woman whom the King delights to honor!"* **(Esther 6:6)**

The enemy will be angry. He will plot and plan, but you, My child, have the victory. Just as Haman's ugly plan was exposed and turned back around on him, I am about to do the same for many of you. My hand has been working all this time. I am going to destroy the enemies who came against you. What was planned for your evil will be their fate; call a three-day fast and come before your King.

January 5, 2012

RESUME

I am the Lord your God. Heaven and nature sing My praise. *In Me you live, move, and have your being* **(Acts 17:28).** I am the Lord of your today and your tomorrows. Yesterday is gone. Today will pass away into yesterday. Live each day to the fullest, relying on Me, seeking My face, asking for My guidance before making decisions. Many are vying for your attention. They seek to destroy, distract, and lead you astray with knowledge and advice that sounds good to the ears of man, but is contrary to My Word and will for your life.

I the Lord your God have spoken, repeatedly. Prepare yourself for the days ahead, as treacherous times are upon you. The hand of My protection has been lifted in the land. Your backs have been turned on the Lord. Idols of man stand, erected in direct defiance of Me and My well-established plans for this nation.

Repent, for the kingdom of God is at hand! Resume the great commission, for many souls hang in the balance. Your job is to reach them for Me. Return to the job at hand! My plans and purposes for you have been distracted by the ways of the world and the evil agenda upon the land. You must focus upon Me instead of thinking you alone can stem the tide of evil that has taken root in this land.

My children have eyes to see and ears to hear, yet there are those who claim to be Mine but do not see and do not hear what the Spirit of the Lord is speaking. They are in danger of following the pied piper over a cliff. He is disguised as an angel of light, full of excuses and flattering words.

As I have said before, you are witnessing how the man of perdition will rise to power, supported by many who call themselves Mine, but they are not Mine. They are deceived. I do not know them. I tell you the truth, men and women must make a choice to stand and serve Me. My hand is lifted, but remains poised over this nation. It has not yet gotten as bad as it can get; corruption is still being exposed. Repentance is always an option. Choose wisely.

January 6, 2012

A REVELATION OF MY HEART

I give you revelation this day of My heart toward mankind. You are My people, made in My image. My spirit lives within you. I've written My name upon your hearts. Wonders and knowledge of Me are stored there. Unlock the potential of My heart within you, for I hold nothing back.

You are flitting here and there, looking for something I placed, knit together, within your very being. I am not distant. I am *in* your heart. Locked within you are the wonders and mysteries of life. I love My children, though I do not love all of their ways.

I am the Lord your God. Today I remind you that you are My child, whom I love. You have captured the heart of the Father. You are a child who seeks after Me, to do My will and follow My ways. Receive a touch from the Holy One to refresh all that is within you, for a new day has dawned and the train has left the station. The train is speeding along the track toward destiny and fulfillment in Me.

Surrender! Surrender it all. I see the things you have been holding onto in secret, thinking I cannot see you. They are exposed by My eyes and the light of My presence. I shed a spotlight to declare, *"Turn, surrender it all to Me."* I will heal you, and we can move on. This secret thing holds you back from your destiny. Close the door to it. Let Us, together, open a window to your future.

January 8, 2012

CHANGE

God's definition of blessing and prosperity is *far* different then the world's definition.

The world as you know it is going to change. Stay humble. 2012 will be a time of prosperity for some of My children. There will be wars, rumors of wars, and famine. My government will be established. I hear the cries of My people; out with the old and in with the new. The people will have peace, not continuous anxiety, as powers shift in the natural and supernatural, as agendas are fulfilled and reversed. A time of relative peace and calm will occur, but do not be deceived, this peace will not last. Security will not last as things are shaken around the world. There will be reversals and upheavals.

My child, you are *Mine*; insulated from much, but not all, as the world spins. Time marches forth and destinies are in the balance. Life as you know it will change. I will restore what you lost. Use what I give wisely. Tithe, for My kingdom must go forth. I will tell you when and where to put My money. Many will need help.

I am with you, My child. It matters not what they say. Hold your head up and walk in My ways. You will receive My exceedingly great reward. Faint not, and don't grow weary, for the kingdom of God is at hand. You will feel My effects all over the world, as mountains tremble and seas roar. The birth pangs have begun and many will faint in fear of what comes upon the earth. The very ground beneath your feet, which you have counted as stable, will shake. Many will cry out to the Lord for the rocks to fall on them, as there is no place to hide from My fury.

The time is not yet. There will be a season of the proverbial calm before the storm. People will get comfortable and be lulled back to sleep. Do not sleep, My child. Use this time of grace well.

Prepare your hearts and minds with My Word. Become one with My Spirit. Learn to hear the voice of the One who calls you by name. Listen for the warnings and danger. Obey My voice. Prepare as you are instructed, for the kingdom of God is at hand.

Love. Allow yourself to be loved by Me. Do not fight Me, nor My plans for you. I know what is best. My plans will prevail. *To whom much is given, much is required* **(Luke 12:48).** My mercy is as endless as the sands in the sea. Position yourself to receive it, and to grow and prosper in knowledge of your Heavenly Father. Night is falling and the winter is cold.

Night is falling and the day well spent. Go in peace, My child, for My hand is upon you ~ speak to nations and to kings. Speak My child, speak. Continue in the ways I have taught you. I have led you to be bold and strong for My kingdom's cause.

January 09, 2012

I Love My Children

I am the Lord your God and today I say this;

I love My children. I am NOT punishing you. I am NOT trying to hurt you. I am trying to get your attention, to get your priorities in order and in line with My Word.

Too many are worshipping mammon. Jezebel is running rampant. People are falling to the right and to the left, fainting out of fear. 2012 is predicted to be the end of the world, but I will not let the earth totter; it will not wobble, it will not totally fall from My grace as the world predicts. They are building bomb shelters and storing up for a rainy day, worried about electromagnetic fields and danger.

Why has there not been a large meteor hit the earth since I planted man in the garden? Because the earth is protected by My grace. I have a covenant with the earth. I made it special and unique. I made it life-sustaining for My glory.

My people bring Me glory. My people fill the earth with praise. It is your praise that lights the world, your praise that ignites the heart, your praise that resounds as all of nature sings along in worship. All of nature sings My praise, and when you join in, the rhythm is complete. The fullness of My glory can be obtained on this earth and it is for you to move and breathe within. A cacophony of sound for My glory!

Do you want to walk in the fullness of My glory? Do you want to walk as My Son did upon the earth, doing the will of the One who sent Him? Praise Me! Abide in Me. Stand firm as the rock of ages. If you don't praise Me, even the rocks will cry out for My glory.

People are numb and paralyzed by their circumstances, but not My faithful servants who are continuing to speak My Word. They are speaking My agenda into existence as they understand more clearly the power of their words upon the earth, upon the future, and upon their circumstances and health.

I have prepared a way for you. I have prepared a way of escape for My children, which is abiding in the shadow of My wings. So few abide; they worry and fear, and look at the multitude of circumstances befalling the world. Did I not promise to provide for My children? Did I not promise I would take care of you and you would prosper? Isaac prospered in the famine. The widow and her son ate in the famine, and My servant received an abundance of oil to sell; it paid off every debt and then some.

I am a God of more than enough; a God of abundance. I am a God who desires nothing more than to show off His children. If you desire nothing but good for your children, how much more does your Heavenly Father, who owns the cattle on a thousand hills, and holds the earth and the Heavens in His hand, long to give His children?

You don't believe in My love. You reject it without even knowing; your words and thoughts come into alignment with the adversary and not Me. Speak life. Speak blessing, and all the world will know you are My children. I am the Lord your God. I have not forgotten about you. You are the apple of My eye and the heart of My very heart. I sing over you words of life. Speak your future into existence as you praise Me.

January 10, 2012

PONDERINGS ON ISRAEL

I was interrupted mid-prayer this morning with a vision of Satan sitting smugly on a throne surrounded by fire, and then there appeared a pentagram in the fire. The fire began to spread. It began coming in waves that were swallowing up people, while Satan sat on his throne, smiling. This vision of Satan looked EXACTLY like one of the pictures of Jesus that someone who says they are a Christian is using on Facebook ®! This is the Facebook picture:

Please find below the original, which according to According to Wikipedia® "is the oldest known icon of *Christ Pantocrator*, encaustic on panel (Saint Catherine's Monastery, Mount Sinai)."

I believe God gave me a powerful revelation about Israel and her leaders.

I watched a video last night about a popular Orthodox Rabbi in Israel who had a revelation of Jesus prior to his death. Before he died, he told everyone that he knew who was Messiah. He wrote it on a paper and sealed it, giving strict instructions that it was not to be opened until the one-year anniversary of his death.

As you can imagine, this caused much controversy after they unsealed the document and found the scribbled name of Yeshua. Many did not believe him, insisting it must be an error. He also had expressed that Jesus told him that the sign of his near return would be the death of Arial Sharon, who is currently in a vegetative state. After watching this video, I sent the video to my Jewish family and friends. I prayed for their salvation and receptive hearts.

As I was praying, my mind wandered to Arial Sharon in the vegetative state and whether he knew the Lord prior his devastating stoke. The Lord quickly responded. I believed He said, "He is mine, they are all are mine. Israel is in the palm of My hand. Golda Meir was mine. After she called Nixon and the United States agreed to help, she had revelation of Me. They all know Me, and know every tribe they are from, and who their forefathers were; Golda is from the line of Deborah, BiBi is from the line of David, and Arial is from the tribe of Judah. Even Ehud Barak knows Me; he is from the tribe of Benjamin. They cannot tell anyone, as it would cause too much turmoil."

The last part of this revelation hit me hard. I felt dread well up inside. I know in my spirit that this was not good. He then pronounced, "The next one will be from the tribe of DAN."

Addendum 2013: With all the events, we have been witnessing since the Lord gave me the above revelation, and with the great evil that has overtaken the nation, I decided it was time to investigate this further. There have been anti-Christ agendas, interesting changes with the last Pope, and one out of four Americans polled believe that Barak Obama is the Anti-Christ. I do not believe Barak Obama is the Anti-Christ because the Lord has been exposing his lies and deceit. These exposures are God's great love and mercy, as many who claimed to be His children were missing discernment and empowered this evil agenda. The Lord was showing us first-hand how many will be deceived. I do believe the next time we see this scenario of a man from nowhere being swept into power, by a flattering tongue, and the media and others lying and hiding rather than exposing the truth, it will be Anti-Christ.

In the 2013 election, Benjamin Netanyahu was re-elected as Prime Minster. The tribe of Dan, in my spirit, rings of evil. Will Israel's next leader stand through the reign of anti-Christ?

According to the Prophet's Dictionary; *The Ultimate Guide to Supernatural Wisdom*, by Paula A. Price, PH.D., "Dan was Jacob's fifth son by Rachel through her maid Bilhah's surrogacy. His name means "a judge." Dan received quite an unfavorable prophecy from his father that threw the tribe into a depth of idolatry and immorality from which it never recovered. According to **Genesis 49:17**, he would become a serpent although his call was to be a judge in Israel. The serpentine ascription referred to Dan's penchant for and ultimate submersion into the ways of the heathen. Jacob's prophesy turned out to be true, for in **Judges 1:34** the tribe of Dan was unable to possess his inheritance and was overthrown by the powerful and cagey Amorites. Dan surrendered to their resistance and became neighbors with them to their ruin.

According to **Judges 18**, the tribe of Dan had succumbed fully to their culture and was an outright Amorite influenced people. Their land later became the hub of the second idolatrous worship center created by King Jeroboam. This was due to their notoriety. As the region settled in the demonic worship forms, Jeroboam drew on Dan's infamy to divert Israel's faith from Jerusalem to his own territory. By the time of Revelation 7, the tribe of Dan is conspicuously absent from the list of the twelve tribes sealed during the Apocalypse era. In their place we find the tribe of Manasseh."

In my studies, I also came across an interview with a pastor who met with Golda Mier and he was convinced she did know Jesus as Messiah. I have not been able to verify the others.

Addendum 2014: Ariel Sharon has died.

January 14, 2012

Washed In A Wave Of My Blood

I am the Lord your God, and today I say, you are butter to My bread and sweet honey to My lips. I love you, My child, and all that the kingdom offers is yours for the asking. Ask and you shall receive. A measure pressed down, shaken together. As you give it shall be given.

Dry your tears, for I am with you. Stand strong and see My mighty right hand work all things for good. You love Me My child, and circumstances have been tough. The rains have not come in their season and there is famine in the land. Famine abounds. There is a famine of love, famines of grace and mercy, and poverty in thought.

As the wave recedes, it removes the debris. Your soul, washed in My blood. Cry mercy for what befalls the land. Cry mercy; behold, I make all things new. Tear down and build up. Let Me create in you a new heart and a new temple for My presence to reside.

I am the Lord your God, and today I say *I love you, My child.* People come and people go; I am removing people who profit you not. I am removing those who drain your resources and close your mind; derailing and distracting from My purpose in you. Do not cry and do not weep, for these things must happen. The dust and the stubble must go in order to create in you a clean heart.

I have not left you. I will never leave you nor forsake you. My plans in your life shall go forth without the interference of egocentric self-seekers who think they know what is best for My children. They are self-centered, only concerned with their needs and agendas; not Me or My agenda. They work toward the fulfillment of their desires and not Mine. They are dragging My good-natured children down a garden path to destruction, filling them with discouragement until they can't ever believe for what I have promised.

Stand tall and strong. Keep your feet firmly planted on the rock of My salvation; the rock of My Word. See the deliverance of your Lord. My mighty right hand uplifts you from the claws of the enemy. I will lovingly clean every wound you have suffered. I will mend your heart, for in My great mercy lies My love.

Woe to those who seek to divert you from My will for you. Woe to those who lie, cheat, and steal from My servants for they are doing it to Me. Everything you have, I have given you. No good thing comes except from your Father above. No good gift comes apart from My hand. The Lord your God has spoken.

January 16, 2012

FEROCIOUS LOVE

I awakened from a deep sleep hearing this;

Your God is BIG. I LOVE My children with a relentless, intense love. He will protect and defend ferociously, like a mother wolf whose babies are threatened. As a lion roars, and a young lion hovers over his prey, I will uphold them in My mighty right hand. I will protect and defend My children, because when one raises a hand against My child, all of Heaven watches. A threat to My child is a direct threat to Me.

You will not fall, you will not stumble, even if you get knocked back a few steps, I am right there beside you to bring you through. Trust and obey; stand in faith. Just stand, and you will see the deliverance of your Lord.

Your enemies are My enemies. You will have to fight, but you have the victory, just like the Israelites when they obeyed, trusted, and stood. They fought in faith and had the victory. Walls fell down, the sun stood still, the Red Sea parted. They even brought home the spoils.

Each battle grew them stronger in faith, stronger in mind, stronger in body. They prospered. There are times when you will escape, and times when you will stand and fight for what is right. You will be called to take more land, to protect your land or all the above. Sometimes you will take refuge in the winepress, but I will call you out.

I call you out into the battle; stand and fight for what is right, open your mouth and speak for Me. My Words contain power. My Angels back them up. Legions fight for you, My child. You cannot see what is going on around you. When you speak, your words contain the power to release blessing or cursing. Angels and Demons remain with baited breath, watching your lips, staying by to hear what you will say. Will it be words of doubt or words of faith? Blessing or cursing releases angels or demons; they respond quickly to fulfill your words.

What you speak prophesies into your own life, as well as the lives of others. There is so much power in the spoken word. I cannot put enough emphasis on your words. Your words create the life you have, and they can help create the life you want. Your Father God has spoken. Broadcast this to My children. I want you to read My Word. Psalm 34 is your word, Psalm 37 your promise.

Psalm 34:

A psalm of David, regarding the time he pretended to be insane in front of Abimelech, who sent him away.

¹ I will praise the LORD at all times.
I will constantly speak his praises.
² I will boast only in the LORD;
let all who are helpless take heart.
³ Come, let us tell of the LORD'S greatness;
let us exalt his name together.

⁴ I prayed to the LORD, and he answered me.
He freed me from all My fears.
⁵ Those who look to him for help will be radiant with joy;
no shadow of shame will darken their faces.
⁶ In My desperation I prayed, and the LORD listened;
he saved me from all My troubles.
⁷ For the angel of the LORD is a guard;
he surrounds and defends all who fear him.

⁸ Taste and see that the LORD is good.
Oh, the joys of those who take refuge in him!
⁹ Fear the LORD, you his godly people,

for those who fear him will have all they need.
¹⁰ Even strong young lions sometimes go hungry,
but those who trust in the LORD will lack no good thing.

¹¹ Come, My children, and listen to me,
and I will teach you to fear the LORD.
¹² Does anyone want to live a life
that is long and prosperous?
¹³ Then keep your tongue from speaking evil
and your lips from telling lies!
¹⁴ Turn away from evil and do good.
Search for peace, and work to maintain it.

¹⁵ The eyes of the LORD watch over those who do right;
his ears are open to their cries for help.
¹⁶ But the LORD turns his face against those who do evil;
he will erase their memory from the earth.
¹⁷ The LORD hears his people when they call to him for help.
He rescues them from all their troubles.
¹⁸ The LORD is close to the brokenhearted;
he rescues those whose spirits are crushed.

¹⁹ The righteous person faces many troubles,
but the LORD comes to the rescue each time.
²⁰ For the LORD protects the bones of the righteous;
not one of them is broken!

²¹ Calamity will surely overtake the wicked,
and those who hate the righteous will be punished.
²² But the LORD will redeem those who serve him.
No one who takes refuge in him will be condemned.

Psalm 37

A psalm of David

¹ Don't worry about the wicked
or envy those who do wrong.
² For like grass, they soon fade away.
Like spring flowers, they soon wither.

³ Trust in the LORD and do good.
Then you will live safely in the land and prosper.
⁴ Take delight in the LORD,
and he will give you your heart's desires.

⁵ Commit everything you do to the LORD.
Trust him, and he will help you.
⁶ He will make your innocence radiate like the dawn,
and the justice of your cause will shine like the noonday sun.

⁷ Be still in the presence of the LORD,
and wait patiently for him to act.
Don't worry about evil people who prosper
or fret about their wicked schemes.

⁸ Stop being angry!
Turn from your rage!
Do not lose your temper—
it only leads to harm.
⁹ For the wicked will be destroyed,
but those who trust in the LORD will possess the land.

¹⁰ Soon the wicked will disappear.
Though you look for them, they will be gone.
¹¹ The lowly will possess the land
and will live in peace and prosperity.

¹² The wicked plot against the godly;
they snarl at them in defiance.
¹³ But the Lord just laughs,
for he sees their day of judgment coming.

¹⁴ The wicked draw their swords
and string their bows
to kill the poor and the oppressed,
to slaughter those who do right.
¹⁵ But their swords will stab their own hearts,
and their bows will be broken.

¹⁶ It is better to be godly and have little
than to be evil and rich.
¹⁷ For the strength of the wicked will be shattered,
but the LORD takes care of the godly.

¹⁸ Day by day the LORD takes care of the innocent,
and they will receive an inheritance that lasts forever.
¹⁹ They will not be disgraced in hard times;
even in famine they will have more than enough.

²⁰ But the wicked will die.
The LORD'S enemies are like flowers in a field—
they will disappear like smoke.

²¹ The wicked borrow and never repay,
but the godly are generous givers.
²² Those the LORD blesses will possess the land,
but those he curses will die.

²³ The LORD directs the steps of the godly.
He delights in every detail of their lives.
²⁴ Though they stumble, they will never fall,
for the LORD holds them by the hand.

²⁵ Once I was young, and now I am old.
Yet I have never seen the godly abandoned
or their children begging for bread.
²⁶ The godly always give generous loans to others,
and their children are a blessing.

27 Turn from evil and do good,
and you will live in the land forever.
28 For the LORD loves justice,
and he will never abandon the godly.

He will keep them safe forever,
but the children of the wicked will die.
29 The godly will possess the land
and will live there forever.

30 The godly offer good counsel;
they teach right from wrong.
31 They have made God's law their own,
so they will never slip from his path.

32 The wicked wait in ambush for the godly,
looking for an excuse to kill them.
33 But the LORD will not let the wicked succeed
or let the godly be condemned when they are put on trial.

34 Put your hope in the LORD.
Travel steadily along his path.
He will honor you by giving you the land.
You will see the wicked destroyed.

35 I have seen wicked and ruthless people
flourishing like a tree in its native soil.
36 But when I looked again, they were gone!
Though I searched for them, I could not find them!

37 Look at those who are honest and good,
for a wonderful future awaits those who love peace.
38 But the rebellious will be destroyed;
they have no future.

39 The LORD rescues the godly;
he is their fortress in times of trouble.

40 The LORD helps them,
rescuing them from the wicked.
He saves them,
and they find shelter in him.

January 17, 2012

I Have Seen It All

You have been faithful through the hurts and the pains, abused and in bondage. The enemy kept you bound, but now you are free. You are free to love in Me. You are free to serve Me; no limits.

Do not let fear bind you, for I know the plans I have for you, plans to prosper you. I remove people you have counted on and become dependent upon; your trust in them was misguided. They took your love and trust, and twisted it into bondage. They said you were not worthy, that you were unlovable. Instead of celebrating your accomplishments and victories with you, they called you unworthy. They turned things around and made it about them instead of allowing you to enjoy victory.

The Lord your God has seen. I have seen it all. I am not blind to the lives and hearts of man. I know every thought, every misdeed, and every plot and plan against you. Cry mercy for the enemy who rose up against the one true God. Cry mercy for the words that pierce like swords through the hearts of My beloved ones. Cry mercy, for I have seen your tears, hurt and pain. I have seen your despair as you huddled in a corner from the onslaught of words sent to accuse, berate, and derail your confidence in Me.

I have seen the faithful wobble under the mighty weight of burdens and bondage heaped upon them. I have seen you standing when others would have fallen. I have seen the mighty become weak, and the weak become strong. I have seen it all. There is nothing new under the sun.

I hold you and sustain you. My angels wield the sword before you to clear the way. They are your fore guard and rear guard.

Your mighty God is with you. Stand strong and tall. Hold your head high and see the deliverance of your God. The wicked will not triumph. The righteous are upheld by My mighty right hand. You will see the victory.

January 21, 2012

YOU WILL NEVER WALK ALONE

I am the Lord your God and you will never walk alone. I am by your side on this journey and I will not abandon you. You cannot lose Me or become separated from Me. I cling to you closer than a brother. You are never alone; step-by-step we travel this journey together. You cannot out run Me.

Listen! The night is long and the days are short before the near coming of the Son of Man on the clouds of glory. Look up, for your redemption draws nigh.

Troubled times are here. The love of many has waxed cold. Hardhearted people have hearts of stone. They have made of themselves deaf and dumb idols, worshiping their very own flesh. Their eyes are blind. They cannot see what is going on around them unless it will glorify their flesh. To idols of sticks and stones they bow, sacrificing themselves upon the altar of self-pleasure and perversion.

They seek to justify their actions. Their lips speak empty words and promises. Lies proceed from their mouths like venom-coated sugar. They hurt those around them by their self-seeking ways, vindictive in heart and mind, always looking for the payback. Looking to justify their actions and taking no responsibility, they blame all around them. I have spoken yet they are deaf to My call. Thinking themselves wise, they are fools lined up for the slaughter. I show them truth, but they see it not. They are blind to My Word and My ways, though I exhibit Myself all around them.

Do not be discouraged in well doing, for out of the mouths of angels speak words of strength to overcome the darkness. Your redemption draws nigh from the enemy of your soul. Rise up and fight the good fight of faith. Depend upon Me for all things.

In this season, be still and know that I am God. Wield the sword of My Word. All good things come to those who wait. As you wait upon the Lord, your strength will be renewed and you will soar on eagle's wings to new heights where the enemy who sought you can never reach. In this season, you will be above and beyond where you need to be to achieve the victory.

People come and people go. Haman has lived among you and he will receive the same fate as he planned for you. Reversals abound; reversals of fortune, reversals of hearts and minds, reversals of man's plots and plans. They cannot curse what I have blessed. Like Baalam, they will stand to curse, but will be made to bless.

Watch Me turn your situation upside down. All will know that I am your God, and you are My people. You have been set apart to fulfill your destiny. Broaden your focus. It has been too narrow; too concerned with yourself and your circumstances. Ask Me, and I will begin to unravel the picture that is your future.

January 21, 2013

DREAM GIVER

I am the God of Israel, and your fore-fathers, who came before you. I am all but forgotten by many in My own land, a land I set aside. This land I am returning to when the Mount of Olives splits. Every eye shall be focused on the eastern sky, and with a shout, pomp and circumstance, all of nature will announce My arrival. I am coming on the clouds and there will be thundering and signs from above. I will announce My presence among you.

Many will run in fear as they look upon whom they pierced as Heaven and nature sing praises to the King. I will rule with a rod of iron. Nothing will be hidden from My view, for I know the hearts of men. Every eye will see and every tongue will confess that I am Lord, Master of all, King of the Universe.

Today I speak to My children, the ones who seek after My heart, seeking Me in Spirit and in truth. You are Mine; heart of My heart. My heart beats within your chest, for I reside in you. I will never leave you nor forsake you. I formed you in your mother's womb and gave you the desires of your heart. I am the dream giver.

Tonight, I anoint your head with oil. I speak blessings over you. I set My angels to guard you. They go before and behind you. I give you new armor, for the armor you have been wearing is worn and you are battle weary. Receive My refreshing. Let My rest strengthen you for the battles to come. The enemy comes at you with great anger.

Fear not, little flock, remnant of My people. You have remained faithful, reserved for Myself. You have not bowed your knee to Baal. Receive My strengthening as I heal your wounds and bruises. I heal your mind of the words that play over and over in your thoughts, spoken by those who know not what they do. I bring healing to you.

Do not think it is strange the trials you endure, for they are not uncommon to those who dedicate their lives to Me.

Persecution reveals what is within you. You will either bow to the bullying and persecution or remain silent. You will conform to those who desire to shut your mouth, or you will be stronger and bolder, walking in more power and authority. Have I not assured you that nothing shall by any means harm you? I have given you authority over serpents and scorpions, and the poison they spew. They can kill your body, they can destroy your strength of mind, but they cannot pluck you from My hand. You are mine, sealed with Holy Spirit, marked for My kingdom. To God be the glory, amen.

January 24, 2012

WISDOM OF THE AGES

Trust Me. Listen to Me, let Me speak to you in the midnight hours, for My wisdom is the wisdom of the ages, not based on man's whim or popular culture. Go in peace My child, resting in Me, for your God is the God of great mercy, who sees and hears, and is intimately involved in the lives of His children. Your cares, are My cares, and your hurts and pains are felt by Me, for We are intimately tied together in heart and mind.

Tune in your thoughts to Me. Train your thoughts to hear what the Spirit of the Lord is saying. I love My children, why do you harden your hearts and your minds to Me? Thinking in all of man's wisdom you know the answers, that you know Me, the one who cannot truly be known; the infinite One and God of the ages. Infinite...in – finite, meaning cannot be understood with the finite mind.

Stop speaking as if you can really know Me or understand My ways, for My ways are not your ways, My ways are higher than your ways. Climb the highest mountain and still you will not be able to see or hear the thoughts of man. Reverence and awe are My due, but I have been reduced to terms man can comprehend. How little man knows is evident every time he thinks he has a small part figured out and it just opens the door to more questions. Awestruck, you should be. It is time to bring reverence back to a Holy God, instead of your familiarity which breeds disrespect and dishonor. If you understood, you would fear the Lord your God with a healthy fear.

Return to Me, all you who are heavy laden. Lay down your burdens in this life and trade your heart of stone for a heart of flesh; soft and pliable, made clean and whole by the blood of the lamb and completely Mine. All of you who wrestle with Me, whether you can serve Me or not, or trust Me or not...give up the fight, for there is nothing on this earth that you can trust to fulfill your heart's desires, let alone your very life.

Come to attention those of you who are lax and lazy, serving Me only when it is convenient and fits into your schedule, or sandwiches between your selfish desires. I am a God who demands more than that. I demand your whole heart, your whole mind, and your whole body be yielded in submission to Me. Not parts and parts together to form a whole; I want the whole being. I desire your whole heart, whole mind, whole soul and body in complete surrender.

Do not be deceived; those who tell you I am not a Holy God to be feared are not of Me. Those who say My grace covers everything are telling you half-truths. Those who tell you that you can live like the world understand Me not. You are called to be holy people, set aside by your love for and desire to serve Me, so all will know you are My children. If the world does not recognize that you are My child, then you must ask yourself...are you truly My child?

All knew whom the Israelites were when they went into battle. All knew that I was their God, and the advancement of their army struck fear into the hearts of men. When was the last time an army of My people, preparing, gathering, or advancing a cause near and dear to My heart struck fear within the hearts of anyone?

What is missing? Is it the amats (boldness), the battle cry, "Rak chazak," or is it fear and reverence...a community, unified in purpose to be obedient to the Lord on a broader scale? A community designed to open the eyes of your heart that you may see what is going on around you so you may hear not just instructions as individuals, but as a corporate body designed to wage war?

The government is changing. The fear of not knowing the way out is opening a door to My Spirit to unleash a tidal wave of My living water in the hearts, and minds of the leaders. Get in line to push through this wave of change. Prepare your hearts and minds and pray. Intercede for the godly change, for seven years of peace or seven years of war (spiritual).

I can hear the cries of My people, but the choice is yours as My body of believers. The anguish of nations not knowing the way out rests upon your choices to come together in one voice to proclaim My change to the hearts and the minds of men.

February 4, 2012

DO NOT ABANDON YOUR POST

I am the Lord your God. Trust Me, My child. Trust Me with all; every hurt and pain, every issue you face, for the Lord your God is one God, all knowing, all powerful and holds all that is, in the palm of My hand. If I can hold the universe and set the laws in motion, something bigger than you can fathom, I can also handle your problems and every minute aspect of your life, for I am intimately involved with every detail.

Decisions you make set wheels in motion. Each decision causes an action and an equal and opposite reaction, which is why you meet resistance when you step out in faith. I am the God of faith. I respond to your faith in Me when you obey and trust that I know what is best to fulfill the plans I have created for you before the foundations of time.

So many have walked away from Me and from My plan for their lives, thinking in all their human wisdom they know best. They have rebelled against My will and My Word. Walking away, abandoning wives, husbands and children, seeking selfish desires and even using My name to justify their actions. I hate being used this way. My Word and Name being used to justify evil acts as if I condone the lust of the flesh and rebellion.

Repent, you who claim to know Me, who claim to know My Word, who claim to be My child, yet have dealt treacherously with your family, the wife of your youth, and gone your own way. When the going gets tough, instead of rising up to fight those demonic powers you have been given authority over in the Name of Jesus, a Name for which they tremble, you roll over, abandon your post, surrender your family to the enemy...all on the altar of self as if it were not your God given responsibility to fight.

Men you are head of your household, but many of you are missing in action. Your wife cannot depend on you; your children cannot trust you. Instead of protecting your family, you just handed them over, yet you think I approve?

There will be a day of reckoning. Have you not read in My Word your responsibilities? Your wife is not your property to control and abuse. She is your helpmeet, a partner in marriage. She brings her own needs and perspectives to the union. Without her, the union is not whole.

You are not to abuse your wife. She is given to you to love as I love My Church; a threefold cord, a covenant partner. I set the example of how to treat your wife. I do not abuse you or leave you. I hold you securely in My mighty right hand.

There is too much justification of your enemy's agenda. Money and selfishness are not reasons for divorce. Did you ever inquire of Me? Did you ever trust Me for the solution before you took it upon yourself to break a holy union, an established covenant? Instead of trusting Me and standing in faith you effectively placed your family in the path of a speeding train; in the lion's den, exposed without a covering.

Turn back from your wicked ways. Have you not heard you would reap what you sow? The forces of evil have been unleashed and are in great fury in the spirit. They "see" a battle won in the hearts and the minds of man to forsake the ways of God. They are running to the finish line.

Do not be deceived and do not justify your actions. The stakes are very high; far higher than the enemy would have you believe. Do not leave nor forsake your God or My ways. Deception is rampant. Blinded eyes and ears deaf to My ways speak from mouths reporting, "Oh I can do what I want, I'll repent later." It is the cry of the enemy's heart to deceive the hearts of man into getting his way; lying and manipulating so that it all sounds just right to the ears of man.

Truth will be exposed. All that is in the dark will be exposed to the light. All that is hidden will be revealed. Do not abandon your post. Do not be deceived by the enemy. Do not be deceived by your own heart. There looks a way right to man but it is not a way right to God.

February 7, 2012

Learn My Ways

The winds of change are blowing through your life and I hear the sound of rain. Change bringing you higher in Me. Level to level and glory to glory in My Spirit, change is inevitable. People come and people go but I am the Lord your God who never leaves you nor forsakes you. This season is about change; changes are in your midst. Things are shaking as I remove everything in your life not founded on the rock of your salvation.

People have set themselves up in your life as your provider, your confidant, your deliver and even your friend, yet their motives are not always pure. I am shaking those relationships now, in the midst of greater shaking of nations not knowing the way out. People who have set themselves up in their own mind as "god" in your life will see that you serve the one true God and their attempts to manipulate you will be thwarted.

I am your God, giver of all good things, Creator of all. So many think they know what is best for you; I, the Lord God alone, know what is best for you. My sons and daughters, look to Me, not man, and see the deliverance of your Lord. People are confused, even ones who claim to serve Me. They are looking to man and themselves to bring the answers; never seeking Me first for guidance, direction and wisdom. If any man lacks wisdom he just needs to ask. Why go off searching for man's wisdom when godly counsel is available from the Creator of all? God have mercy as foolishness abounds in the hearts and the minds of man. What looks like foolishness to man is wise in My eyes. Step by step follow Me. Listen for My voice of instruction and obey. Follow Me in word and deed.

It's always darkest before the dawn, so hang on to Me. Anguish of nations not knowing the way out; they do not cry mercy to Me, still looking for their own solutions. Do not be one of these. Cry mercy before My throne. The enemy is attacking, warfare is increasing. Where you were silent you cannot afford to be silent. Where you spoke, you will have to be silent and not attempt to vindicate yourself. You must listen for My Spirit and obey. Speak, fight, and be silent when told. Let Me fight for you. Like computer animation, you are an extension of Me. When the operator moves, the character on the screen responds with the same movement that is how we should move, together in unison ~ My instruction immediately responded to.

Spend time in My presence and learn to hear. Learn to see what the Spirit is saying and doing and follow suit. Time is short and the stakes are high. Many are falling away. Many who claim to know Me do not. Like a dog going back to his vomit, they cannot keep up the pretense any longer that they serve Me. There is no fruit, no true love in their heart. Concerned with appearances rather than substance and truth, they give the appearance of a relationship with Me, but I tell you I know them not. They refuse to allow My Spirit and Word to change them. Happy and content with the way they are. Sitting in church wasting time in order to create an appearance that makes them feel better about themselves and their true heart motives.

I see past the outer appearances, I see the heart of stone in the chest of man. Let Me replace your heart of stone with a heart of flesh that is soft and pliable to Me. It is what you desire but you cannot surrender. The pride of life blinds you and you seek to justify your actions, words, and behaviors, but the correct response is surrender; unconditional surrender to the Lord your God, for I am God of all I created. Help Me to help you. Help Me to bless you. You cannot stand in defiance to Me and My Word with a stony heart and expect Me to move on your behalf. If you do what I require, I will do what I have promised. Too many expect blessing just because they are created by Me, but that is not how things work. "You owe Me" does not work with Me. Man created a system of blessing and entitlement mentality, but that is not My way. I do not bless just because one is breathing if he is slothful and lazy. Learn My ways. Surrender to Me, the Lord your God. Heed My ways.

February 8, 2012

VICTORY CRY

I am the Lord your God and today I say shout the victory cry over all of your circumstances, over every enemy that has risen up against you. I am about to intervene in the circumstances which have had you bound, living with pain and rejection, for I want My children free. Rise up in your spirit and hold your head high. Prepare for battle with the confidence of David who challenged, "Who dares rise up against the Lord My God? My God is with me!" Stir it up inside yourself. Stand in confidence.

My angels surround you and victory is assured when you are in Me. The enemy has had the upper hand in the lives of many of My children for too long. I am exposing the deeds being completed behind your back to sabotage and to destroy you. Many of you will be hurt by the revelations coming forward from darkness into the light, but as I said yesterday, I am dealing with relationships in your life, and many set themselves up as "gods" in your life to keep you looking at, and in bondage to, them.

Victory is here, but there will be a trail of broken hearts as these exposures come forth. Be quick to forgive, be quick to love, but do not go back into bondage when I set you free. Change your mind-set. Many will leave you when the exposure is made. Do not be sad, for these things must come into your life to be dealt with to move into the next season. There are those going with you and those who are not. Seek My discernment in the future as Jezebel lays many traps and leaves many victims in her wake. Be set free in Me to fulfill your destiny. Hearts and minds are being exposed with motives that are not pure. Cleanse yourselves from all unrighteousness and seek Me with a pure, undefiled heart, in worship and praise. The door is open to the temple. Kneel before My throne of grace.

Show mercy for those who have been deceived; the enemy prowls around like a roaring lion, seeking for whom he may devour. The roars are loud, you can feel the hot breath, but I will shut the mouths of the lions and the Lion of Judah will come roaring through you in all My power and authority to silence those who have sought to destroy you. They have met their match. They picked on the wrong person; ME, because I live in you!

You are an extension of Me and you are no longer going to be feeling the sense of defeat you have felt in these past seasons. Rise up all that is within you and establish who you are in Me. David, you are not too small, you are not too young nor too old; you are My warrior King, destined for greatness in My Kingdom and no Goliath can defeat you when you come against him in My Name.

Shout the battle cry! You, My child, fight in the name of the Lord your God. Victory is sure, victory is won and when you defeat this giant who has been taunting you in the name of the God you serve, the rest will flee. The strongman is out front, mocking and shouting to intimidate you into running or surrendering, but I am with you. Run boldly toward the giant in My name and finish him off.

February 11, 2012

SING PRAISES

The Lord your God loves you with an everlasting love. I sing praises over My faithful ones who obey and do My will as they bow their hearts and heads in worship and praise to their King.

Does it sound funny to you that I praise My children? You bring such joy to My heart, My faithful ones. Your Father looks down on you with joy. I rejoice over you with singing and I long to spend time listening to you; your hopes, dreams, and fears. I know that even with your expressions of doubt, in your heart you are resolute to stand with Me, come what may. It's funny how you express a fleeting doubt, yet I see your heart, and you stand in faith. Faith that I am your Abba Father, that I am your all and all, that I am your provider, your redeemer; the author and finisher of your faith.

So is the nature of man; I am your Abba Father. I am your deliverer and your protection. I am the provider of all good things. The seasons have been tough. Fear and doubt have crept in. People are falling out of faith; trusting in man rather than Me. Their hearts will faint out of fear for what befalls the earth, but you, My child, are safe in My arms.

People make decisions to know Me or refuse Me. With lip service they bring Me onto the altar of self-pride, but I do not want lip service. I want a heart completely mine; A heart that grieves over what I grieve over, and rejoices over what I rejoice over. I seek a heart that discerns the things of God, a heart that looks above and beyond the natural and sees the finished work of Christ in all those around them. A heart completely mine, that longs to see as I see, to hear as I hear, and to love as I love; not with the world's definition of love, as tolerance, but God love that speaks the truth kindly while pulling people off the wrong road and ushering them to right path. It is a love that does not condone sin, yet helps them work through sin issues into freedom. It is a love that does not condemn or condone them, but longs to see man set free in Me.

Listen to me, My child, and do not let the words of the enemy condemn you. My soft-hearted ones who long to hear the voice of your Father, I see. I see everything. I have cried with you over the hurts and the pain, the lies and deceit you have faced; I understand, as I endured the same thing. When you cry, I cry. When you love, I love through you. When you tell the truth, My truth is in you. When you speak My Word, My Word comes to life. You live in Me and I live in you...we tabernacle as One.

February 12, 2012

GO IN PEACE

Go in peace, My child, My peace. Not the false peace the world offers, for they cannot guarantee you tomorrow, let alone your next breath. My peace I leave for you; My peace that surpasses all understanding. Choose to walk in My peace. Let it envelope you as the warmth of the sun on a cold day. The night is long and the day is well spent. Kingdoms are rising and falling, and there is anguish of nations not knowing the way out.

My peace I leave with you to see you through the difficult times. It is the underlying current that wells up, whispering, "I don't know how, but I know I am going to be okay." This peace comes from trusting Me to fulfill your destiny in Me.

Do not look right. Do not look left. Look at Me. Abba knows best. I can see what is coming next as the nation's line up and the people take sides; the fence line is clearing of people going to the right or the left. Do not fear, My child. Go in peace, for these things must happen. The night is long and the day is short till the coming of the Son of man on the clouds of glory. Know that your future is in My hands. Not one hair will fall from your head without My permission. Trust Me in all things, even when you do not understand, for I am the God who rejoices over you with singing. My love for you is extravagant.

Trust Me in all things. I only desire to do good to you and bring you safely home, but you must understand the world does not love you, just as it does not love Me. They persecuted Me and recognized Me not, and they will persecute you. A servant is not greater than his master, but I set the example and you can do all things in Me.

February 14, 2012

BE STILL

Behold! Be still! I am with you! I am your God who heals you. I saw your every heart break. I held it in My hands, for I am the God of all comfort who is near you. I saw! I saw it all! It was not directed at you, but at the Spirit of God Who lives in you.

The darkness overcomes the light, it seems, in a season, but the light of My love and presence can never be extinguished. I am the light of the world, and all things will bow before Me on that dreadful day of the Lord. It is a fearful thing to fall into the hands of a Holy God and not be in right standing before Him.

I weep when My children weep and I rejoice when they rejoice. I am with you, My child. I am with you. I will never leave you nor forsake you. I am with you in the midnight hours. I am with you when you feel alone. You are *never* alone. When the world rejects you, I am with you. When those around you do not understand you or appreciate you, I do! It is going to be all right. Whatever you are going through, it is going be all right, for I am in the midst of all, working it out for My glory. Just choose to be still and know that I am God, the God of your todays and your tomorrows. The God who heals you, yes, it is I, your Abba Father, who speaks comfort to you.

Rest, stop striving. Go when I say go, stay when I say stay. You are coming out of the bondage that held you. You will look for the enemy, but he will not be found. Soar in My spirit as an eagle soars. Rise above the fray and soar peacefully in the stillness and quiet, riding on the winds of My Spirit. Soar to great heights in Me. Leave it all behind; gain a different perspective, a higher perspective, My perspective. Count it all joy when you fall into various trials for this is a temporary affliction. Evil will not prosper. Be still and know that I am God.

February 16, 2012

THE HAMMER

The victory assured. The hammer has fallen and the case closed in Heaven's court. I have already decided; the angels are in motion. The stage is set for victory. Where the enemy thought he would prosper, he will fail. Where he thought the victory was sure, the tables are about to be turned. I resist pride, arrogance, and a haughty heart. When they rise up, they rise up against Me.

When will you figure out that when you do things I detest and act that way, you are not rising up against other people, you are in fact rebelling; rising up against Me, for I am God of all. You come into rebellion against Me and My ways. It is so easy to believe poorly and think it is nothing, but understand, how you treat others, what you do or do not do to represents Me, reflects on Me.

You are Me on this earth. You are My advocate, just as I am your advocate before the Father in Heaven. Just as an attorney represents you in a court of law, speaks for you, defends you, you do the same for Me before those I place around you every day. How do you represent Me? How good an advocate are you? Are lives being changed because I live in you? Would you pay an attorney who represents you the way you represent Me?

Hearts touched, lives changed for My glory and power of My name. Conviction to make My agenda yours upon the earth. The days are getting darker and the night will be long; there are many hurting people to reach with My love and mercy. Changed lives from hopeless to hopeful, from lonely to belonging, from unloved to loved by the power of My blood and the cross. Lives will change.

Life is changing. The hammer has fallen in Heaven's court and My people have been found wanting. Do not keep your love to yourself. Proclaim My name, changing one life at a time. Let Salvation ring!

February 19, 2012

NEW BEGINNINGS

It is the time of new beginnings. Trust Me to bring you through. All is well My child, all is well; I will never leave you or forsake you. I am the God of your Fathers and I love you. People will come and go, but I will never leave you. Trust Me for a new beginning. Hope abounds. Wipe your tears. How long will you mourn Saul?

February 20, 2012

MY REMNANT

I am the Lord your God and the Son shines brightly on My children, for I am the light of the world, a light to nations, the salvation of man. Kingdoms come and kingdoms go, but the kingdom of God endures, standing through it all.

My hand is upon you, My child. What I have established no man shall put asunder. Man devises plans in his own mind that seem so grandiose. Man plans, not including Me, as if he can control his next breath, let alone a promise for tomorrow. The best laid plans of mice and men as they say, but a plan founded on Me, a firm foundation, in obedience to My will and My ways, will prosper through time indefinite; eternal purposes for the kingdom.

Your God is with you, My child. I am not a God of flesh and blood, nor sticks and stones. I am alive in you and I have come to bring you home. Feel My heart beat in your chest? You are alive in Me. Breathe Me in. Let My Spirit rest upon you afresh and anew, for I have come so you may have life and life more abundant. The world's ways are not My ways and the differences are becoming widely apparent, for where can you go that sin does not abound? Even inside the "church," sin abounds. They know Me not.

My remnant, I hear you crying out. Rise up in Me and see the salvation of your God, for behold I make all things new, and today I renew your heart in Me. I give you fresh dreams and revelations which are mine to share, not with all, but a few. I selected a few to go with Me to higher heights and greater glory. The three went with Me to the mount and they saw My glory; the others did not see. Secrets I long to impart to you, new and deeper revelation of My Word. As My words come to life on the pages I share with My faithful few, not all eyes will see and understand; not all eyes will enter in, for they see Me not.

The times they are changing. Behold I make all things new in the lives of My devoted, called out ones, whom I have selected, and set aside in a time of preparation for such a time as this. You will emerge from your cocoons. A glimpse of My glory will change you; it will provoke fear in the hearts of many as it did the Israelites.

People will look to you knowing you have been with Me. They will look for answers, prayer and intercession; point the way to Me. Preach the basics, as the apostles did. Do not deviate from My message. It is the same message. It has not changed. Tell them I love them, but cannot tolerate their sins. Share with them that I desire all to "Come to the cross and let Me free you, it is only then you can get a glimpse of My love for you."

Surrender. The key is surrender; surrender to the Lord your God for the hour is late, and the time is short and there is much to accomplish upon the earth. Rise up My faithful remnant. Call yourselves blessed.

February 21, 2012

TRUST ME MY CHILD

Trust Me, My child, trust Me. All is not lost. Transitions are always difficult. It is in these times I draw you closer to Myself. You must trust Me to work it all out for your good and My glory. The times, they are changing, and if you cannot trust Me now, how will you trust Me through what is to come upon the earth?

February 24, 2012

ANGELS GATHERING

Today I had to go to the store. I was coming down Countyline Road, when I saw a huge flock of white birds. They looked like sea gulls to the north. They were flying in a circle, diving and looping. They were beautiful.

I looked to the south, and there was another flock of white birds flying in a similar pattern. When I arrived at the end of the street, another flock flew into the city.

This is NOT a common sight here.

I pondered, "Lord, you must be trying to tell me something here?"

He said the angels were gathering, and I knew in My spirit it was for battle.

I am not sure what that all means or looks like, but I think this goes along with the previous word about the new beginnings; there is a shift in the Spirit and God is admonishing us to trust the Lord.

February 25, 2012

PREPARE FOR BATTLE

The Angels are gathering. The wheels are in motion. The troops assembled. Prepare for battle. Prepare for war. Good and evil, right and wrong, truth and falsehoods square off.

The battle is for the hearts and minds of the next generation. Vulnerable, they have been raised with lies and know no other way; thinking the lies are normal, when societal lies are anything, but normal.

They fight for wrong, thinking it is right. They denounce right, thinking it is wrong. A backwards and perverse generation that needs to come into line with the truth of My Word, to reverse the tide willingly and knowingly rather than out of fear from what befalls the earth.

February 26, 2012

I HEAR YOUR HEART

I hear your heart. I hear you crying. I feel your heart breaking, but you have not lost faith in Me. Your heart still sings to Me. It's a new song. Out of brokenness comes victory. Out of humility, I can move. You cling to Me and I cling to you; I will not let you go. I will not let you dash your foot against a stone, for I am the arms that uphold you. I am the arms that love you.

Go in peace, My child, go in peace. I will never leave you nor forsake you. I am the one who clings closer to you than a brother. My right hand uplifts you. Do not fear the threats by day and evil by night, for they will not come near thy dwelling. Those who oppose you, oppose Me. You will face persecution for My namesake. The road is long, and many are tired and battle weary. I am sending reinforcements. They will listen for you to speak My Word. Go forth.

Psalm 34:

I will bless the LORD at all times;
His praise shall continually be in my mouth.
² My soul shall make its boast in the LORD;
The humble shall hear of it and be glad.
³ Oh, magnify the LORD with me,
And let us exalt His name together.

⁴ I sought the LORD, and He heard me,
And delivered me from all my fears.
⁵ They looked to Him and were radiant,
And their faces were not ashamed.
⁶ This poor man cried out, and the LORD heard him,
And saved him out of all his troubles.
⁷ The angel of the LORD encamps

all around those who fear Him,
And delivers them.

⁸ Oh, taste and see that the LORD is good;
Blessed is the man who trusts in Him!
⁹ Oh, fear the LORD, you His saints!
There is no want to those who fear Him.
¹⁰ The young lions lack and suffer hunger;
But those who seek the LORD shall not lack any good thing.

¹¹ Come, you children, listen to me;
I will teach you the fear of the LORD.
¹² Who is the man who desires life,
And loves many days, that he may see good?
¹³ Keep your tongue from evil,
And your lips from speaking deceit.
¹⁴ Depart from evil and do good;
Seek peace and pursue it.

¹⁵ The eyes of the LORD are on the righteous,
And His ears are open to their cry.
¹⁶ The face of the LORD is against those who do evil,
To cut off the remembrance of them from the earth.

¹⁷ The righteous cry out, and the LORD hears,
And delivers them out of all their troubles.
¹⁸ The LORD is near to those who have a broken heart,
And saves such as have a contrite spirit.

¹⁹ Many are the afflictions of the righteous,
But the LORD delivers him out of them all.
²⁰ He guards all his bones;
Not one of them is broken.
²¹ Evil shall slay the wicked,
And those who hate the righteous shall be condemned.
²² The LORD redeems the soul of His servants,
And none of those who trust in Him shall be condemned.

February 26, 2012

THE ANGELS ARE GATHERING CONTINUED

The Angels are gathering. The night is falling. There is confusion of nations; not knowing the way out, anguish of hearts and minds.

Look to the one true God. He is the only way out. The only way out is a changed mind-set. The only way to be really free, is to be free in Me, even in the midst of bondage.

The Angels are gathering. Fear will grip the heart of man. Anguish of nations, not knowing the way out, nations cannot save themselves. No amount of talking, no laws, no policy, will be able see their way clear of what befalls the land.

Pray for the leaders. Pray that blind eyes be open, for they cannot legislate their way clear of the situation. They must seek the One, true God, for it is only My hand that can change the tide of policies that have sought to destroy this nation I have blessed. Your own leaders have pronounced judgment on this nation. Your own leaders must humble themselves and seek My face.

I hear the cries of My remnant. Rise up and stop thinking. Act upon your convictions and speak. There is a man seeking My heart and the choice will be black and white, right and wrong, for Me or not; the hearts of the people will be exposed. One way is blessing and one way is cursing. Do you recognize Me when you see Me? Do you recognize Me when I am speaking through a person? Do you recognize Me at work in the world today?

I still choose to use people. There are many true and false voices speaking. Many did not recognize My chosen. They did not recognize Me when I walked the earth. My chosen will be persecuted and even killed. Are you ready to speak? Are you ready for what will befall the earth? Will you stand when others fall?

The time does not have to be yet; the earth has a chance to pick a different path ~ a path that leads back to Me. A decision is coming. That decision will choose which future this nation will walk; to continue on the path you have been on for the past four years, or choose a new path that will lead back to Me, the one true God. The choice is clear; the decision is yours.

February 27, 2012

DRY BONES WILL COME TO LIFE

I am the Lord, your God. Your King of all desires to bless you. The tide is turning in your life. In the midst of chaos, this is a new season, a new beginning. The Angels are gathering. They will soon take flight to meet you in the darkest night of your soul. I will bring resurrection power and resurrect those things you thought were dead.

The dry bones will come to life. They will live again to declare the glory of your God. The dry places became bleak, but the rivers of living water will begin to flow into those places in your heart that were parched. You will live again. The enemy sought to distract you, derail you, even to destroy you.

Where you were bound in shackles, you will be set free. The enemy of your soul did his best to keep you in bondage, but you are free in Me. To resurrect the dead places in your soul, I bring life. I bring light to the darkness, to set you ablaze with the fire of My Spirit; to love and be loved. Let love take flight. Do not fear to love again.

Cry mercy for the ones who sought your life. Cry mercy for their eternal being. Cry mercy for them to love and be loved by the Lord, their God. Cry mercy, for the enemy of their soul is seeking whom he can devour and they are blind to the bondage they live in and join in with others.

Break free! Break free of the old mind-sets, old ways of seeing your world. Be surrendered to Me and wait. Watch, and you will see the glory of the Lord surround and invade your circumstances. Break free and run to the Lord your God. I will send the warriors to fight for you while I protect you in My arms.

The war is won, but the battles still rage here and there. Stand strong. Stand tall and see the deliverance of your Lord.

February 28, 2012

WILL YOU TRUST ME

I am the Lord your God and I have your best interests at heart. I know what is best. Will you trust Me in this? Will you trust Me in this entire situation you find yourself in, even though you cannot find your way and all seems confused?

Will you trust Me? Will you trust Me to heal you? Will you trust Me to save you from the enemy's hand? Will you trust Me with your very life and all that you have? Will you trust that the Lord your God knows best, that the Lord your God loves you? I want to know that you trust Me, even when it makes no sense and it is a struggle to stay in faith.

Jehovah your God *does* love you, My child. Trust Me to do what is right and in your best interest. Things may look like they are going in the wrong direction, but I know the end from the beginning and I made you a promise that I will work all things together for good for those who love Me.

March 1, 2012

VAPOR

I am sending My strength to your heart and mind to give you hope. Do I dare dream again, you ask? I am the God who gave you those dreams, for they reveal the desires of your heart, and it is I who gave you those desires. They are like seeds planted in your heart that you grow to discover.

Dare to dream again. Some will say, "No, it's the wrong time. No the economy is bad," but what does that have to do with Me? They may have abandoned My plans, but I still have My plans for you, and I will bring others alongside you to affect these changes. My plans do not change because of the disobedience of one man (person); all will reap what is sown, but for My mercy poured out on a humble heart.

You all have that one man (person) whom the enemy has used to do you wrong; to try and destroy My plan for your life, but I am here to say, those plans of the enemy will not prosper. Let no bitterness take root, forgive, and you will be forgiven, for it is I, who changes the heart of man. I give grace to the humble and I am can harden a heart.

There is a window of opportunity passing by, fleeting as it may be. It is an open door to all I have to offer in the life of man. A choice must be made to accept or reject this. The life of man is but a vapor in view of eternity. A vapor...as David asked, what is man that I am mindful of him? I set before you blessing or cursing; an opportunity to accept or reject. Do you seek My hand, My face, or My heart?

March 3, 2012

SPRING FORTH O' WELL

I am the Lord your God who needs you. I need your hands and your feet to be an extension of My heart in this dry and weary land where there is no water, and the people are thirsty.

Spring forth, O well of mine! Let the living waters flow through your belly to revive the parched hearts and minds of those in need of My presence and My healing touch upon their lives. Struggling in their own strength, they plod along and their days are long; the ground is hard, for they know Me not.

It's time for a change, time for a change; a change in circumstances, a change in lives. It is time for a change in how you allow Me to move through you. Surrender your hopes and fears. Surrender all to My lead.

Obey the Lord your God and you will see the glory of your God invade your circumstances in ways you have only dreamed. Be My hands and feet. It is not over till I say it is over. Do not let the lies of the enemy deceive you and cause you to lose heart; I am is with you, My child.

Take that step of faith. In faith is where I will meet you. You will rediscover Me and see Me in new ways. The Lord your God has spoken.

March 4, 2012

BURN

Rediscover Me. Let the fire of your first love reignite in you. Burn with the passion you once felt. It is still there. The flame within you is burning. Stoke the fire. Fan the flame until you are enveloped in the fire of My Spirit; an all-consuming passion. The Lord your God desires you burn with love for Him.

March 7, 2012

UPSIDE DOWN

The Kingdom of God is upside down. If you give, you will receive. The last will be first and the least are the greatest. This is a day of upside down. Where the enemy thought you were bound, He is in for a surprise as the hidden hand of God moves in your circumstance.

I am a God of mercy and grace, and I give grace to the humble. The key to your deliverance is seeking My face. I am the Lord who loves you, the Lord who upholds you, and turns the tables that are the hearts of man. Lord, have mercy. I hear your cries and My hands are in motion. I am working behind the scenes of your life to work all out for good.

March 8, 2012

THE TRANSITION

Life as you know it is about to change. Changes are in the air; the transition, the new beginning. What I warned about is coming to fruition. Trust Me, My child, to see you through.

Where the enemy thought he would win, he will lose. Where he thought you were bound, you will be free. What he has said is a lie. What he did is inexcusable, but the Lord your God saw it all and I mete out justice. The Lord your God forgives you for giving it attention. Now, walk forward in Me, keep your eyes upon Me. I will not let the enemy win. I will pick you up when you fall. I will be with you when you lose heart and the pains of life seem insurmountable, for I understand your pain.

I can see through the eyes of eternity. I can see the end from the beginning. You won the battle. Give Me praise! Praise your way through the narrow place. Praise is the battle cry that gets the angels to mount up on your behalf. Shout from the roof tops, the Lord your God is God. He is the God of your today, your tomorrow, and even your yesterday. Shout to your God for restoration and vindication; bring My Name back into your life. I will show Myself strong. I am the lifter of your head and the holder of your hand.

Cry mercy, for the enemy of your soul has deceived many. Blind and deaf they think their actions are approved by Me, but they know Me not. My ways are not the ways of man. My kingdom is upside down. It is a foolish thing to the world, but it is My way. This is the way I intend for My people to live.

Cry mercy for the deceived ones who think they are right; I desire none will be lost, but many will be. The pride of life and arrogance prevents them from the humility I require which opens the door to receive Me. Pride of life, standing on the ways of the world rather than My Word. Cry mercy.

March 10, 2012

CONCERTO

I give you guidance and direction. I give you peace in the way you should go. The steps of a good man or woman are ordered by Me. Seek Me in the quiet place. Seek Me with your very heart. Let us connect Spirit-to-Spirit and heart-to-heart for the battle is wearying and the days are long.

How about a line change; let the weary warriors rest and I will send in My angelic reinforcements. Are you in need of a line change? Are you in need of rest?

Come to Me, all who are weary, heavy-laden and I, the Lord your God, will give you rest. Stop the worry and the striving. Lay it down at My feet. The world tells you it's all up to you. You must perform like a trained seal and meet the worldly expectations, but I am the orchestra leader of your life.

I have written a beautiful concerto for your life. You can't be a part of the orchestra and not follow My lead for you will sound like a clanging symbol rather than a beautiful symphony that makes one's heart soar, allowing you to rest in My arms.

Stop your striving. I cannot love you more than I already do. You have spent your life trying to earn the love of parents, children, and spouses, and you continue to strive to earn My love. Your Heavenly Father is not to be compared or held to the example of the world. The love you experience is but a shadow of the love I feel for you. Yield to the passion and desire I feel for you. Accept it. Stop trying to earn it.

The world would tell you that you are unworthy to receive the vastness of My love for you, but you are worthy of all I have to offer. Every good thing comes from My hand; you will not truly

130

comprehend the depth of My love for you in this life, for you have nothing to compare it with. My love for you is all-consuming, fire tempered with great gentleness and mercy, covering you like a soft blanket with My Spirit. The depth, width and height of My love cannot be measured in human standards. How can it be, when I measure the universe with the palm of My hand? When you enter into My presence, My love will overtake you. It is indescribable.

Trust Me, My battle weary warriors. Hold on tightly to the sword of My Word. God have mercy on the enemies who have risen up against My children, for your Heavenly Father loves you, and He stands watch over you. He sees all that has been done to taunt you.

The bullies are about to be silenced; the mouths of the lions shut. The "prayers" of the unrighteous rise up as a clanging symbol to My ears and interfere with My symphony, the beautiful melody of your life. I will silence your adversaries for a time, long enough for you to recover your strength, but you must use this time well. It will be short-lived, for your enemy roams around like a roaring lion and he will make his rounds.

There is no shortage of people he can use; those who willingly respond and obey his evil desires towards you. Pray for the ones who will answer when he comes, that they will be strong in that day and not yield to his wiles, schemes, and plans. Pray they will have eyes to see and ears to hear what the Spirit of the Lord is saying, and thence choose to follow the giver of life, rather than the enemy of their souls. Can you hear the music I wrote in you, telling the story of your life?

March 11, 2012

STAND

You love the Lord your God. Your love for Me will not go unrewarded. Blessed are those who follow My Word wherever He leads you. In good times and bad, I am your refuge and your hope to time indefinite.

You have had faith. You have never seen Me or touched Me yet you believe in the Lord your God. That is faith! You pray and stand through life's circumstances expecting Me to move in them. That is faith! You are unafraid to share the truth about My love, grace, and mercy. That is faith!

You love, stand, and speak, despite persecution, even among those who call themselves your brothers and sisters. You endure it all. The tears may flow, the heart may hurt, but you endure it all with a future and a hope. Standing beside Me, shoulder to shoulder in the trenches, you have come through the battles stronger than before. Face to face, you fix on Me. Heart to heart, your heart breaks when you feel mine break. You grieve when I grieve. You think it is you, but it is our connection that causes you to respond, reflecting the emotions, and the heart of the Father.

You are in Me and I am in you, a reflection of the heart of the Father. Stand! When all is lost, stand! When you do not know how you will make it, stand! When confusion fills your mind and the road is unclear, stand! When you have done all there is to do, stand!

Your Heavenly Father will see you through. He will bring streams in the desert. He will give sight to the blind man, and ears to hear. He will make a way where there seems to be no way. You serve a God of faith. I respond to faith. I give in faith. I move in faith. It is impossible to please Me without faith. Let your faith soar. Do not be afraid to dream again. Let your faith soar like a kite on a windy day. Let the string out and fly to new heights.

See the glory of the Lord descend upon your life to work all things for good. You love Me, My child. So few do. How much more do you think I love you and desire to pour out My Spirit in abundance that you may be an extension of Me upon the face of the land? Believe it. Receive it. It is the heart of your Father in Heaven toward you, My faithful ones. The love of the Lord your God is alive in your heart.

March 13, 2012

ALL IS WELL

I am the Lord your God, and all is well. It may not look like all is well, it may not feel like all is well, but if I am in it, you can be assured, all is well. Do not fret. I know things are overwhelming and the way has become unclear, but I have sent reassurance, after reassurance that I am here with you in the midst of the storm. With a word I can rebuke the wind and the waves, but how much better is it to know I am in the midst of your circumstances.

I have allowed a perfect storm to remove the debris from your life branches that have attached themselves to you, took root and are draining your resources, your time, energy, and finances. I cut those branches off, those branches that seemed to flourish, off of you. Scavengers and parasites they are; soon those who were draining your resources and nutrients, leaving you dry and thirsty, even dead inside, will be cut off from their life source. They will have to set root in different soil, to grow and flourish on their own or die.

Those dried branches growing on you, those dried branches of your life will then come back to life and sprout green leaves, growing much fruit. The birds of the air will seek refuge among them and you will live once again.

The vision of the evil hand stealing the money represents the enemy. (The Lord showed me a vision of a hand with long nails and thin crooked fingers; it looked like something out of a horror movie. It reached out and grabbed a stack of money). The parasite branches which have been stealing the resources and the blessings I have poured out have intercepted and interrupted the flow. I am pruning the dead branches of people who benefit you not, and even bring harm. You will soon thrive again in due season. Trust Me, I know exactly, what needs to be removed. Spring is approaching.

March 15, 2012

DON'T MESS WITH HIM/HER

I am the Lord your God, King of the Universe. Everything revolves around Me. My hand is the source of every good thing. My eyes travel to-and-fro, looking for a righteous heart in those who serve, justified by faith and righteous in My blood. My eyes pierce the darkness and nothing can hide from My sight, not the darkest of hearts and minds, for I see every thought and every plan hatched in the dark nights against My children. Your God is a God of mercy. Your God is a God of grace to the humble.

To the weary heart; I have seen. I have seen you struggle. I have seen your desire to please the Lord, your God, for righteousness sake, and I have seen the enemy at work in your life. I have seen the actions that have tried to destroy you and the words that have pierced your heart like the sharpest of arrows. I have seen it all.

Your job is to hold fast to Me and My Word. To hold to My promises made to you. I have not forgotten the dreams and visions, for I gave them to you, and I am faithful to perform My promise. I am re-orchestrating your life; altering the circumstances that had you bound. The enemy will not prosper, but will be brought to naught.

Where he thought he would win, he will lose. Where he thought he would prosper, he will fail. For I, the Lord your God, will frustrate his way. All will know that I, the Lord your God, am with you. They will point here and there saying, "There is the man/woman of God. God is with him/her. Don't mess with him/her because you will have the Lord to contend with," as I strike fear in the heart of the enemy. Go in peace.

March 16, 2012

MY SERVANT JOB

The Lord your God is one God. The Lord your God is a God of love, but I am also a God of justice, and I mete out that justice with a firm right hand. I am the God of all mercy and grace, and I beckon you to come and sit at My feet and hear the words of My very heart, for mercy reigns supreme. The rod of judgment is falling in your midst for a disobedient nation and a people who have brought this upon themselves.

The questions I asked My son Job, My faithful one, I ask each and every person today. How can you not trust Me when faced with those questions, knowing that I, the Lord your God, has the answers?

I am the only one who knows the end from the beginning and the beginning from the end, for I created the beginning, and I orchestrate the end and everything in between.

Man, I give you free will to accept or reject Me. Your decisions every day in this regard affect not just your life, but the lives of all those around you. Your rebellion knocks them out of place and creates storms in their lives.

What is man that I am mindful of him, that I allow those who think themselves wise to make decisions that tear apart lives and families? To those who think themselves wiser than Me, as I said to My servant Job...

Job 38

The LORD Challenges Job

1 *Then the LORD answered Job from the whirlwind:*

² "Who is this that questions My wisdom
with such ignorant words?
³ Brace yourself like a man,
because I have some questions for you,
and you must answer them.

⁴ "Where were you when I laid the foundations of the earth?
Tell me, if you know so much.
⁵ Who determined its dimensions
and stretched out the surveying line?
⁶ What supports its foundations,
and who laid its cornerstone
⁷ as the morning stars sang together
and all the angels shouted for joy?

⁸ "Who kept the sea inside its boundaries
as it burst from the womb,
⁹ and as I clothed it with clouds
and wrapped it in thick darkness?
¹⁰ For I locked it behind barred gates,
limiting its shores.
¹¹ I said, 'This far and no farther will you come.
Here your proud waves must stop!'

¹² "Have you ever commanded the morning to appear
and caused the dawn to rise in the east?
¹³ Have you made daylight spread to the ends of the earth,
to bring an end to the night's wickedness?
¹⁴ As the light approaches,
the earth takes shape like clay pressed beneath a seal;
it is robed in brilliant colors.
¹⁵ The light disturbs the wicked
and stops the arm that is raised in violence.

¹⁶ "Have you explored the springs from which the seas come?
Have you explored their depths?

17 Do you know where the gates of death are located?
Have you seen the gates of utter gloom?
18 Do you realize the extent of the earth?
Tell me about it if you know!

19 "Where does light come from,
and where does darkness go?
20 Can you take each to its home?
Do you know how to get there?
21 But of course you know all this!
For you were born before it was all created,
and you are so very experienced!

22 "Have you visited the storehouses of the snow
or seen the storehouses of hail?
23 (I have reserved them as weapons for the time of trouble,
for the day of battle and war.)
24 Where is the path to the source of light?
Where is the home of the east wind?

25 "Who created a channel for the torrents of rain?
Who laid out the path for the lightning?
26 Who makes the rain fall on barren land,
in a desert where no one lives?
27 Who sends rain to satisfy the parched ground
and make the tender grass spring up?

28 "Does the rain have a father?
Who gives birth to the dew?
29 Who is the mother of the ice?
Who gives birth to the frost from the Heavens?
30 For the water turns to ice as hard as rock,
and the surface of the water freezes.

31 "Can you direct the movement of the stars—
binding the cluster of the Pleiades
or loosening the cords of Orion?

^{32} *Can you direct the sequence of the seasons*
or guide the Bear with her cubs across the Heavens?
^{33} *Do you know the laws of the universe?*
Can you use them to regulate the earth?

^{34} *"Can you shout to the clouds*
and make it rain?
^{35} *Can you make lightning appear*
and cause it to strike as you direct?
^{36} *Who gives intuition to the heart*
and instinct to the mind?
^{37} *Who is wise enough to count all the clouds?*
Who can tilt the water jars of Heaven
^{38} *when the parched ground is dry*
and the soil has hardened into clods?

^{39} *"Can you stalk prey for a lioness*
and satisfy the young lions' appetites
^{40} *as they lie in their dens*
or crouch in the thicket?
^{41} *Who provides food for the ravens*
when their young cry out to God
and wander about in hunger?

Job 39

The LORD'S Challenge Continues

^{1} *"Do you know when the wild goats give birth?*
Have you watched as deer are born in the wild?
^{2} *Do you know how many months they carry their young?*
Are you aware of the time of their delivery?
^{3} *They crouch down to give birth to their young*
and deliver their offspring.
^{4} *Their young grow up in the open fields,*
then leave home and never return.

⁵ "Who gives the wild donkey its freedom?
Who untied its ropes?
⁶ I have placed it in the wilderness;
its home is the wasteland.
⁷ It hates the noise of the city
and has no driver to shout at it.
⁸ The mountains are its pastureland,
where it searches for every blade of grass.

⁹ "Will the wild ox consent to being tamed?
Will it spend the night in your stall?
¹⁰ Can you hitch a wild ox to a plow?
Will it plow a field for you?
¹¹ Given its strength, can you trust it?
Can you leave and trust the ox to do your work?
¹² Can you rely on it to bring home your grain
and deliver it to your threshing floor?

¹³ "The ostrich flaps her wings grandly,
but they are no match for the feathers of the stork.
¹⁴ She lays her eggs on top of the earth,
letting them be warmed in the dust.
¹⁵ She doesn't worry that a foot might crush them
or a wild animal might destroy them.
¹⁶ She is harsh toward her young,
as if they were not her own.
She doesn't care if they die.
¹⁷ For God has deprived her of wisdom.
He has given her no understanding.
¹⁸ But whenever she jumps up to run,
she passes the swiftest horse with its rider.

¹⁹ "Have you given the horse its strength
or clothed its neck with a flowing mane?
²⁰ Did you give it the ability to leap like a locust?
Its majestic snorting is terrifying!

²¹ It paws the earth and rejoices in its strength
when it charges out to battle.
²² It laughs at fear and is unafraid.
It does not run from the sword.
²³ The arrows rattle against it,
and the spear and javelin flash.
²⁴ It paws the ground fiercely
and rushes forward into battle when the ram's horn blows.
²⁵ It snorts at the sound of the horn.
It senses the battle in the distance.
It quivers at the captain's commands and the noise of battle.

²⁶ "Is it your wisdom that makes the hawk soar
and spread its wings toward the south?
²⁷ Is it at your command that the eagle rises
to the heights to make its nest?
²⁸ It lives on the cliffs,
making its home on a distant, rocky crag.
²⁹ From there it hunts its prey,
keeping watch with piercing eyes.
³⁰ Its young gulp down blood.
Where there's a carcass, there you'll find it."

Job 40

¹Moreover the LORD answered Job, and said:

² "Shall the one who contends with the Almighty correct *Him?*
He who rebukes God, let him answer it."

JOB'S RESPONSE TO GOD

³ Then Job answered the LORD and said:

⁴ "Behold, I am vile;
What shall I answer You?
I lay my hand over my mouth.

5 Once I have spoken, but I will not answer;
Yes, twice, but I will proceed no further."

The LORD Challenges Job Again

*6 Then the LORD answered Job from the whirlwind: 7 "Brace
yourself like a man,*
because I have some questions for you,
and you must answer them.

8 "Will you discredit My justice
and condemn me just to prove you are right?
9 Are you as strong as God?
Can you thunder with a voice like his?
10 All right, put on your glory and splendor,
your honor and majesty.
11 Give vent to your anger.
Let it overflow against the proud.
12 Humiliate the proud with a glance;
walk on the wicked where they stand.
13 Bury them in the dust.
Imprison them in the world of the dead.
14 Then even I would praise you,
for your own strength would save you.

15 "Take a look at Behemoth,
which I made, just as I made you.
It eats grass like an ox.
16 See its powerful loins
and the muscles of its belly.
17 Its tail is as strong as a cedar.
The sinews of its thighs are knit tightly together.
18 Its bones are tubes of bronze.
Its limbs are bars of iron.
19 It is a prime example of God's handiwork,
and only its Creator can threaten it.

^{20} *The mountains offer it their best food,*
where all the wild animals play.
^{21} *It lies under the lotus plants,*
hidden by the reeds in the marsh.
^{22} *The lotus plants give it shade*
among the willows beside the stream.
^{23} *It is not disturbed by the raging river,*
not concerned when the swelling Jordan rushes around it.
^{24} *No one can catch it off guard*
or put a ring in its nose and lead it away.

Job 41

The LORD'S Challenge Continues

^{1} *"Can you catch Leviathan with a hook*
or put a noose around its jaw?
^{2} *Can you tie it with a rope through the nose*
or pierce its jaw with a spike?
^{3} *Will it beg you for mercy*
or implore you for pity?
^{4} *Will it agree to work for you,*
to be your slave for life?
^{5} *Can you make it a pet like a bird,*
or give it to your little girls to play with?
^{6} *Will merchants try to buy it*
to sell it in their shops?
^{7} *Will its hide be hurt by spears*
or its head by a harpoon?
^{8} *If you lay a hand on it,*
you will certainly remember the battle that follows.
You won't try that again!
^{9} *No, it is useless to try to capture it.*
The hunter who attempts it will be knocked down.
^{10} *And since no one dares to disturb it,*
who then can stand up to me?

11 Who has given me anything that I need to pay back?
Everything under Heaven is mine.

12 "I want to emphasize Leviathan's limbs
and its enormous strength and graceful form.
13 Who can strip off its hide,
and who can penetrate its double layer of armor?
14 Who could pry open its jaws?
For its teeth are terrible!
15 Its scales are like rows of shields
tightly sealed together.
16 They are so close together
that no air can get between them.
17 Each scale sticks tight to the next.
They interlock and cannot be penetrated.

18 "When it sneezes, it flashes light!
Its eyes are like the red of dawn.
19 Lightning leaps from its mouth;
flames of fire flash out.
20 Smoke streams from its nostrils
like steam from a pot heated over burning rushes.
21 Its breath would kindle coals,
for flames shoot from its mouth.

22 "The tremendous strength in Leviathan's neck
strikes terror wherever it goes.
23 Its flesh is hard and firm
and cannot be penetrated.
24 Its heart is hard as rock,
hard as a millstone.
25 When it rises, the mighty are afraid,
gripped by terror.
26 No sword can stop it,
no spear, dart, or javelin.
27 Iron is nothing but straw to that creature,

and bronze is like rotten wood.
28 Arrows cannot make it flee.
Stones shot from a sling are like bits of grass.
29 Clubs are like a blade of grass,
and it laughs at the swish of javelins.
30 Its belly is covered with scales as sharp as glass.
It plows up the ground as it drags through the mud.

31 "Leviathan makes the water boil with its commotion.
It stirs the depths like a pot of ointment.
32 The water glistens in its wake,
making the sea look white.
33 Nothing on earth is its equal,
no other creature so fearless.
34 Of all the creatures, it is the proudest.
It is the king of beasts."

And Job's response to me, was the right one;

Job 42

Job Responds to the LORD

1 Then Job replied to the LORD:

2 "I know that you can do anything,
and no one can stop you.
3 You asked, 'Who is this that questions My wisdom with such ignorance?'
It is I—and I was talking about things I knew nothing about,
things far too wonderful for me.
4 You said, 'Listen and I will speak!
I have some questions for you,
and you must answer them.'
5 I had only heard about you before,
but now I have seen you with My own eyes.

*6 I take back everything I said,
and I sit in dust and ashes to show My repentance."*

Job was restored. The accusing mouthpieces of the enemy were forced to give unto his bosom gold and livestock. The very ones who accused Job of wrongdoing were forced to give an offering on his behalf. They were dependent upon the heart of Job, the one to whom they did wrong, for mercy. They were dependent upon Job's intercession before My throne. That is just like God to cause our enemies to come to us to make restoration.

The Lord continued; This is a two-fold lesson; repent for thinking yourself wise, trying to second-guess My plans, accusing My servants of wrongdoing during hard times, thinking yourselves wise while living in ignorance of the fullness, greatness and majesty of your God.

Know that it is sometimes blind faith that will see you through when you cannot find the way. Do not second-guess or try to figure it out; wasting time in worry. Have faith that the Creator, the Master of all, knows the answers and will work all things together for good for those who love Him. Do not worry about what others say or do, for they are fools, thinking themselves wise in their own eyes. They cannot answer My questions but refuse to repent on their own. They, too, will be dependent upon your prayers and intercession, your heart of mercy. Restitution will be made. I, the Lord your God, will see to it. Tables will turn and restoration will come.

PONDERING GREATEST BATTLES

Some of the greatest battles I have ever fought were with those in my own household. Some of the most vicious, hateful words that have ever been spoken to me or over me, have been from members of my family.

We all have wounds in need of healing. Those scars don't go away. I will wear them until Jesus returns. However, the blood of Jesus heals those gaping wounds of the heart and mind.

You are NOT who *they* say you are! You are NOT those things! You are God's precious child, His betrothed, His beloved. He holds you in the palm of His hand. He will *never* let you go!

If we allow Him, if we choose to forgive, He heals the pain. A painless scar remains; a reminder of where we came from, the battles He has brought us through, whose we are, and why every day, in every circumstance, we can lift our head high and fight the good fight of faith. When we get knocked down, we stand back up dust off our feet, going forth in His strength when we can muster none of our own.

Those who chose to become mouthpieces of the enemy are threatened by your faith. When they see the anointing on you, the depth of your love for the Holy One, they come face to face with their lack of faith. When they come face to face with the anointing, it is an Isaiah moment; "*Woe is me, for I have seen the Lord.*" It either leads to repentance and humility, or lashing out at the servant of the Lord.

Matthew 24 tells us offense will abound in the last days, and we are seeing this come to pass. People are offended over the slightest things, all the while insisting out of one side of their mouth that we must RESPECT *all* views. They throw stones when the view does not coincide with theirs, or when they are convicted by the Word written upon their heart.

Matthew, Chapter 10, confirms that Jesus did not come to bring peace but a sword. He said our enemies would be in our own households.

34 "Do not suppose that I have come to bring peace to the earth. I did not come to bring peace, but a sword. 35 For I have come to turn "'a man against his father, a daughter against her mother, a daughter-in-law against her mother-in-law— 36 a man's enemies will be the members of his own household.' 37 "Anyone who loves their father or mother more than me is not worthy of me; anyone who loves their son or daughter more than me is not worthy of me. 38 Whoever does not take up their cross and follow me is not worthy of me. 39 Whoever finds their life will lose it, and whoever loses their life for My sake will find it.

Have heart, you are not alone in your struggle. I am praying for all of those out there receiving this, whoever you are. There may be more than one.

God loves you so much that He sent this word from a fellow traveler of the narrow road to speak to you. He desires to confirm that you are not alone. We all have struggled with this. The Almighty is *with* you! You are *already* victorious. The enemy is just messing with your mind, trying to discourage and distract you from keeping your eyes on the face of God.

I pray this word from the heart of God reaches you and brings you comfort.

March 19, 2012

THE TIME HAS COME

The time has come for change. The time has come to stop your weeping and move forward in Me. Hiding out is not an option. Withdrawal is not for this season. This season is for boldness; to go after the enemy and push him back. The more you withdraw, the bolder he gets.

Sound the battle cry, "*Rak Chazak!*" Use the weapons of your warfare to push him back. As David said, "*You come to me with sword, spear, and javelin, but I come to you in the name of the LORD of Heaven's Armies, the God of the armies of Israel, whom you have defied.*" (**1 Samuel 17:45**).

I heal your heart and mind. You will move forward in My Spirit, in heart and mind. Level to level and glory to glory, you will stand. In My presence you will move, breathe, and have your being. The abuse has ended. The past is the past. The future is now. The end is a new beginning.

Behold, I make all things new. Go in peace, My child, knowing no weapon formed against you will prosper. The Lord your God has spoken from His throne to His children, yet you continue to fear and doubt. What will it take to convince you that My words are true?

Have I not proven Myself time and time again? My faithfulness is like a mighty mountain; My presence is like sweet perfume, strong yet delicate. Your God sees. I am not an idol of sticks and stones. I see your heart break. I see the end from the beginning. Have faith in Me, the One who is the lover of your soul, the One who died for you to that you might be reconciled and set free.

March 21, 2012

PULL BACK YOUR BREAST BONE

I am the Lord your God, King of the Universe. The world is changing. This is not the country you grew up in. Innocence is gone; a demonic agenda has taken control. The heart of man is not mine. I speak that you will know them by their fruits; their fruit stinks. It is putrid and rotten, a stench upon the land.

It is not too late for your nation to reverse course; not too late, YET. The heart of the people will be revealed in due time. Their hearts' desire for evil or good will become clearly evident. Woe to the nation who turns its back against the Lord, who calls evil good, and good evil...and every kind of blasphemous thing. The heart of man and the heart of the matter will soon be exposed. Will you stand for good or evil? You will give an answer on the day of reckoning.

Do not just look at the nation; what about your own life? How are you living? Are you willing to pull back your breast bone and allow Me to extract the tares from your heart and mind? May I give you the mind of Christ to see and hear as I do? Will you choose to do as I command, so that My ways will be your ways, My heart your heart? Can you love like Me, telling the truth and not condoning or excusing sin and, abominations against Me?

Blinded eyes and ears are comfortable, thinking a little prayer is all that it takes to save your eternal soul. Did I not tell you to work out your own salvation with fear and trembling, even though it is by My grace alone you are saved? How do you reconcile the two?

Seek My face. All the answers are found in Me. My heart pumps in the chest of those who are truly mine. Do not be afraid, My child. Pull back the breast bone and let Me extract the tares. Behold, I make all things new.

For those in battle, truly this is the battle for your life. The enemy will stop at nothing to destroy My called out ones. You are the ones I hid for a season, called aside in a time of preparation. The enemy has identified you and stepped up attacks, waging war and seeking to destroy in rapid succession, just as he did to My servant Job. Hold on.

Haters will come and blame you. They will tell you that you are not in Me, and I not in you. They will tell you your sin has found you out, but that is not truth. The enemy painted a target, and he has you in his sight. Stand tall. Fear not. Hold on to Me through the storms. You *will* have the victory.

Just as I said to Satan, "*Have you noticed My servant Job? He is the finest man in all the earth. He is blameless, a man of complete integrity. He fears God and stays away from evil,*" I will say the same thing about you; "Have you noticed My servant____? He/she is the finest man/woman in all the earth. He/she is blameless—a man/woman of complete integrity. He/She fears God and stays away from evil."

March 22, 2012

YOUR HEART

Your heart is ever before Me, says the Lord of Hosts. Your face is what My dreams are made of, My child. My beautiful bride, how My heart longs to hold you; to feel your embrace, your kiss. I yearn for the day We will be together as man and wife. We will never be separated again. You will see Me face to face. You will be able to touch Me and feel the warmth of My love.

THE STEPS

You are My friend. As you stand in faith for Me, your faith multiplies. You are counted into the faith Hall of Fame. Isaac, Jacob, Abraham, and David were all men just like you. They had fears and insecurities. They made mistakes. They all had an excuse as to why they were not the one I should choose, but they were the one. I do not look at external appearances, I look to a heart completely Mine; a heart humbled before Me, ready to have the tares extracted...a heart of surrender.

You are a woman/man of faith. You have stood when others would have fallen. You continue to stand, come what may, through the circumstances of life. I have a plan. I give you a future and a hope. I work all things together for good because you love Me; not because you plead, not because you beg Me, but because you love Me.

Circumstances may change; the road you are traveling may feel like it is all uphill and the valley may feel like the shadow of death. Yet you cross through. You pursue the path laid out before you, knowing that the steps of a good woman/man are ordered by Me ~ the Lord, your God.

I am with you, My child. I am with you and the time is coming when your circumstances will turn around. Trust Me for the answers, instructions, and guidance. You will then make your way through the darkness. The battle is strong. The road is long and marked with potholes. Persevere through. Watch the suddenlies of life come upon you; answers out of the blue, from whom and where you least expect them.

Heaven's court has convened. The hammer has fallen, the case decided. The verdict is to be announced. For My faithful, who serve Me in Spirit and in truth, I exclaim, Well done, good and faithful servants, but this I hold against you; stop searching for answers from the wrong places and wait on Me. Stop second-guessing. Stop trying to force an issue. Stop trying to manipulate to get your way, for your ways are not My ways. What looks right to a man is rarely right to the Lord, your God. Wait on Me. Be still and wait on Me for the outcome, for I see the end from the beginning. I know what is best. Your lack of faith in Me to make the right decisions is like looking at one puzzle piece and trying to figure out what the picture looks like. Surrender to Me, but do not cave in to the enemy's demands.

Put on the whole armor I have provided. Wield the sword of My Word; pray My words, not your own. Speak My words over yourself, your life, and circumstances. Watch things change. My word used properly, as I intended, are the greatest weapon you have to change your circumstances. Your greatest enemy is the very words that come out of your mouth. The enemy and the angels wait upon every word, seeking to hear either faith or doubt. They take hold of your words and run to fulfill the assignment based upon that which you have spoken. Stop idle chatter. This is sabotaging for yourself and your future. Speak My Word and watch all of Heaven and earth align to My intentions. Speak in faith.

March 25, 2012

ONLY FOR MY GLORY

The storms of life are gathering. Darkness is increasing, but it is only temporary, My child, for soon the sun will shine again. You will then emerge from the hiding place beneath My wings into the dawn of a new day.

Though the enemy rages, the wind blows, and the water threatens to overtake you, it is only a threat. It is designed to make you fear. Be secure in yourself by being secure in Me. I will give an answer to the wind and the waves. I will respond to those who rise up against you.

Sometimes that answer is silence. Vengeance is mine, says the Lord. You owe no man an explanation for why you obeyed Me. As a soft answer turns away wrath, silence can speak volumes. Silence turns the battle around; minds begins to run wild with excuses and explanations, guilt and conviction. Silence allows for introspection and you do not get drawn into a battle that you were not meant to fight. You are not Holy Spirit; He is your warrior.

The rain falls and the winds blows through your life; this allows a cleansing to take place, giving room for new growth. As spring approaches and the grass that was dry and withered comes back to life, as the plants and trees begin to grow new leaves and the flowers begin to bloom, you, too, will bloom in due season. As what was dormant springs back to life, seeds long forgotten resurrect in Me. The old becomes new, the dead arise.

Truth emerges from the shadows of your heart, mind and life. You see with eyes of angels, for behold, I do a new thing. I bring restoration and life for My glory. *To God goes the glory*, you will shout after the transition is complete and you are perfectly positioned in that place called "there"...which is where I wanted you all along. You did not know how you would get there, but suddenly you'll be there; it will have happened for My glory alone, because of My grace.

I will cancel the bad decisions you have made. I will also terminate the pain you have endured on behalf of bad decisions others made, who betrayed you. For I love you, My child. My grace and favor; one touch from the God your King, and behold I make all things new.

March 27, 2012

I JUST CAME TO TELL YOU

I just came to tell you that I love you. No weapon formed against you shall prosper. You are blessed in the field and out. You are blessed going in and blessed coming out. The grapes are ripe, and you will reap in due season if you faint not.

The voice of the accuser taunts and ridicules, but you are not who they say you are. You are My beautiful bride says the Lord, and I protect what is Mine. I protect and uplift. I am the giver of all good things. It is I who gives and takes away.

March 29, 2012

THE PAST IS THE PAST

I am the Lord your God, and today is the first day of the rest of your life. Today I say, start fresh. My mercies are new every day. The past is the past; it does not define who you are.

Your future is in Me. I am the God of your future. I am the God of your promises. I am the God of mercy. I am the God who does not hold your faults against you. I see you cleansed in the blood of My son. Your future awaits; it is now. Your future is whole and complete; replete with My plans which were established for you from before the foundations of the earth were created.

The God of all mercy and grace calls out to you. Stand in faith. Believe Me! I am the One true God who holds you in His hand. You are My beloved and I am yours. No weapon formed against you shall prosper. It is always bleakest before the dawn.

I already decreed the dawn of a new day and the transition continues. Transitions are hard and transitions are long, but there is a necessary stretching that must take place. This is that you fit into the new place I have prepared for you. Otherwise, you would not fit; you would be out of step and out of time, too small to fill the space.

Hold on, help is on the way. Hold fast and you will soon see better days. Pray for those who persecute you. Pray for those who did not have your best interests at heart. Pray that they will release their selfish desires, thoughts, and deeds, so all will be well with your soul. The enemy agenda has been fierce. He has been working overtime on your thoughts, heart, and mind. He is seeking to destroy your faith in Me.

This time is crucial in the Spirit that you do not fall in your faith. Speak life. Speak mercy. Decree and declare that all is well with your soul. Let your Spirit soar in Me. Forget the past and break those thought patterns that do not glorify Me or your future. You have power in My Spirit, and authority in the Name of My Son to change lives. You are capable of speaking to nations ~ to change the tide and create a new future.

March 30, 2012

PIERCE

Pierce the darkness with the light of My presence. Pierce the silence with the sound of My Word. Decree and declare My words into the atmosphere and watch the tide begin to turn; the tide of darkness that has surrounded you, the tide of the enemy who came in like a flood to destroy you. Turn him back with My Word. Raise the sword between you and the enemy of your soul. Draw a line in the sand. Enough is enough.

Now is the time. You are the one to confront darkness in the authority of My name. Know when to speak, know when to be silent. Every battle has a different strategy. Seek Me for instructions in which way you ought go. You are a mighty warrior, a man/woman of valor called to confront the darkness and speak light into hurting souls around you. Stand and support one another. When one is weak, another is strong. Contend for the victory; persevere and push through.

The authority of My name is not used as I intended. Too many afraid to contend, not believing My Word. **Luke 10:19** reads, *"Behold, I give you the authority to trample on serpents and scorpions, and over all the power of the enemy, and nothing shall by any means hurt you."* In your fear and slumber, the enemy overtook and overwhelmed you, but feel My strength rising. Can you feel it stirring in your belly?

Arise mighty warrior, arise. Heed My strategy to defeat the enemy. Decree and declare; see the salvation of your Lord. Stop talking about the battle. Understand you are in transition and fear not, for I am with you. Fear not for I am your God and you go nowhere without Me. When you wield your sword, My angels do too. When you decree and declare My Word, angels are set in motion by your voice speaking forth My truth; they prepare the way and remove obstacles, completing your words of faith.

The key to effective prayer is to pray My words, for in My Word you have power to create; power to receive what you say, for good or for bad. You have weapons of warfare; use them. Your select weapon in this season is to decree, and declare My Word. Pierce the darkness with the light of The Son.

March 31, 2012

INNOCUOUS

The Lord your God has spoken many, many times to bring you hope and encouragement, yet doubts and fears still linger. You are more than a conqueror! How can it be any other way when I am with you? Shout praises from the rooftops. Shout praises from the valley. Shout praises from the street corner and give glory to your God.

Do not fear the evil that comes by day, or the terrors by night. Do not fear the reaper who threatens to overtake your harvest and steal all which you worked so hard to plant. You *will* reap your own harvest. The locusts will not steal it.

The God of all mercy loves you. The God of all mercy sees and hears everything that goes on in the hearts of man; those who plot and plan against you, those who threaten and intimidate... but their clanging symbol is just for show. There is no substance. Just like Gideon, I will confuse their way. The enemy camp will be scattered with the crack of an earthen vessel and a torch. Fear will descend upon them and they will not be able to run fast enough. They will know they made a mistake, thinking they can plot, plan, and succeed against the One true God. When they come against you, the Lord, your God, is your rear guard.

As the enemy soldier dreamed of a barley loaf rolling into camp and causing destruction, you, too, appear innocuous, innocent as doves...yet the Lord of Heaven and earth has your back. You will not go alone. Decree and declare victory, as I instructed yesterday.

Sit silent before your accusers and watch the victory of the Lord. Further instructions will follow as you move and breathe and have your being in Me. Total surrender to Me avoids the enemy snare. Rest in Me, for the God of all mercy will see you through.

April 1, 2012

EMBRACE THE DAWN

Embrace the dawn of your new day. Do you feel the change in the atmosphere? Did you feel something shift? Do you feel strength building, your body healing? Did you feel that subtle shift in your focus? Did you feel the nations tremble?

I am with you, says your God. You will rise from this place and be healed. You will preach with the fire of God in your belly, blessing the nations. Go forth in the power and glory of My name.

April 3, 2012

LIVING WATER

The dawn of the new day has broken through the darkness and My Spirit is ministering to the broken hearted. Behold, I make all things new. No weapon formed against you shall prosper. Every voice that rises up against you, will be silenced. Like Baalam, every time the voices try to curse, they will have to bless, for I control the tongue of man. I can cause it to cleave to the roof of his mouth, or even silence his voice, as I did with Zechariah. I can cause tongues to speak blessings as they strive to decree curses upon you. For I, the Lord your God, am a God of blessing to My upright ones, the remnant of My people. I control the heart of man and I can turn it right or left, making it soft or hard.

Seek Me in the morning and command your day to fall in line with My Word. Watch the changes come to pass as you replace your negative thoughts with mine. The God of all mercy sees your struggle, trials and pain. I am not blind to your hurts. I have not turned away.

Stand firm, be still, knowing that I am your God. See the victory. Your struggle is not against flesh and blood, but against the enemy working through people and circumstances to destroy you. He is against the God in you; those he uses are blind to this fact. They cannot see the things that they say and do in My name, are not of Me. The pain is worse when it is done in the name of the true and living God, but I tell you the truth, they are of their father the devil, for the love of God is not in them. They neither know Me nor recognize Me. My Spirit is not within them.

Pray for your enemies. Let forgiveness flow through your heart and the oil of gladness will flow out of you. You will be a well of living water; an endless supply to quench the thirst of those I bring upon your path. I am your supply, your King eternal, the true and living God.

Living water never stops flowing from My throne of grace. Do not be stingy with the water; do not hoard it. Let it flow through you into the lives of all whom you meet. They will then be refreshed and come to the throne, becoming another well and fresh supply of My living water to all whom they meet.

April 5, 2012

VICTORY NEEDS TO BE WON

Today victory needs to be won in your heart and mind, for that is the battlefield the enemy has been scourging in this season. The battle has left you weary, worn out to the point of listlessness. You are inactive, sitting in a hovel of self-protection as the war rages around you. The winds howl and intimidation builds to a crescendo.

The enemy has stopped at nothing. He has held back nothing that can be used to hurt My chosen vessels. Let Me rise up within you. Let the authority you have forgotten that you possess, in My Name, build within you. Line up your thoughts with My heart and mind. Speak My words over your situation, for I am the God of your words, I am the Word of your heart. You are in Me, and I am in you. Sing to the Lord, your God. Dance, rejoice and watch as the heaviness breaks off.

April 8, 2012

I RESURRECT

I resurrect your hope. I resurrect your dreams. I resurrect My love in your heart. I resurrect your health. Behold, I make all things new. I am turning the tables. Where the enemy thought he would win, he will lose. Where he thought he had you bound, I break the chains. You are alive in Me and I am alive in you.

You have been though a long, dark night. The light is breaking through to push back the darkness. Feel hope arise in you, feel My love ignite a passion. That fire within you that was "lost" for a season will restart. You lost your way for a season on the storm tossed seas, finding no direction. You could not find the shore.

I am pointing the way home. A beacon of light breaking through the darkness with the light of My presence and love, pointing the way home. The path you are to travel will become clear again as I resurrect you to new life by renewing your mind. I make all things new.

Quickly come into agreement and alignment with My Spirit within you. Many of you have become off track in this season, unable to find your way. All roads seemed to lead nowhere. All roads seem to lead you away from Me. Now all roads, no matter where you find yourself, will lead you back to Me. I have made a way where there seems to be no way, ready to turn your situation on its ear, forever and ever, amen.

I re-ignite fire. I re-ignite passion. I re-ignite favor in the lives of My children. Behold, I make all things new. I renew your mind and heart with My resurrection power. I cover you with the blood. To every hurt and every pain, I apply the balm of Gilead.

I send people to minister to you; to encourage and ignite passion that is contagious. Do not overlook the people I send to you in this season, for I use people to fulfill My purposes. My purposes will go forth. My passion will spread like fire though you. Watch your words, allow Me to renew your mind that it will come into line with Mine.

A beacon of hope to lost hearts, minds, and nations. A spark; it just takes a spark to ignite a brush fire. Burn the dross and you remain a new creature in Christ. Stand firm for Me and do not let the enemy tell you who you are and who you are not. The dross of old mindsets, old ways of viewing the world, old ways of looking at yourself, I burn away that you may see, who I see. My special child, you are the heart of My heart, the one I love, the one I died for, the one I call Mine.

Behold, I make all things new. I raise you to new life in Me. You have been through the bowels of Hell for a season. I raise you to new life in Me this day. I am giving you new life.

April 10, 2012

You Will Soon Forget

Be still and know that I am your God; the God of your present, the God of your past, the God of your future. I am the all-knowing, all-seeing God.

Gods of sticks and stones neither see nor speak, but the Lord, your God, is alive. I raise you to new life in Me. I raise you to new hope.

You will soon forget the pain of this season. There will be a restoration of praise when you look at all the good things I have done for you. You will see all that has blossomed out of the hurts and trials of this season. You were a dormant seed in a dark place; it's time to spring forth into new life.

April 13, 2012

DRAMATIC SHIFT

I am the Lord your God and today is the first day of a dramatic shift in the Spirit. You may not feel it in the natural, for changes will come slowly as I move and have My being among My people. I decreed the dawn of a new day. I decreed new beginnings, but the changes have not been seen.

The land I start with, the land you will begin to see change in, will first be your hearts. I will prepare their soil to receive what I have in store you. Hearts have been hard in this past season as losses have multiplied. However, My Spirit is moving among the wreckage of many lives, marriages, and finances to bring them into line. Prepare your hearts and minds for the new thing I have been speaking about.

It will come to pass as surely as a new day dawns. The sun rises among My people to restore hope and faith, as hearts and minds that have been used and abused in this season are mended. Behold, I make all things new. Hearts and minds will become pliable again. Those who lost faith will be given extra measure, to overcome the discouragement in this season.

The status quo will no longer be acceptable as fire from Heaven falls upon My children who have stood faithful in this season; faithful through the hurts, pains, and all the enemy has thrown at you. You could not see which way to go, but you stood and looked up toward Me, seeking My face. You were faithful.

Your Father from Heaven has seen and will reward His children in due season, for the Lord, your God, proclaims, "Well done, good and faithful servant. You stood when others fell. You refused to compromise. You stayed on the narrow path when others walked away, and the Lord your God is well pleased. You have been beat up, bruised, and broken by the attacks, but you kept your eyes on Me. Turn. I shall turn your situations and the enemy will not prevail."

April 17, 2012

I Do Not Condemn You

I am the Lord, your God, and I am on your side. I am cheering you on, encouraging you to make right decisions and to keep your eyes on Me. Keeping your heart in My hands through faith in Me and My Word. Do you know that I am with you, that I am for you?

I am not against you. I want what is My very best for you. I desire to see you prosper and thrive in the things of the kingdom. My will is that you see My kingdom come, birthed and grown into fruition on earth, just as it is in Heaven.

I am the Lord your God, and many are serving Me haphazardly; wobbling in faith. They are struggling in the flesh to serve when it is all about My grace and not condemnation. I do not condemn you. I am faithful and just to forgive you when repent before Me, I remember your sins not when you confess them. It is you who remembers. It is the enemy reminding you of your failures and transgressions.

The enemy invades your eye and ear gates. He bombards your thoughts. Keep, your thoughts stayed on Me; you will see the victory. I cleanse your heart. I cleanse your mind of all unrighteousness and restore vision; a hope within you of where you are going.

The giants loom. The mountains tremble at the thought of the Holy One of Israel coming forth in battle array, planting My foot in front his (the enemy) brigade and saying enough is enough, while the little barley loaf (you) rolls into camp and achieves the victory.

Unsuspecting, unexpected, who would have thought little ____ (your name here) would have achieved the victory? Look at all that came against. You have the victory, for the Lord your God is with you, My child. It will not come by flesh nor by might, but by My Spirit says the Lord. By My Spirit you will achieve, by My Spirit you will conquer, by My Spirit you can do all things. By My Spirit you will have victory, thus sayeth the Lord. Go in peace, My child, go in peace.

April 20, 2012

TIME TO FALL IN LINE

May the God of all comfort bring you comfort and peace in your hearts, for you alone cannot solve the problems of the world, but your hearts grieve for the least of these. Your hearts cry out; you feel My grief in the Spirit for My children to rise up and leave the four walls of the "church." You are called to go forth, healing the sick, raising the dead, cleansing the lepers, and casting out demons.

I decreed signs and wonders would follow My children. Too many are chasing the signs and wonders rather than the One true God. Pray, so they will be in order; signs, and wonders will follow them.

Time to fall in line with My plans and purposes; to heed My Word. Who is this god so many claim to serve? Why do they call Me Lord when they do not obey Me? The words of their mouth sound right, but their hearts are far from Me. Call them out, for by doing so you snatch them from the fires of Hell. I am not a God of tolerance. I am a God of love, and love speaks truth and does not condone sin. The people have lost sight of this God; preachers are preaching what feels good, but it does not lead to heart changes or bring repentance.

You are My chosen, My ministers; speak what I speak. Do what you see your Father in Heaven doing, for by doing so, all will know you are Mine and I am with you. I long to restore signs and wonders to follow My children. As it was in the early church, it will be today.

I want to shake the status quo, shake the mausoleums of dead religion and meaningless words and action. I long to replace the false signs and wonders enticing the body of Christ with true signs and wonders. I want My children to operate in discernment, returning their eyes toward seeking My heart and not My hand, for by doing so, all will be added.

As it stands, many are following the Pied Piper, the deceiver. He masquerades as an angel of light but brings destruction; all in My name, they claim. My heart is grieved by My church gone astray.

I am calling My remnant out, to stand, to speak, to love, to move in My Spirit and bring deliverance; to set the captives free by the truth of My Word.

Remnant, Arise! Remnant, arise in Me. Arise in My Spirit. Hearken, your ears to hear and your eyes to see what the Spirit of the Lord is sharing. Do not fear. Do not hesitate. Obey, for I desire to use you mightily to set the captives free. You shall heal hearts and minds by directing their way to Me. I am God. I am here. I am with you. Never doubt My presence, for I live in you.

Draw from the well of living water and give a drink to all who are thirsty. Living water ignites a spark of life, giving hope, healing, and freedom. The salvation of the Lord will come upon the people, and the land will be set ablaze. As hearts come ablaze you will have a new fire; the joy of your salvation will return to develop into an overwhelming fire that cannot be extinguished.

April 29, 2012

SOMETIMES

I am the Lord your God, Master of All, King of the Universe. I hold all things in My hand. I control your destiny when you yield to Me and give Me free reign in your life. You have been given a choice to go on *in Me*, or to go on *in your own way*. Those choices are presented to you each and every day.

The enemy seeks to destroy, seeks that inroad where you choose to compromise My Word, and in deed. If you are not careful, wham ~ you are headed off upon a rabbit trail. I give you mercy to show you how to live in accordance with My Word. My mercies are new every day.

You sin "big," you sin "little." No, there is not one righteous, but by having faith in My Son. Man classifies sin into categories. I do not. Sin is sin. You condemn yourself for the "big" sins, but not the "little" ones, yet they are the same to your soul. Adjust your thinking. If all sins are the same then you cannot make yourself more justified, a better person, or more closely Mine. You cannot control sin through work in your flesh.

Stop the condemnation of the enemy. You are a sinner. You can be a sinner saved by grace, justified by My blood, righteous through faith in My Son, or you can continue to look at yourself as a sinner, trying to earn grace, living in condemnation, under religion, never being good enough to be My child, never able to receive and walk in the fullness of My mercy. My son died that you would receive life abundant from Me. You can walk in the liberty of My Spirit, or subscribe to bondage to man and the ways of religion.

Stop beating yourself up over your wrong thoughts and wrong desires. The enemy will not relent in His pursuit of you, but know that nothing will come against you that is not common to man. I am a God far bigger than those thoughts and sin issues you struggle with. I will never leave you nor forsake you.

I am going to love you through the storms, temptations, and the sins you commit. Sometimes you will succeed and sometimes you will fail, but that does not mean I will love you less. I am going to love you home to My arms. Stay in Me, abide in Me, by My grace you *will* overcome. You cannot make yourself good, better, or holy. Holy Spirit convicts, Holy Spirit transforms. Rest in Me.

May 4, 2012

FAN THE FLAMES

The hearts of the people have grown cold, careless, not even caring for blatant sins and deceptions. They go ignored, rather than exposed, excuses rather confronted, dealt with and made right. They take no responsibility for their actions and seek to lie and blame.

Impure mouths speak out of hearts that know Me not, the things of Me, the kingdom and the values of the fore Fathers. The foundations of this nation have been left behind, altered, the truth removed and replaced with lies.

My remnant is alive and well. My remnant, My children, My praying people, I will honor you in the midst of great turmoil, for I know the ways of the hearts of men. Great miracles and provision will come out of the darkness that surrounds you as I move in your midst.

Fan the flames of revival in your hearts and it will be contagious and spread as the darkness and oppression increases among those who know me not. I have called you to be the light, the love of My presence to a hurting people with hurting hearts and anguish of nations not knowing the way out. My light will shine. It will invade the darkness and drive it back. Wherever you go, drive out the darkness.

Your authority will increase in the land as you start to move in Me and speak My Word over all your situations. My Word is a changing force. My authority resides in you. You may not have seen the results you wanted, but things are about to change as My authority increases within you, and you learn how to walk in My presence. Fan the flame within yourself, the flame of My presence within you, so you are neither hot nor cold but set ablaze, a fire that no man can quench.

Let Holy Spirit flow and do not hinder His presence in you and His movement through you. As danger increases, His guidance and direction will be critical to your survival as the darkness increases. The world is a dangerous place and the agenda is against you, but you have victory in Me.

May 9, 2012

STOP STRIVING

The Lord your God is with you wherever you go. I am the Alpha and Omega, the first and the last, the author and finisher of your faith. Fret not. Strive not. My hand is upon you, My child.

Death will not overtake you; My mercies are new every day. My favor is upon you, for you are blessed and highly favored in the kingdom of God. Do not strive, for it is not by might, nor by power, but by My Spirit. My children are striving in their own strength to try and fix their situations, but the doors have remained closed.

The key to the door is not striving, it is by My Spirit. I open the doors no man can open and I close doors no man can open. I am the key. I am the door. I am knocking on your heart.

Stand still and usher in My presence; see the glory of your Lord overtake you. Your deliverance draws nigh. Seek first the kingdom of God and all else, will be added, unto you. You have it backwards in this season, striving and distracted by the things around you and your situations.

The enemy took his best shot to get your eyes off of Me, but now I tell you the truth, I am the author and the finisher of your faith. I am the great I am. I am the one who created you and formed you in your mother's womb and I am the one who will deliver you from the hands of your enemy.

April 11, 2012

BRING HIM PRAISE

I am the Lord your God, your King and I control all that goes on around you. I orchestrate the details. I bring people in, and I take people away. I manipulate your circumstances for ultimate glory to be poured forth through you.

Do not despise small beginnings and the work I am doing within your soul, for in crushing the olive, an abundance of oil flows. In pruning and crushing, My glory pours forth in greater measure. My glory fills the earth and all of creation shows My love and beauty ~ from the ocean shores to the mountainscapes, from the lion on the Serengeti, to the mouse who may run in your home.

My beauty shines forth like the noonday sun and all of creation sings My praises. The oceans roar, Holy, Holy, Holy is the Lord God almighty; the birds chirp beautiful praises to your God and King. Praise changes your world and the lives of those around, bring me glory. My glory fills the earth.

You are not insignificant. No one is insignificant in My Kingdom. I love the least of these and I love you. Let the praises ring in the midst of this transition and watch My glory shine through. Watch My Spirit move in your midst and circumstances for it is not by might but by My Spirit says the Lord your God.

Bring Me praise. Bring Me praise, for I am the Master of all. Praise breaks yokes of bondage, sets the enemy fleeing, and ushers in My presence. Praise Me from the depth of your heart, let your whole being praise Me without regard to what it looks or feels like and you will shine like the noonday sun in the midst of your circumstance. In the midst of your pain, My glory shines through.

May 13, 2012

Over Flow

I am the Lord your God, and today I speak to you from Heaven above, to your heart of hearts. Come to Me, seek Me, abide in Me, for how I long to have you near Me. I long to whisper in your ear how much I love you and see you respond in praise. When I speak over you, My children whom I love, every cell in your body is listening and responding in praise.

Do you know I speak praises over My children? *Well done, good and faithful children* is not just something I will say, but something, I do say, when you obey.

I see you righteous; I see you Holy, off spring of My spotless lamb, for you multiply the Spirit within you and the Spirit can be multiplied ad infinitum and still remain complete in each one. The fullness of the Spirit does not dissipate in you unless you refuse to be filled and to keep a continuous river of living water flowing from your belly.

The overflow allows you to move in the gifts, signs and wonders. You are called to minister, but you cannot give what you do not have, and you have nothing to give if you are not overflowing. Overflow in Me; there is a thirsty world waiting for what you have to give. I send you out 2 x 2 to bring Me praise, to bring Me glory, to heal the sick, cleanse the lepers, and cast out demons.

This is your calling. This is your purpose ~ to lead people to Me, unashamed, unafraid, with the glory proceeding out of your mouth like the sharpest of swords to break the chains that bind and set the captives free. Free in Me, for My glory fills the earth.

May 19, 2012

EYES OF ETERNITY

I am the Lord your God, Master of all, King of the Universe, and today I say; do not let the changes and the transitions of life cause you to lose heart. Life is full of changes. People will come and people will go, but it is the Lord your God who orchestrates the seasons of your life for maximum growth and glory. I expand My kingdom purposes.

All things work together for good for those who love Me. All things work together for My kingdom purpose and plans for your life. You know in part, you prophesy in part. The how's and why's will not be answered until you can see with eyes of eternity.

So, for now, accept with the faith of a child that the steps of a good man/woman are ordered by your Lord. Obey. Watch the glory of your God unfold around and move through you. Give Me praise, for the Holy One of Israel is worthy to be praised.

May 21, 2012

I WILL NOT RELENT

I will not relent in My pursuit of you, My protection of you, My love for you. I will not relent in pursuit of justice and mercy for My children who seek to please Me and operate in faith. Through the good times and hard times, they pursue Me and do not relent, come what may. They stick to the ways of their God. They believe what I have spoken is truth and they stand on the promises. They are shown, great mercy.

Grace poured out to give you the strength to stand and endure the trials and storms you face along the way. I will not relent in doing well to you. I will not relent in making your enemies, who are My enemies, My footstool.

Time served; I mark you time served. I declare you not guilty. I open the prison doors and set you free from all that had you bound, for I know your heart, My child. You will not relent in chasing Me and seeking Me. Quiet endurance, steadfast through the ebb and flow, stand strong.

May 28, 2012

MEMORIAL DAY

Today, remember. Erect a plaque in memoriam on your heart that the Lord your God is one God. He is not the multiple gods that man created to satisfy their soul's lust for power and greed.

The Lord your God is one God, and wants to rule and reign over His Creation. A Sovereign God over a nation set apart, as a light to the world, but that light has been snuffed out by greed and power hungry individuals who pay no mind to the Lord your God. They have hijacked this great nation and the people follow along like three blind mice, the Pied Piper, and sheep to a slaughter.

Silence; the silence is deafening. Raise a banner of love. Raise a banner that proclaims, "In God We Trust." Raise a banner to your King. Take a stand and publicly praise your God. The silence is deafening. The enemy has gagged the mouths of My children.

People everywhere are being intimidated into silence by the loud voices of condemnation that demand rights and privilege they are not entitled to, for it infringes upon the rights of others. One's right is no greater than another man's right. No sin is worse than another sin; certainly no sin should be magnified and glorified, condoned from the highest office in the land, or tolerated and glorified in My house.

The world is backwards. The heart of man has waxed cold, calling good evil and evil good. Woe to you, a perverse and godless generation, but I am less concerned with the state of the world and its ignorance than I am with the state of the "church" living like the world. You look no different in My eyes.

There are dens of thieves and robbers stealing from My children. Lies and more lies; a perverse generation you are, having a form of godliness and denying My power. Woe to you, for you have known Me at one time, but you turned from Me; adulterous, the harlot, prostituting yourselves at every turn.

Where is the "church" triumphant? Where is the power, and signs and wonders, that I intended for you to move in to change the world? I will tell you where - nowhere! So, you invent them, and fake them. Men speak with fanciful words and deceit. They lead the innocent in and get caught in a trap of Satan, lured by the lust of the eyes and ears, rather than true anointing from on high.

They flock to have their ears tickled but they would not know truth; they would not know Me, if I was standing in their midst. The Sadducees and the Pharisees knew Me not.

I am not welcome in most of these buildings called "church." If I showed up they would not recognize Me. When a move of the Spirit does start, they quench it immediately as out of order. Holy Spirit is not welcome, but how can you be born again without Him? You can't, yet you claim to know Him to be saved. You then deny His working in your life. You deny His gifts as not for today. You impotent and insolent (insultingly contemptuous in speech or conduct) "church."

The Lord your God rebukes you this day. Stop going your own way. I was no different in the early "church" than I am today. Seek Me. Prostrate yourselves and seek Me, you blind and perverse generation, before it is too late. You have abrogated (declared null and void) your post. Walked away from your assignment, disqualified yourself. AWOL, but My plan is still My plan, and I can redeem the time if you turn and repent. Follow the Lord your God as I intend to be followed, not on your terms, but on Mine.

That is where restoration lies, that is where true power resides and can move; where I intend for you to live, in the center of My perfect will for your life. I change not. I never moved, but it is time for you to move. It is time for you to change or the banquet will be in full swing, with you on the outside looking in.

June 1, 2012

RESURRECTION

I am the Lord your God, and today the sun shines as a sign that I never change. I am consistent and faithful. The laws of the universe change not. Just as you count on the sun to rise each morning, I am faithful to watch over My Word and perform it. I am your faithful God, your port in the storm where My anchor holds you tight and safe.

Watch as I overshadow you with My presence, watch what seems impossible come to pass, and watch those dreams you thought were dead resurrect to new life. Watch as new life explodes in My Spirit to bring those dry bones to life.

Where there was loss, there will be abundance. Where there was bondage, there will be freedom. Where there was dryness, there will be streams of living water. Where there was death, there will be life. The dream giver, your God, is alive and well and I am still on the throne. Though things look bleak in some areas, nothing is too big for Me to bring into submission to My perfect will.

Will you trust Me with the impossible? Do you have faith to believe the impossible is possible with Me? Watch! I say watch as dead things come to life; the dead parts of your heart, the dead parts of your faith.

Restore! I restore the years the enemy has stolen and the cankerworm devoured. I set your feet on the rock of your salvation.

The Lord showed Me a vision of a person standing on a boulder that was wobbling and Jesus was placing shims under it to stabilize it.

Where there is doubt, there will be assurance. Where there was fear you will rise up, mighty warrior, and push back the darkness. All things belong to Me. Release. I speak release from the chains that bind. I speak a mighty move of Holy Spirit into your life to call things that are not into being.

Speak to the abundance of rain from the cloud the size of a man's hand. Speak to the few fishes and the loaves and feed a multitude. Speak to a few with flames of fire over their heads and watch as multitudes come to Me from the fire of a little flame, for My spirit burns brightly in your heart.

As the darkness increases, you will be a target for some, but the light of salvation to many. Let your light shine, step into that authority I have given you. There is power in your words far beyond what you understand, and even further beyond what you exercise. It is vital that you understand your authority as a believer. Do you not know you have the authority to make demons tremble? Walk in it, talk in it, watch things change around you.

June 12, 2012

EMPTY PEWS

I am the Lord your God, Master of all, and My heart is grieved for the status of My church. So many empty pews; bodies fill the seats but they are empty of My love, grace, and mercy. They are empty of My Word, empty of Holy Spirit living and breathing in them, content to sit; listening but never hearing. Never changing, never applying My Word to their lives; empty of Holy Spirit, trying to teach what they do not have, do not live, do not know. How can they give what they do not have to give?

Holy Spirit multiplies. When the Word is preached, with Him involved, He is the life transformer, the giver of life to the word on a page, in season and out of season. He is the source of power in your life to move mountains, to work great miracles in My name. To see the lost found and the dead live.

Arise. Arise to new life in Me. A life in My Spirit, following, neither left, nor right. Eyes on Me, run with the one who lives in you. To see My will done on earth as it is in Heaven. To see the dead in the pews come to new life, proclaiming My Word. To do My works in faith, in obedience to My lead, then the church will become My Church.

The body will work together, for what is an ear without a head, an eye without a face, a foot without a leg? Stop serving man; stop glorifying a man behind a pulpit and fix your eyes on Me. I am the giver of life. I am the giver of life-sustaining words that truly transforms. Let Me transform you from a shell into a mighty warrior who carries the Spirit of God with you, to affect change wherever you go.

Your very presence in a room floods My presence into the atmosphere to affect change. The light that transforms, the light that changes all that it comes in contact with, the light of My presence, the light of My love, the light of My mercy, the light of My grace ~ touch My children and bring them to repentance.

Dead in the pews, I resurrect you to life. Blind eyes be open, heart of stone be soft; look upon the one you have cursed. The one you claimed to know, but knew not. Do you not know I am the same yesterday, today and tomorrow? I have not changed.

My gifts are for you, for today, and for tomorrow ~ to empower you to do the work of the kingdom, but you deny the source of that power. You deny the Lord your God and the Spirit who longs to come upon you with power from on high, to move you into your calling, to give you revelation you do not have, to allow you to prophesy and speak in tongues of the Heavenlies.

How can you deny Me yet claim to know Me? How can you claim the Father and Son but not Holy Spirit when we are one? Jesus told you to wait in the upper room but you left and grew impatient, deciding it was not necessary after all. I tell you clearly; it *is* necessary.

Seek Me until you find Me, for I am truth. My Word is truth. Not one jot or tittle will fade away. Every word reveals My true nature; My responsibility to you and your responsibility to me ~ relationship, clearly spelled out.

Come to Me on My terms, not your own. Come with a repentant heart; I resist the proud. You are of your Father the devil, speaking lies and perverting My Word while manipulating My children. Come out of her (Harlot church), come into the truth. Come into the light of My truth and I will set you free.

June 15, 2012

Don't Give Up

Don't give up. The road you are on seems all up hill, but the Lord your God has not abandoned you. I am with you till the end. Brighter days are coming and My glory will be revealed in your life. All will know that I am with you.

Those who spoke discouragement and accusations will be silenced as My glory is revealed. Conviction will fill their hearts of stone for a life transforming revelation of My sovereignty. I call you blessed, My child.

June 17, 2012

INSIGNIFICANTLY SIGNIFICANT

Behold, I set before you an open door of My mercy and grace; an open door of My presence, an open door to see the glory of the Lord shine through.

What is man that I am mindful of him? If you could see through the vastness of time and space, in and out of the Spirit, you would see you are insignificantly significant. Insignificant in the vastness of the universe, but significant to be My children who capture My heart. Significant enough for Me to send My Son to die for you that we can be joined together in eternal relationship. You are insignificantly significant.

Insignificant to a government run amuck. Insignificant in a sea of faces, yet I know your face; every detail. I numbered the hairs on your head. I set eternity in motion through you. They say you do not matter, but you matter to Me. They say your life won't account for much, but its counts unto righteousness. They say you are too small or too weak, too fat or too tall. They say you are too old or too young and you just don't have what it takes, but I created you. I called you unto great and mighty things; the insignificant things of this world become significant across the sands of time.

So rise up mighty warrior, know that you are blessed. The God of this universe has called you blessed and chosen you for such a time as this. A giant among men/women for such a time as this; yield to Me, the Lord your God, and watch My glory surround you.

The Lord your God is with you. The Lord your God has set things in motion for a mighty move of My Spirit in your midst. You will see signs and wonders, great miracles from above. All will know you are My child, for My hand rests upon you. I want you to love Me. I want My mercy to flow through you, to reach out your hand of compassion in a dry and thirsty land.

June 22, 2012

COLLISION COURSE

I am the Lord your God, King of the Universe. Every knee will bow to Me. No one can stand in the glory of My presence. Nations will shake and seas will roar; anguish of nations, not knowing the way out. The people will tremble in fear, asking the rocks to fall on them to hide them from My presence.

My children, SPEAK while I can be found so those who have an ear can hear the Word of the Lord, your God. Bring them to the light of My presence. It all comes down to speaking. Will you speak the words I give you to speak? Faith comes by hearing and hearing by the word of God. The Lord your God is almighty. Is there anything too small that it escapes My sight? Is there any need too great that I cannot meet it?

If My people will humble themselves and pray, and turn from their wicked ways, I will heal their land; the land of their hearts. The nation is on a collision course with destiny ~ the Lord your God. It won't be pretty. Wayward individuals intimidate and bully. They are on a collision course with the Lord, your God; the Almighty One, the Giver of Life, the Maker of Heaven and Earth. Evil men and woman have left Me, thrown Me aside like yesterday's garbage; the precious treated as vile rather than Holy. I am a Holy God and I cannot tolerate sin in My presence.

A covenant broken, a land dedicated to My name run amuck. Evil ones have erected altars, offering sacrifices to their gods. The people watch in silence, condoning; the smoke rises to Me as a vile stench.

Knock down the altars to the gods, My people. Smash them to bits. In their place, erect an altar to Me, a Holy sacrifice with a

197

Holy heart. Walk righteous in Me, in faith, believing the Lord your God is one God and able to restore all the enemy has stolen.

I am able to heal the land. Where My presence is, there is life; abundance of joy as the ground springs forth with abundant fruit. Hearts will be fertile and receive the seeds of hope to harvest an abundance of joy, for the joy of the Lord is your strength. It will set you free from the ties that bind.

June 27, 2012

I NEVER FAIL

Trust Me. Trust in Me, the Lord your God. I never fail. I never fail to lift your head, I never fail to turn everything around for good for those who love Me. I never fail, because I am love. Love never fails to accomplish what it sets out to do; Love never fails. I will never fail to accomplish the plans and purposes I have for your life.

It may not look like YOU think it ought. It may not be what YOU planned, but the best laid plans of man cannot compare with what I have prepared for you. Your eyes have not seen, nor your ears heard and your mind cannot imagine, the wonders and beauty you will behold when you come into the fullness of Me.

Store your treasures in Heaven where neither moth nor rust can destroy. Trust Me, to accomplish the plans I have for your life. Trust Me that I work evil for good; ashes for beauty. You will come out of the kiln red hot, but when you cool you shall be a beautiful empty vessel, ready to receive the fullness of My Spirit.

I want to move and breathe through you. I want your thoughts to be My thoughts, and for you to do what you see the Father doing. I want your hands to be My hands, to comfort the hurting. Give a drink of water to the least of these, then give them a drink of the living water. They will never thirst again. An endless supply is available to flow through them into the lives of others. Reach them. Reach the ones who know me not.

Come out from the walls that confine you. Step into the world and be My light. Chase back the darkness. Confront the giant and take the land back from those who taunt you. You are a mighty army, get dressed for battle. March around the walls and see

Jericho fall. What is too great for your God?! Nothing, says the Lord of Hosts. I give and I take away. Through it all, you learn to depend on Me. I am your source. The provider of all your needs. Look at Me. I never fail.

June 29, 2012

I Am

I am the Lord your God, King of the Universe. All that was, all that is, and all that will be is of My making. Fear not, little flock, for the Lord your God is one God. I am mighty to save. Mighty in the Kingdom are those who have given their hearts in surrender; those who hold nothing back from Me, who long to serve Me in Spirit and in truth. Mighty are those who sacrifice their wants and desires to a Holy God in order to see My dreams, the ones I have given you, come to fruition; those who lay up their treasures in Heaven rather than filling their storehouses on earth where moth and rust destroy and the enemy hands can reach.

The Lord your God is with you. The Lord your God is one God. Look to Me for your salvation. I will fight against all that dares raise its head against you. I am salvation. I am grace. I am mercy, and I am, is I am. I am in your midst to provide for your every need. Lean not on your own understanding, for your heart can be deceived. Look to Me ~ to My Word. Say what I say; think My thoughts, and never stray.

The Lord your God is goodness and mercy, and I am in your midst. Think on thoughts that are lovely and true, life-giving truths. Seek Me. Seek My Word in Spirit and in truth. Let My words come to life in your midst. In the midst of My presence is fullness of joy and every good thing.

Seek the truth of My Word. Do not rely on words of men who seek to deceive you with flowery speech and doctrines of demons. These have just enough truth to seem reasonable, but not enough for you to come to a saving knowledge of Me.

Deceit and ravenous wolves are everywhere, but they appear as gentle as doves. Do not be deceived. Seek My face, and My truths. My truths are not the world's truths. The world has perverted My Word and intent. Doctrines of demons with just enough truth to sound reasonable, but a half-truth is not truth; it is a lie, for they are of their father, the father of lies.

Seek Me while I can be found, while freedom to speak is expected. Share truth, confront the lies with My Word and watch them disappear. Resist the enemy and he will flee. Resist him with My Word. My Word is power. My Word is a weapon of change, to change the atmosphere, to change your heart, to change nations; one life at a time.

Do not underestimate My power to affect change, even when it looks like there is no way. I am a God who makes a way. I am a God who gives you hope. I give you a vision for change, a purpose in Me, a stirring, a restlessness within your soul that longs for something more, something greater than where you are at this moment.

Yield to the stirring; it brings you hope. It will restore your vision. It will energize you for the days and weeks ahead. It will bring revelation. The fire of My presence will fill your belly and My plans will go forth.

July 1, 2012

HOLY

Think on those things that are conducive to the Holy life you want to live, not on those things that are preventing you from coming to a Holy life. I am the One who makes you Holy.

July 3, 2012

WHITE HOT

My wrath is white hot. The stench is rising up to Me and it is foul. Rise up, oh warrior, rise up! The time to fight is here. Silence and apathy have drawn you into this battle. You were silent when you should have spoken, and spoke when you should have been silent. The outcome will be utter destruction, for My anger mounts against you.

The false church rose in a way not pleasing to Me. It has led many, many astray. Many have fallen away from Me, and are no longer serving the One true God. Whom do you serve? Who have you been serving? Take a good look at your life. Examine your hearts. Who have you been serving? Is it the father of lies, the enemy of your soul? Mercy speaks to you this day. Choose whom you will serve.

July 11, 2012

GO TELL THE PEOPLE

Jeremiah 1:6-7 (NLV)

6 Then I said, "O, Lord God! I do not know how to speak. I am only a boy." 7 But the Lord said to me, "Do not say, 'I am only a boy.' You must go everywhere I send you. And you must say whatever I tell you.

Go to the people and tell them what I have to say; judgment is coming to America, judgment for turning her back on Me. The church who knows Me not, the people who worship themselves instead of Me. All of creation is groaning in anticipation of My coming. Others are groaning from the mess they have gotten themselves into by ignoring Me.

My remnant believers arise. Your Father is calling you out, calling you deeper. Stand and speak, humble yourselves in prayer for your fellow man. I have saved for Myself a remnant who have not kissed the image of Baal and have not bowed their knee except to Me. That remnant includes YOU.

I am calling you out. I am calling you to come up higher; I am calling your name. Can you hear Me speaking? There is a world out there, a sea of people who know Me not, a sea of people who claim to be a follower of My Son; "Christians" that know Him not.

What does it take to be a follower of mine, to be My child? It takes brokenness, humility, and repentance. It takes honor and obedience. It requires respect toward the ones I call, and greater respect for the ones I send.

I call you out, remnant of My people. I call you out. Are you listening? Are you listening even though the beat of the enemy's drum sounds louder and louder? Look to Me, the God of your salvation. Miracles abound for those who are mine, miracles in the desert places, miracles in the rest, miracles in the uphill struggles, and miracles in the downhill journeys. There are miracles where you expect them not. Watch for miracles, watch for the suddenlies of God as I move amongst the remnant; miracles of provision and miracles on the highways and byways.

Remnant, will you believe Me for miracles as in the days of old? Can you believe your God is not dead and that He is a miracle working God; and I have never changed? As darkness increases around you, My light will shine brighter through you and people will flock to you. They are attracted to the flame within you. Lead them to Me. Miracles will abound, defying even your mind and what you thought I would do, as My words come to life from the pages of time.

If you can believe it, you will see it. You will command and it will come in My name. I restore authority to My chosen ones. The authority of My name has always been there, but you have not walked in it and have doubted. Watch as My Word comes to life. Watch as the sea of faces look up to Me. Watch as I restore power and authority to My Church; not buildings, but to My people who walk in truth ~ you are the Church, not mass assemblies of hypnotized people who are looking for lies, half-truths and deceit, but truth-seekers...God seekers. Those after My heart, those who seek balance between My face and My hand, will see the heart of God.

I am restoring authority. The authority never changed, how you perceive authority is what will change. Feel it rise up in you. Feel increase as you spend time with Me.

July 14, 2012

Whom Do You Serve?

I am the Lord your God. Kings will bow to Me. Watch as I expose the wolf in sheep's clothing who has perpetuated a huge deception upon this nation, against those who have no eyes to see, nor ears to hear; enticed by flowery words and a flattering tongue.

Expose, for grandma is not who she claims to be. Now all will unravel, the tangled mess that the enemy has woven into these United States. I am still God. Judgment has fallen, but My goal is restoration of a great nation that was founded upon My Word, going where I told them to go, settling the land I told them to occupy, believing in Me, and My Word, that though they came from humble beginnings, they would become a great nation. You did just that as I was kept foremost in men's minds and hearts.

The wicked consumed the harvest. Like locusts, they devoured the beauty and heart of this nation. My heart still beats in this country. It is the remnant that will rise to take back what belongs to Me. Can you feel the power rising within you?

Support those I have chosen to bring about the change. Those whom I have called to lead the charge, to turn back the tide, to re-dig the wells of your ancestors who knew Me and stood in faith. Your ancestors fought on their knees and on the battlefields to worship Me in Spirit and in truth. Men who stood for what was right and fought for rights to worship Me. They overthrew tyranny in whatever form it came. Now it is your turn. There comes a time in every man's/woman's life they must choose whom they will serve. This is your time. Who do you serve, God or man?

July 20, 2012

"Church" Triumphant

No matter what the enemy has tried to convince you of, no matter how many things he has taken from you as a nation, as a "church," and as individuals, you are the "church" triumphant.

July 25 2012

Fog

The future is Mine, the grain is Mine, and the firmament is Mine. The dust is Mine. The world is in chaos; spinning on its axis is order, but the people are in disorder. There is anguish of nations, none knowing the way out.

What was once abnormal and sinful is now normal; my creations lead empty lives, blind to their own condition. They smile on the outside, glorifying their sins and evil ways, but I see what is on the inside and they are empty; dead. The cessation of their breathing will mark their natural death, but they are already dead inside, empty where I should be dwelling in their hearts.

I want the world to know that I love them. I want the world to know that I care. All they see around that is beauty is of Me, and they blame Me for the evil, yet cannot see their own wicked ways. They blame Me for the lack of love, but I am love.

A fog has settled thickly over their hearts and minds, clouding their vision. They cannot see. Their ears cannot filter truth from lies, but you are the light. You are the fire that will burn away the fog, for where you trod demons flee. Where you speak, demons fear. They may rise up to harass you, but keep standing, keep speaking.

It is a game; who will blink first, who will flee first. Do not let it be you. Speak My Word, for there is power in the Word. Speak My Word in faith, believing. Darkness will tremble. I tell you the truth, I am the way, the truth and the life, and no man comes to the Father except through Me. There is power in My Name. Even when you do not know what to say, call out the Name of Jesus. Watch things change.

July 27, 2012

MOVE THAT MOUNTAIN

AND THE LORD WOULD SAY TO YOU:

If you have faith the size of a mustard seed, you will work miracles. You can move mountains. There is no obstacle that can stand in your way; not a jail cell, not a mountain of debt, not sickness or disease. Your healing waits on the other side of faith.

Speak to the mountain and watch it move. Stand in faith and see miracles; miracles of provision and healing. They said it was impossible, but I am the God of the impossible.

If I am your God, then you are a child of Mine, you can do what you see your Father doing. You have the power to change lives and circumstances, to change the atmosphere. Christ lives in you. No matter how large the mountain and no matter how impossible it seems, your faith to see it happen is the door to your miracle.

I turn everything meant for evil into good for those who love Me. I turn ashes into beauty, mountains into mole hills. Step out in faith knowing I am there to catch you. Speak words of faith over your circumstances, release your control and watch Me move.

I am your Father in Heaven. You can trust Me. I know the desires of your heart. You can release to Me your hurts and bitterness, unforgiveness, and fears, those things that color your view of Me, and realize I am the Lord, your God, who loves you. I will not harm you. I desire for you to receive all that I have to give you.

August 1, 2012

HEAD AND NOT THE TAIL

I have made you the head and not the tail. Even though many of you feel like you are the tail, you are blessed and highly favored children of Mine. All things will work out for My glory and your honor among men.

The days are long and the nights are short. There is no shortage of worry and fear in the earth today, but I am the Lord your God, King of Mercy, and I pour out to you this day My wisdom of the righteous.

Do not fear what the nations will go through. Do not fear when nations tremble, for the earth is My footstool and all you see that is beauty is of Me. Let the nations roar; they cannot roar their way out of this. Let them fear, for they have made the bed of their circumstance, but let *My* people rejoice with singing. Let them erupt in praises to their God; the Holy One of Israel, for I love My children. I rejoice over you with singing. My rock establishes you as Kings and Priests in the nations. Do not fear. What can man do?

I am the rock of your salvation and My heart reaches down to you. Do not fear, do not fret, the Lord your God is near. Nothing shall by any means harm you, and nothing shall come near your dwelling.

The Lord your God, is *your* God, Maker of Heaven and Earth. Your God is mercy, but they call Me not. I wait, but they are a rebellious lot, shaking their fist at Me. I am a patient God. I do not desire any be lost, but lost they will be, in all their foolishness, thinking themselves wise.

Your God is a God of mercy, not slow concerning My promises. I am waiting. I wait upon you to rise and be My people on earth, to move in the authority I have given you, to be the apostles of this day, disciples, called out ones...My representatives. I desire you to be My ambassadors, My hands and feet; workers of My miracles.

Children of the most high, you are. Rise up. Speak like it, act like it, and don't let the devil tell you any differently. You are set apart, a chosen people, called before the foundations of time. I call you Mine. Rise up and let Me use you in ways you never imagined, in ways you have only dreamed, for I am a merciful God. I give grace for the humble.

August 2, 2012

HOPE OF NATIONS

I am the Lord your God. All that is, held by My hand. My hand of righteousness upholds you, for you are made righteous by My Son. Grace eternal, justified by the blood of the lamb slain before the foundation of time. I called you. I called you to Myself and you listened. You heard My call, for MY sheep hear My voice and will not follow another. You felt Me drawing you near and you accepted My love, My grace and My mercy.

You inherit the kingdom. You inherited grace, for without grace nothing can be done. A bridge between God and man; I long to give My children every good thing. My kingdom is yours.

Keepers of the light within you, shine like the beacon of light that you are. Unashamedly shine forth. Light the way, for many are in darkness and confused. They walk in fear not knowing the way out they withdraw into their shells.

You have the answers. Stop running, stop being busy and take the time to look around at who is standing next to you. Join forces to affect change, to reach the lost and hurting, to bring them into the kingdom. Exchange truth for lies and darkness for light. Change cursing to blessing; transform a life, a heart, with My Word.

My people stood up for one of their own yesterday (Chick-Fil-A). Sleeping giant, arise, you contain great power. One person, empowered by Holy Spirit and taking a stand, can effect change. Multitudes standing, speaking My words and walking in My deeds can set the course of this nation back on track.

My people, you have been silent too long. You have allowed the enemy to run over you. You have power in your words when they are Mine, spoken in faith. Change the course of this mighty nation. There are things for you to do.

I empower you afresh to speak. Raise your hands and let Me fill you. Open your mouth and I will fill it. Do not be anxious about what you will say. I am the Word, and the Word is God and you are My vessels of change to reach the lost and hurting. You are change agents. You are the change people need to see.

You are the hope, for I reside in you, and I am the hope of nations. I reach out to you this day and encourage you to stand, to speak truth, to be a beacon of light. Reach out to the lost, hurting, weary, and fearful. They will see your peace in the midst of the storm. It will draw them to you. Lead them to Me, My child, lead them to Me. Tell My children I love them.

August 5, 2012

Go Forth

Go forth, My child, go forth. Do not let the lies of the enemy, the words spoken, detour you from the path I have placed your feet upon. Our enemy is a liar, seeking to derail you from your destination in Me. My hand is upon you, child, and I am not letting go as you cling to Me and My Word.

The Son rises upon you, My child. The light of the world floods in bringing hope, new life and a new perspective. The light will let you see things in a new way, for your God has mercy upon all that He has His hand upon. His light shines through.

Do not be afraid to go forth in power and might. Confront the enemy forces, for I am your front and rear guard. Nothing will, by any means, harm you. One by one the angels will be set to flight to drive the enemy back home, forced to leave your land. Your God has spoken.

August 9, 2012

EXPOSED

There are many people going their own way, trying to achieve salvation by the works of their hands. They sit in churches, they may even call upon My name, but they know Me not.

They may say or even do the right things, but I know them not, and the numbers of people who claim to know Me is staggering compared to the number of people whom I know. The remnant, the true followers, are but a fraction of the number who claim to be My children. They are on the road to Hell and they do not even know it.

Lying spirits, pride and arrogance have blinded them to their true condition. They refuse to surrender, preferring to live like the world with a little bit of Jesus thrown in. This is why the church remains impotent. This is why signs and wonders do not follow. This is why they know Me not, and I in that day, will tell them to depart from Me, I never knew you.

On the slippery slope to hell and they care not. They will care one day, but for many it will be too late, doomed for eternity. Many voices are crying out in the wilderness, bearing witness to truth that will set them free, but they are deaf to the call, unable to discern truth from lies, thinking they know best.

You can tell them nothing. Their hearts are hard. The world spins into the future. Time is short. You love the world and the things of the world more than you love Me. Pretenses are there; Pharisee's who act in piety and religion, but I do not look at the outward appearances, I look at the heart. I know people's hearts, and many are far from Me.

I hold your heart in My hand. I control your next breath. The universe fits into the palm of My hand and you fear Me not. You are not taught about My holiness. There is no fear of the Lord. I am a rabbit's foot to bring you luck, a blessing. You take Me out when it is convenient; you rub My foot and make requests. You believe it is a game called life; most do not see the gravity of their situation.

I am a holy God. I will not tolerate sin in My presence. In that day so many will cry out, "Lord, Lord did we not do this in your name or that in your name," but I will tell them the truth, I never knew them. Words and actions are cheap. Man can be fooled by outward appearances, but I cannot be fooled. Your hearts need more of Me and less of man's wisdom, more of My presence and less of your games.

Surrender to Me this day. You know who you are. I am convicting you right now. Stop the games. Stop pretending and surrender to Me. Stop holding back, making areas of your life off limits to Me. Bring down the walls. If you say you can trust Me with your salvation, then why can't you completely surrender to Me?

I am waiting. I desire none to be lost. I am opening your eyes to expose the false sense of security that has come over the body who claims to be in Christ.

August 10, 2012

Go Forth

The Word will go forth. You live, breathe, and have your being in Me. Let the chips fall where they may. Correction is of Me. Holy Spirit, move through the crowd and remove the stops from ears. Let them hear what the Spirit of the Lord is saying. Give them ears to hear. Much is at stake and the price is high to follow Me.

My burden is light. Spiritual versus natural, the race goes on slow and steady, a sprint to the finish. I will work all things out for My glory. Your Lord has mercy. Continue on, fight the good fight. Love your neighbor, and love your God. Watch as I turn the road from rocky to smooth and you glide through time and space in My Spirit.

August 11, 2012

THREAT

Things broke wide open in the spiritual realm and the enemy knows you are a threat. Stand strong, stand tall, face to face with Me. All will know you are My child, My real child.

Unafraid to speak what I tell you to speak, you will go and proclaim My Word and restore the foundations, as that is what you prayed to do, to speak with power and might. All of Heaven backs you up. You have power. You are worthy to walk in this calling, fully obedient to Me.

The release of the anointing is yours. It will be coming upon you to do greater things than you saw Me doing. All will know your God is real, and reigns; they will see the power and the might.

As you go forth from this place to speak truth, not all will want to hear truth, but I desire none be lost. I desire you speak. I give, and take away, and the world around you spins into the future. For many it is a future without Me. What was your detriment as a child is turned around, as a benefit in the kingdom. They said you were too blunt, but people need to hear the cold hard truth. You do it in a way that they know you care. You cry, Lord have mercy, and I will. When you dust off your feet and move on, taking your blessing, your peace will go with you.

I will back you up, as I backed up Paul and Peter. Their words contained great authority and so do yours. Watch as things change and do not falter. The Lord your God is pleased with you. You have pleased your God, and it is My good pleasure to pour out to you a blessing you cannot contain. Things are about to change in the Spirit. Your Lord has mercy.

August 13, 2012

PEACE BE STILL

You are My pride and joy, My children. Though the going gets rough and the sea rages, the boat rocks and the winds blow...though you feel tossed about and fear tries to come in, know that the Lord your God is One, the God who loves you. I am the God who upholds you, the God who will never leave you nor forsake you. I know the end from the beginning. All things will bow in submission to Me.

All of nature praises My name, for I am the Creator of life and Giver of life eternal. Do not fear the storms of life. Even the winds and the waves are in submission to Me. Today I speak, "Peace, be still," and the stillness of the water will be at first an eerie sight as the seas have raged for so long. Allow My peace to overtake and surround you.

It is a conscious decision to receive My peace, to walk in My Spirit or to walk in the world and the world's wisdom. Peace does not, and cannot, come through man or his devices.

Peace is a gift from a Holy God. It is not natural in the world. The world is a world of disorder, but I am a God of order and the world revolves around My Word. Allow Me to use you. Allow Me to be your only One. The One who anoints your head with oil, the One through whom all blessings flow. Allow Me, the Holy One, to come in like a flood and change your circumstances. Allow Me to come in like a flood and wash away your tears, your fears, and all that is not of Me.

August 16, 2012

Pure As Crystal

The Lord your God is with you. The Lord your God is one God. The Heavens and earth will by no means pass away until I am accomplishes My plans and purposes.

Water as pure as crystal flows from My throne. Living water for the asking is yours to partake; water that fills you, water that sustains you. Enter into what I am doing in this place, for I wish to bring changes to hearts and minds, changes to your perspective.

I am in your midst. I am in this place. My power to heal, save, and deliver is in this place. Enter in. I long to bring changes. I long to bring answers to questions and revelations to your prayers. Settle yourselves. You are too busy to hear Me; an encounter with the Holy One awaits.

August 17, 2012

Fresh Oil

Today is the first day of the rest of your life. Actually, every day is the first day of the rest of your life. My mercies are new every day, and the depth of My love for you ever increases.

Silly child, you fear and you worry too much. If you trusted Me as much as you worry, life would be a far different place. The execution of faith would be far different from a place of trusting the Lord your God. The ultimate trust is that you can see your circumstances and just put your hands in the air and praise Me instead of working in your own strength to fix things, to stop sin, or to change your behaviors. The battle is Mine, says the Lord.

It is not by your strength, nor your power. It is by My Spirit that changes are wrought in you. All of Heaven sings praises for one sinner turned around. My grace is sufficient for you. My mercies are new every day. No one can move the hand of God unless I choose to be moved. I chose to pour out upon you an anointing of fresh oil of My presence that breaks the yoke. It breaks the chains. I set you free tonight. Walk in it by faith and fruit will follow.

August 17, 2012

WHOM DO YOU SERVE?

I am the Lord your God, and nations are burning in the fires created by their disobedience. They embrace foreign gods instead of the one true God. All of nature is crying out, moaning and groaning for the day of the Lord, but that time is not yet.

There are things that must take place before the awesome and terrible day of the Lord. People are not ready. They claim to know Me, but know Me not. They go farther and farther away from Me.

They believe truth for lies and lies for truth. They cry out to a god created in their own image rather than the one, true God. All of nature moans, and there are birth pangs. There is anguish of nations not knowing the way out. In all their wisdom, they will fail, for I confuse their way. They cannot see the end from the beginning. They see in part and know in part. Confusion reigns.

Seek first the kingdom of God and its righteousness. Seek first the Lord your God in all things and watch the tide turn as the darkness flee and blessings are restored upon this nation.

This is still a nation under God for I honor those who came before you. I honor their prayers and their dedication to a Holy God, for they stood and fought. They believed for what was right; freedom to worship the Lord their God. They did not fear what man, would do, they feared the Lord their God. They had the Victory! Whom do you fear, God or man? Your future is with one of these. Whom do you serve? You make the choice.

August 19, 2012

RAIN

The sky cries out to the Heavens above, seeking rain for the land, but choices have been made and consequences are expected. You live in a fallen and fractured world. Cry out for mercy on the dry and parched land. I long to not just bring the rain, but to reign in your hearts and minds.

Repent, and I will heal your land. Seek first My face and all will be added. Once you were a nation of abundance; you could be again. I am God who loves to bless, but I am also a God of justice. It rains on the just and unjust. Seek first the kingdom of God. Repent of your wicked ways.

August 20, 2012

TAKE OFF YOUR SHOES

I am the Lord your God and the nations are Mine. The earth and the things therein are Mine. My Word set them forth into being, and in "that" day, the earth and the Heavens will roll up like a scroll.

I speak to you now from Heaven; earth will bow because it is Mine and the nations tremble before the Lord your God. You, My child, know your Father. You hear My Word; the voice of another you will not follow.

I set you in motion. I set the task before you as a mighty nation to rise up, call Me blessed, bring your Father glory in Heaven and on earth. Sing praises to your God, lift and magnify the Name of God in all the earth. All of nature sings praises to Me, and whether there is 1 or 100 listening, not one word falls to the ground. My Word goes forth to accomplish its purpose, bringing Me glory in the land.

Have heart, My heart. Nothing is wasted in the kingdom. Even if it was meant for evil, I turn it around for My glory. The enemy is defeated; no matter the plot, plan, or means of attack, I turn it around for your good. I am a mighty God, a God of mercy; I have pronounced blessings over you My child. I will not leave you nor forsake you. I will bring you through.

Surrounded by angels, filled with the power of My might, you will conquer the land. You will drive the enemy out and all will know that you are My child and I am with you. Our enemy is a defeated foe. Rise up and act in this truth. You wandered in the wilderness, but you have crossed the Jordan on dry land. The enemy will relent. He will turn back. My angels are with you. Take off your shoes; you are standing on holy ground.

August 21, 2012

MIGHTY ARMY

The strength of a thousand men is rising within you. A mighty army is emerging from the shadows of time. They will come into the light, strong and true to their God, igniting a fire in the hearts of men, wielding the sword of My Word to bring the captives into submission to Me. I am the Lord, your God.

The enemy has taken captives believing every kind of evil, he keeps them in bondage. They cannot see their chains, but they are chained and in stocks none-the-less.

Rise up, army of one, the One true God; speaks. Drive back the darkness. Drive back the enemy. The Lord your God is One and I long to see My people free in Me, bound to My will, My plans, and purposes for their life. Each is a seed planted in My kingdom, ordained to set the captives free, to set a neighborhood and a city free.

Promote My agenda. The Lord your God loves to see you speak and do what you see your Father in Heaven doing. Wield the sword of My Word, listen to the voice of Holy Spirit, and rise to new heights. See Me move in a tangible way in your midst. Those things you long to see, those healings and miracles, they start with Me. Surrender to Me and allow Me to move through you. Soon it will become second nature to be doing the will of your Father in all things.

Read Proverbs; know how you should live. Understand the choices you should make. There is only one choice; My way. Choose to see the coming of the Lord your God in the clouds of Heaven. Choose to allow the Lord your God to overshadow your hearts and minds that you may become kings, and priests in the land I gave you. Come grasp your piece of the promised land that has been set aside just for you. Your treasure lies in the field of your obedience. Your provision is where I have called to you to walk out your assignment, to set the captives free.

August 23, 2012

I WILL KILL YOU

I woke to the words, "I will kill you Kerrie - you are the keeper of the flame."

God responded; *The threat is an empty threat for My hand is upon you My child. My hand of righteousness upholds you and nothing shall by any means harm you. No weapon formed against you shall prosper. Hold on to this; My Word.*

The nations tremble and there is a city a flight that needs to come back to Me. It was dedicated by people who sacrificed and loved Me, but though there are buildings given My namesake, they have strayed from Me~ the Lord, their God.

I call the people home. I call them back to Me. The city trembles and the demons are angry. People are confused as they believe what is right is wrong and what is wrong is right.

Arise warriors, push back the darkness. They do not want you among them; they fear Me, in you because deep down they know you are right. They have compromised; it's a large ship to steer back into port and eat humble pie, but it must be done.

I call back into unity the body of Christ, the way it was intended. I broke down the dividing wall between Jews and Gentiles, yet they erected a dividing wall among themselves; monuments to man and man's way of doing things rather than the pure faith and power of My Word.

Pray for the churches. Pray for the pastors and leaders who made Me a competition rather than a body of believers. You broke down the wall and moved out of the four walls; and the resistance has been high to a move of My Spirit. You have heard the same excuses they give Me for not coming together as a body, preferring to remain separate.

Remaining separate is less threatening; ideas are safe and never challenged, everyone is comfortable. It is time to break down the walls erected between churches as well as walls between doctrine and people. Resistance continues, but that resistance is not of Me.

My plan is to draw all men unto Me; I am not about drawing them into this building or that. The time is short; My children need to get on board with what I am doing, what the Spirit is doing. The ways of man surely lead to regret.

My children need to be told not to miss what I have put in front of them; not to miss a move of God, a move of My Spirit in this city. Just because it does not look like you thought, or sound like you thought does not mean it is not Me. Man's ways are not Mine own. They say to you "it's not the way I would do it" and they said the very same thing about Me.

My Son was a stumbling block to many. They did not recognize Him. Many are in danger of not recognizing Him and the things of Me, again. Few recognize the things I am doing in their midst. The people past did not recognize My Son; He did not look like they expected, He did not say what they thought He ought, He did not do what they anticipated, nor did He sound like they thought...but He was no less My son.

I choose the seemingly foolish things to confound those who are wise in their own eyes. Cry out to God for mercy. Gamaliel was right when he said, "I say to you, keep away from these men and let them alone; for if this plan or this work is of men, it will come to nothing; but if it is of God, you cannot overthrow it lest you even be found to fight against God."

August 24, 2012

RAISE A BANNER

You are not alone. It feels like it at times, but you are not alone. The Lord your God is with you.

Interpretation of tongues; "Strengthen your people, Lord. Strengthen your people in the things of you. Remove their burdens and tares of the heart that are not of You. Move and breathe in our midst in a mighty way. Let the earth shake and your kingdoms rise for glory of the one true God."

The Lord your God is with you. I am in your midst and My timing is perfect in all things. Trust Me with your heart and lean not on your own understanding. The Kingdom of God suffers violence, and the violent take it by force.

It is not going easily. The power of darkness is stirred up and has taken to flight like a flock of birds, making effort to push back My light. Rise up, people of God. Rise in your authority in Me. Push back the darkness that longs to take over the light.

The Kingdom of God is advancing; voices are rising to My ears. My people cry out. They are finding their voice again. The enemy gags have been removed; he is not happy. My people are talking. My people are hearing truth. Lies are being exposed; games and deceit are being exposed to the light.

Do not stop, My children. Do not stop. Do not stop speaking and praying. There is power in your words. You are planting seeds and bringing the darkness to light. It is not just the demons who affect you; not just single demons rising up, but territorial spirits and principalities over cities and nations. They are feeling threatened, for they had become complacent; arrogant that they were in control of this nation.

They see My people awakening; speaking and standing, believing for change. Change belongs to Me. It is not the world's way to turn the direction of this ship back into the port of safety in Me. A blessed and glorious nation it can be again. I am coming soon, but the time is not yet.

Souls hang in the balance. Eternity is at stake. I desire none to be lost. Rise, My children, rise, stand, raise a banner to the Lord your God. Your banner is love. Your banner is truth. Let it roll out across this land.

August 26, 2012

DEAL WITH THE DEVIL

This nation is at risk. This nation is in a challenge; a fight between light and dark, good and evil, and evil has risen. The enemy has risen up and taken to flight across this land. Push back the darkness and proclaim My name. Proclaim My agenda to the masses.

In the name of Jesus, every knee shall bow. Principalities and leaders will bow too, for I am God of this nation. I founded this nation for such a time as this, to protect My Israel. To be a light in the night, a beacon of hope; to exemplify the values I, as your God, hold dear.

The enemy has sought to destroy. He has made great inroads as My people slept. They were so sure I would handle it all and keep My hand of protection upon this nation. They thought they had to do nothing. While My people slept, the enemy went on the offense and took much ground. He poisoned the minds of the people and perverted the youth of this nation.

I call light into darkness. I call a return to holiness, a return to My Word as final authority, I call My hopes and dreams back into the heart of the people. Where there is hope, there is life. Without it, people perish. Our enemy perverted the word hope; counterfeited hope to bring destruction upon this nation.

In a world where people want hope and change for the better, they made a deal with the devil and sold their soul to Muslim "terrorists" who are bent on your destruction.

Terrorist does not just mean weapons, fear, and blowing things up. Terror can be wrought and inflicted by power hungry moguls who wield the sword, through a pen, and make unilateral decisions, for what is best for this nation. This people and the pen, in this case, has been mightier than the sword of My Word in the land. With a government run amuck, and corrupt not seeking what is best for the people, they promote their ungodly agenda to drive the multitudes further from Me.

I expose the plot and plans, the agendas of darkness, I have risen up voices to speak and do the "impossible;" to do what others refused and were in fear to do, the hard work, the dirty work to expose. Evidence is placed before you yet you still do not see. This is not surprising, for the blind see not. Deceived, believing lies for truth and truth for lies, the enemy mocks and bullies My voices into silence.

Speak, for the day is at hand. Rise up and speak to this nation; be blessed, for in God we trust, not man. Rise up and shout the Lord your God *is* your God and in HIM we trust. Rise up, people of God, for this is your hour. This is your moment to set the captives free.

Let the blind see and the deaf hear; shake off the spell that has been placed upon them. Hear what the Spirit of the Lord is saying. Rise remnant, arise. Your day is at hand to be the people you were created to be. Speak My Word. Let Me live in and through you. If you cannot find your voice now, how will you find it when the persecution intensifies and you have to choose Me, or the world, as your final answer?

August 28, 2012

PLOTS AND PLANS

The Lord your God is one God and the nations tremble at My feet. The rumbles have begun. The birth pangs, anguish of nations not knowing the way out, but I am the way out. I am the truth and the life. No one comes to the Father except through the Son.

Many have devised plots, plans, and formulas to come to Me. They, in the foolish wisdom of man, have sought to make it more complicated than it is, refusing to believe it could be so simple; a heart surrendered to Me, the Lord their God. In pain and foolish pride, they press on, looking for what is right in front of their noses. They miss Me, because they refuse humble submission and cling to foolish pride; a stumbling block to many.

Nation will rise against nation. There will be anguish, not knowing the way out. For all My good intentions, they will be lost; off base and out of line, making the simple things difficult, and the difficult things simple. A backwards world, the carnal mind is. Thinking themselves wise in their own eyes, destruction awaits, but I give grace to the humble and strength to the weak.

I work all things for good for those who love Me and are called according to My plans and purposes; those who place faith in Me, who seek Me while I can still be found, those who reach out to grasp My hand as I reach down toward them.

Hearts cry out, "Lord, have mercy," and I do. For those who need help when they see no way out, I come down with all My glory to change a life, to change a nation, one life at a time. I reach down with humble grace to show you the way home to the Lord your God. I want you; heart, mind, body, and soul.

August 29, 2012

GAME CHANGER

The clock is ticking. One by one, the hands of time move across eternity. The future is now, and the things I have spoken will come to be. Naysayers will rise in the face of My Word to the contrary. My logos and My rhema words will come to pass, for I do nothing without telling My prophets.

My prophets have been warning. My prophets have been speaking. There are so many deaf to the call; asleep and content, they wander along the path of life, but they refuse to take a risk, and obey. They will never fulfill that one great thing they were put upon the earth for; that one great kingdom life changer.

My obedient ones change lives. My obedient ones change cities, towns, and nations, bringing the kingdom to its knees in praise and worship of the one true God. Game changers; My obedient ones are game changers. They are not busy with the things of life and distracted, but busy with the things of Me. They are seeking for more of Me in every situation. Hungry for the things of God, not just content with the status quo or the things they have been told, they press ahead in the things of Me.

Obedient to My call, you may see little fruit for your labors. It seems nothing is changing in the natural, but this is a lie from the enemy. It remains true that for every action, there is an equal and opposite reaction by the kingdom of darkness to stop the power of God from going forth into the world. You, however, are victorious. You conquer by faith and the word of your mouth.

Let the words of your mouth rise like a sweet savor to your God and King. When you speak, all of Heaven backs up My faithful ones. All of Heaven backs you up. You are the game changers, the ringers, the ones I planted and entrusted My kingdom to.

Yours is the glory in Christ Jesus, for you do it not to make a name for yourself but to lift high the King of Kings, and Lord of Lords, your God and Savior. Your hard work has not gone unnoticed. I see. I see your toils. I see your strengths and your weariness. I see your joy and your pain. I see your laughs and your cries. Press on; the hands of time are marching forth into eternity.

August 30, 2012

TRAIN

The train is rolling down the track. It has no brakes. It is My people who stand between Me and disaster. Pray, My people, pray. You stand in the gap. You stand in time, for such a time as this. Nations tremble and bow to their knees, either in reverence or in fear.

Fear has gripped this nation, but so has blind arrogance. The need to be right and to lead without example has become the mainstay of American politics. Children follow the Pied Piper over the cliff to their destruction. They are blindly following; without eyes, they cannot see. They are deaf to My call; without ears, they cannot hear what the spirit of the Lord is saying. Vitriol they spread, lies they portend as truth and the world revolves around fallacies, half-truths, and out and out blatant lies.

Can you hear Me calling? I am the way, the truth, and the life. Man cannot save you. Government cannot save you. The One, true God, can save you and radically transform your life.

Change is of Me; true change to affect the destiny of this nation and its people. True change only comes from Me. All other changes are temporal and fleeting.

God have mercy. Cry out from your soul. God have mercy on a backwards world. They see no other way. They see lies as truth and truth as lies, but their hearts cry out from within their chests to be delivered from bondage. The truth is written on their hearts, but they are blind and deaf to its truth. The heart is a compass, always pointing at the Word. It is My Word that will always lead you back home to Me. The world may get loud, but the one who remains in perfect peace is the heart who is stayed on me. May My grace and love be with you...

Father God

September 2, 2012

MISSION

I am the Lord your God. I sent you on a mission to share in the harvest of another, to reap fields in which you have not sown, to share in the rain in season and out of season, and to celebrate the mercies of the Lord, your God. The wealth of the wicked is laid up for the righteous, faithful to obey in the big and little. The Lord, your God, is with you.

September 3, 2012

CARRIERS OF THE DUNAMIS

The time has come to decide, whom you will serve, and who do you say I am? This is not revealed to you but by the Spirit of the Lord. The Spirit of the Lord is calling, drawing all men to the Father in Heaven. Who do you say that I am? You were created for such a time as this, to walk in My ways and to be a godly example in the Earth. You were created for such a time as this, to speak My Word into existence, to move among the people. My Word will not return void. It will accomplish its purpose.

We need more speakers and less complainers. We need more doers of the word and less dreamers. We need more power and authority in the Earth, less fear of man and his ways. We need more who will rise up and do as I said, unashamed to heal the sick and raise the dead, unafraid to cast out demons.

Satan roams the streets; a roaring lion. My people hide in fear. Why do you fear what I have given you authority over, that which I have commanded you to control? The winds and waves are in your control. Calm the seas of your life. Speak "Peace, be still," so it will go well with you. Peace in the midst of the storm is about you and your attitude as the storms rage. The one who is kept in perfect peace is one who abides in Me, for in the shadow of My wings there is protection.

Make your voice heard in the land. Joshua, take the land, the Promised Land. It still flows with milk and honey, though it does not look like you expected. See through My eyes, not with eyes of man. You crossed the river Jordan on dry land and the enemy pursued, but he will not be going where you are going. There are vineyards that you did not plant which are ripe for the harvest. Look unto the fields, for they are ripe unto harvest.

Reach the hurting and the lost with the power of My words spoken through vessels of love. I desire none to be lost. Pump up the volume of your voice to speak; know that when you decree and declare My words, all of Heaven backs you up. My Word is your sword and shield; push back the enemy.

Your beliefs are looked at like nostalgia, for the enemy has gained much ground. The world these teenagers grow up in is a far cry from the carefree life you lived as a child. They grow up too fast. There is so much evil in the world. There are no absolutes, no right or wrong; the wisdom of the world, such foolishness. Time marches on, but I raise up a mighty army of youth to spread from coast to coast that will contain the fire of God within them, burning the chaff wherever they go. They are called to set the demons to tremble, and angels to flight. They will carry forth My mercy as a weapon of their warfare; a mighty army of power. They will be carriers of the dunamis, carriers of the power; great signs and wonders will follow them and the people will be amazed.

September 4, 2012

WHAT WILL YOU DO WITH ME?

The Lord your God is One God. Nations are spinning on the globe, out of control, choosing to go their own way. As I have attested (previous prophetic word), they march towards eternity like a passenger train out of control...towards their eternal destinies oblivious and unaware; blind to the truth that stands before them which could protect them from eternal destruction.

My heart breaks. I desire none shall be lost. Rise up, oh people of God. Speak. Be who I created you to be, for such a time as this, as Esther did. She fasted and prayed; she broke protocol and spoke to the king, beseeching him to protect her people. You, too, are in the kingdom for such a time as this. The future of your people, hangs in the balance. The future of your children and grandchildren is precarious; won't that cause you to rise up and raise a banner to the Lord your God? Will you not speak, knowing as Esther did that if she perished, she perished, but she still did all she could do to save her people.

What will you do with Me? Who do you say I am? How big am I, in your eyes? Can you believe and have faith for big things? Can you believe and have faith, that as it was with Esther, the hidden hand of God is with you? It is at work, just waiting for the people who call themselves mine to pray and seek My face. I do not intervene without permission. Pray, people of God. The Lord your God demands you speak and pray; rise up or will you exercise your free will to do as you please? Choose this day whom you will serve. Who do you say I am? What will you do with Me?

September 10, 2012

BIRTH PANGS

The Lord your God is with you. The Lord your God is One. I would move Heaven and earth for you to love Me as I have loved you. The Heavens shake and the oceans roar; there is confusion in the land, the land of your fathers. There is deception. People are afraid. They have no way out but through Me.

All of nature is groaning; birth pangs have begun to birth a new nation. One nation under God, with Jesus as the head. It is coming soon. It is coming fast, as a thief in the night. My horses are prepared, the armor is ready to wage war against the beast. All of Heaven waits. No one knows the day or the hour, except the Father in Heaven.

I sound the battle cry. A mighty army is rising up on the Earth. The remnant of My people will make changes in the Earth. Return to your God, the God of Heaven and Earth, the one true God. All of creation can feel the rumbling. They are grumbling and complaining, moaning about the state of the nation. Cry out to Me you peoples, for I am the rock of your salvation. There is no other way. Not one of your gods will save you, stubborn prideful lot you are, thinking all your wisdom can turn the tides.

The seas of humanity are being stirred up in a cauldron of boiling oil and you cannot see the danger that is about to befall you. You cannot fix this mess. No man is strong enough, no man is good enough, no man has wisdom enough to fix this mess.

I, the One true God, will not leave you orphaned. Cry out to Me all you peoples, cry out to Me to save you from your mess. Cry out with a true heart towards Me; acknowledge My ways. Belong to Me, leave your other gods. See them for what they are, sticks and stones, powerless to save you. Acknowledge Me in all your ways. Repent, and I will heal the land.

I give, and it is I who takes away. The sun shines and the storms gather in due season. The sun will shine again in due season, depending upon what you do in the storm. Cry out to Me, people of Zion, cry out to Me. I am the Lord your God, King of Heaven and Earth. The New Year is approaching. It is time for a fresh start; fast and pray. Seek the Lord your God and see what I will do to change the tide.

September 12, 2012

POINT OF NO RETURN

Again, it is clear, we have a choice to make as a nation, as a people, as a remnant of God. Be silent or speak...

Point of no return. The Arab Spring has begun (back in 2010). Satan is stirring up the Muslims and the people of this nation. Many are deceived, believing Allah is YVHV.

The mighty Satan is rising. Many in this nation think he is their friend. The current administration is ill-equipped to handle this situation. They are apologists, condoning the behavior and actions of the enemy in your midst while snubbing My children, the children of Israel.

Woe to you who call evil good, and good evil. Woe to you who turn your back on Israel, the apple of My eye. When will you rise and speak truth? When will you stop apologizing and running in fear? You have no need to apologize for the Lord your God. You are condoning every sin that comes your way, condoning the agenda of the Muslim people; there is no peace in their hearts.

Allah is not Me. Allah, is not a god of love. He is Satan, and he stirs up the people to come against Me and My children in the earth.

September 13, 2012

OFFENSE RUNS RAMPANT

I am the Lord your God and nations are in an uproar, rebelling, with Satan fanning the flames of that rebellion. Nations rise and fall, but My hand is upon you, My child, My hand is upon you. Though nations rumble and roar, the peace of God can fill your heart when your eyes are fixed and stayed upon Me.

Treacherous times are here; the earth is shaking and all of nature is crying out to Me, when will the end be, what will be the signs of your return? I tell you the truth, you are living those signs right now. Offense runs rampant in the land, over small and inconsequential things. Look at what the enemy has done with offenses; blown them up, way out of proportion, and selfishness to the extreme. Only their hearts matter, only their lives are important, only their beliefs are correct...anyone who does not think like them is automatically an enemy.

The beauty of this country was in the diversity of color and culture, but the enemy perverted everything good. Those differences have become a point of contention which has spun out of control. Blind people promote a satanically influenced agenda to divide and conquer.

There is no tolerance, yet they cry out for tolerance. When they state, "We must have tolerance," they only mean tolerance for their sins and beliefs. Gods of self, they have made idols of man. The world spins and the hands of time tick. Blind and deaf to their deception, they are blind and deaf to the truth that is staring them in the face.

My people, are you prepared for what is to come? Prisoners in your own houses, in jails, and concentration camps? Life as you know it is changing. The enemy has made great inroads to erode the life you have been free to enjoy. All is changing; how fast that change occurs depends upon you.

I have been exposing a reflection of hearts for evil, yet you refuse to hear. You make wrong decisions. You will wake up one day and discover where you have been led astray and you will wonder how you got there, but you have no one to blame but yourselves.

Now is the time to speak; rip off the blinders and earplugs...listen. Hear and know what the Spirit of the Lord is doing and repent of your wicked ways. Do so now, while there is still time to change the future path this nation is taking.

The only true freedom is found in Me. Governments, idols of man, sticks, and stones cannot save you. I am the God of angel armies and I am mighty to save. I am mighty to heal, mightily able to reverse the course and consequences of your decisions, but you must turn to Me.

September 14, 2012

FOR GOOD IS EVIL

I am the Lord your God and nations are trembling; light is battling against darkness. The divide is opening more clearly every day as I separate the sheep from the goats. Lambs are being lead to the slaughter by the evil one who is pushing his agenda on this earth. He fans the flames of unrest in the hearts and minds of men.

His ammunition is hate which he uses to stir the hearts and minds of men. He whips up the evil that is already in their hearts; seeds planted from generations before. The rivalry between brothers, Isaac and Ishmael, continues. Like jealous brothers, they are stirred up with envy disguised as hate; hatred against My blessed, chosen ones.

You are still chosen, but disobedience and impatience birthed this conflict. I turn everything around for My glory. As I have told you days ago, the birth pangs are unpleasant. You are living in this time and you are watching the pages of My Word come to life in the lands.

I desire none be lost, but man has free will. I send out the fire of My Spirit to meet the hearts of men who are willing to hear. I send out the Spirit of truth to speak to the minds of men, to affect change and spread wildfire in your midst.

The times are changing. The days of old, the innocence of days gone by, has faded into the sands of time, never to return. For good is evil, and evil is good in the minds of men. They have no desire to serve Me in Spirit, and in truth, preferring half-truths and lies to condone their sins and tickle their minds. They desire to live as they wish, double-minded men in your midst, filling the land with their poison.

Look to Me, the One true God. I am the author and finisher of your faith. I began a good work in you, and I will see it through. I will not abandon you, for I am in your midst and I hear the sound of rain. I hear the sound of thunder; rain in the Spirit to water the dry land until it is fertile soil.

September 18, 2012

SOUND THE TRUMPET

The Lord is the blessing and glory of Heaven and Earth. To Him is all glory forever and ever, amen. Rock of Ages He is, and will forever be. Give God the glory forever and ever, amen. Give God honor and praise. Worship, for the King of Kings is worthy to be praised. With all you have inside you, every fiber of your being, live to bring Him praise.

Command the trumpets to sound in Zion for THE God and King is stepping into your season of despair and turning it around for His glory. The hidden hand of God has been working all things around for His glory. Even when you could see Him not, His hand was upon you, His child. All of Heaven backs Him up when He makes a decree.

Sound the trumpets in Zion, for the miracle worker God is on the throne. Sound the trumpets in Zion, for the God of Mercy, your today and tomorrow, is with you till the coming of the age.

Sound the trumpets in Zion, for the King of Kings and Lord of Lords is God of all. You are His child, His inheritance, a mighty nation, a people free in Him.

Sound the trumpets in Zion, for the King is on the throne of righteousness. He holds you in His right hand, sustains you, loves you, and protects you. God of all mercy, I will extend My hand, My invitation to all who are willing to humble themselves before Me. My hand is extended that they may take up their cross and follow Me. I invite all to serve Me as they depend upon Me in all things.

All of nature is groaning; crying out to the Lord, their God, for mercy. Mercy will be extended to those who are My children, called according to My purposes, My namesake, in the land of My people. Nations rise and fall, shaking before your God. People have hearts of stone, trusting in man's wisdom to deliver them from evil and the frightful day of the Lord, when all will bow at My feet, and their veils be removed. The hearts of the people will be revealed. At that time, there will be no denials, no excuses, and no turning back; it will be too late in that day. Foolish virgins you are, you will miss the coming of your King. It will be as a thief in the night, I shall arrive at an hour you least expect. The people will be living as in the days of Noah, full of sin and violence, distracted by the things of this world, wholly unprepared for what will befall them. It will be too late when the son of perdition is in the earth.

Make My name known among the peoples, plant seeds into their hearts, one heart at a time. Reach them for Me. Tell them I love them, that I desire none be lost. The hour is at hand to turn and repent for wicked ways. The Lord your God has spoken.

September 19, 2012

HORDES OF HELL

I woke in middle of the night with a vision and hearing the words:

"They are coming as hordes in the night, scores of them to do battle with the King."

Vision: I saw the hordes of Hell coming out of a portal. They looked and moved very similar to the way the enemy moved in the movie *The Matrix.*"

The Lord spoke the following:

The Hordes of Hell are riled up. They hear a sound of a distant thunder; the thunder of a mighty army waking up and assembling ranks. It is the army of the Lord, the remnant people, waking up across the land. The enemy (Satan/demons) has taken to flight to push back his enemy (the remnant) that is rising.

Lies and deceit abound; they will use every trick they can to stop you. Do not be dissuaded from My plan. Do not fear, the God of the angel army armies is with you. Did I not tell you the angel armies would be passing by and you had a choice to join rank or watch from afar?

My voices are rising in the land; they are being minimized and ignored, but they are rising, none-the-less. The voices are small, like the size of a man's hand, but about to rain down in a torrent. If you believe, stand, march, cry out to the Lord your God and move as I move. Do as I do, be still when I am still, and watch the tide rise and fall at the sound of My Word.

Repent and I will heal the land ~ the land I gave you, the land of your fore-fathers, the land that is still flowing with milk and honey. You crossed the Jordan, now fight the battles to possess the land I gave you. There are many battles to fight. Drive the "ites" out. Watch some walls fall. Choose this day who you will serve. I call you to drive the "ites" out from among your midst.

Hittites: (Sons of terror. Subliminal torments, phobias, terror, depression, deceit)

Girgashites: (Clay dwellers. Focus on earthliness, unbelief in what cannot be seen)

Amorites: (Mountain people. renowned, Obsession with earthly fame and glory, domineering)

Canaanites: (Lowlands people. Addictions, perversions, exaggerated people-pleasing)

Perizzites: (Belonging to a village. Limited vision, laziness, low self-esteem)

Hivites: (Villagers. Vision limited to enjoying an earthly inheritance, hedonism)

Jebusites: (Threshers. Suppression of spiritual authority in fellow believers, legalism)

(http://www.shamah-elim.info/girgash.htm#The_7_types_of_evil_spirits)

Drive out the "ites" - take your position of authority; pray, draw the sword of the Word...refuse to back down. Resist the enemy and he will flee. This applies to all that has risen up in this nation. Fast and pray, repent before the Lord your God. Every one of you has played a part in things getting this far away from Me. Whether through silence or apathy, you have run like the world, caught up in the things they are caught up in, reverencing the things they reverence, doing the things they do, and saying the things they say. Now is the time to turn and run towards the enemy; send him to flight.

The enemy will not expect you to rise up and speak. He will not expect you to decree and declare, let alone pick up 5 smooth stones and run toward him in My name. They will mock and taunt, yell and scream, and do their best to intimidate, but let them; it is the best they have to use against you. Do you see the difference? They walk in darkness and smokescreens.

Words will not harm you. When you counter them with My truth, they fall to the ground and lose power. Use words for My glory; change the tide, take the land. This is the country that was given to you to occupy and subdue, but there are enemies in the land.

Drive them out with My Word. Talk to them about Me, exercise the authority you have been given; My words. If you do not stand with the God of Angel Armies, you will be held captives in the land you were given to occupy. Do not take the spoils unless I command it; some spoils will be the end of you and some will be laid up for you as treasures of darkness.

The Lord God is a God of mercy, but I need to see which side of the fence you are on. Let the doubts flee, make a commitment, take a stand in the land. Raise a banner to the Lord your God.

September 20, 2012

REFLECTION OF THE HEART

The Lord God, Son of Man, will be coming in the clouds in all His spectacular glory, but that time is not yet. Nation will rise against nation and tongue will rise against tongue. All of nature will cry out to the Lord their God, Creator of every living thing. Then the end will come.

I will rule and reign with a rod of iron. I will subdue nations, tribes, and peoples. It will be a grand and glorious time for a while; a day is like a thousand years. Then evil will run its course to reveal the hearts of man. Many will choose the way of destruction rather than the way of true peace.

When the Lord spoke the words above to me, He demonstrated that it was in context with all the other recent words. I am crying, in mourning, begging God to forgive us. I asked the Lord if He would tell me who the next president would be.

I was given the answer; "Man of sin," and the caveat; a corrupt election. This next election will be a reflection of hearts. What more can I do, God asked, indicating that He had exposed the corruption, the wolf in sheep's clothing, the lack of a birth certificate and nothing mattered. The media and the people are deaf, dumb, and blind.

I asked the Lord if we could change the path. He said, if we would respond as I preached on September 7, 2012 (see link to video sermon below). He said, the next election would be a reflection of the hearts of the people. If the people voted for more of the same destructive change, then this nation would see judgment.

I preached per the Holy Spirit on that date; "I am not sure if we can change this, but it is up to us, HIS people to REPENT, SPEAK, PRAY, STAND! God relented with Hezekiah. He said he would not destroy Sodom and Gomorrah if he could find a handful of righteous. God have mercy! Your remnant is crying out to you! We will do it your way. Forgive us Lord for our apathy, our silence, lack of prayers and not trusting You.

There are more than ten in the land, who serve the one TRUE God. I know what I heard the Lord say, this next election will be a reflection of the hearts of the people and it grieves me to know that people who claim to be GOD'S children will vote for one who supports the things that God hates and calls an abomination (abortion, homosexuality). I can hardly speak when I think of these things. I just frankly do not understand. The stakes are so high and yet people do not see.

You can watch the video Whom Will You Serve and all our videos at www.youtube.com channel bearwitnessmin.

http://www.youtube.com/watch?v=gxbBiMnLJ5o&list=UUa1Y_U w_pXuSF1D--8q-5Xg&index=6

September 24, 2012

HEAR AND OBEY

This day I call you out from among nations, to speak My voice of victory to the captives. They will run and not grow weary for I will lead them with My right hand. All will know you are My children. Children birthed of Me and My Spirit, for this is a new day, in a new season.

The tides of humanity have changed, but the hearts are the same; evil and corrupt, yet they also contain knowledge of Me, for I have written My words upon their hearts and they know I exist. Going their own way to fill a void that cannot be fulfilled with the things of this world, they die empty and alone, never experiencing the love of their Heavenly Father. They are doomed for eternity, never knowing Me.

They could have had it all. Every good gift comes from the Father above, but they did not recognize My hand when I gave them good things. I am God. I am the God of your today and tomorrow; the nations tremble and people are fainting out of fear, wanting to run, but there is nowhere to go. For so many, I am is not an option. Pray for your fellow man to wake up, look up, and seek Me while I can still be found.

The author and finisher of your faith has spoken. The One true God of Israel, Who formed you in your mother's womb to serve Me. You were birthed for such a time as this; you were raised, and I command the army of My children to arise. I speak Spirit to Spirit and heart to heart, arise. I call forth in My Name to fight the good fight, knowing you never fight alone. My angel armies make up your front and rear guard.

Whom do you fear? Fear the Lord your God and obey My instructions. Obey the call I put on your life. For such a time as this you were called, fully equipped in Me to carry out the assignment I laid before you. No man can stop My plans unless you let him. Ignore the noise and chatter. Ignore the distractions. Tune in to Me. Hear and obey My instructions. Pray, did I not tell you to pray?

Get out of that slumber the enemy has put you in; you allowed it. Shake off the sleeping powder and rise. Put on your armor and stand for what is holy. Let the chips fall where they may in this life season. At least you stood, at least you spoke and heeded the call of the Watchman; their blood will not be on your hands.

September 25, 2012

TODAY I BLESS YOU

Today I send legions of angels to move and act on My behalf in the earth. They are already moving the obstacles at your feet to make your path clearer. Move, My people, move. Speak, My people, speak to the mountains with words of faith and watch them tremble; watch the mountains move.

It is going to become clearer, the way you are to go, the path you are to take. In My mercy, I see your struggles to find the way. You call out to Me for guidance and direction, and I will not leave you orphaned. Even in the desert times, I am with My children. I sent My pillar of fire by night and My cloud by day. It may not be the way you thought you were to go, but follow Me, nonetheless, for I know the way home. I know the way to the Promised Land; the land of your youth, the land of milk and honey.

Do not faint with fear for what is to come upon the earth. You, My child, are safe in My arms. My hands are upon My children. In love, I cradle you. I caress your hair; you are Mine, and nothing shall pluck you from My hand. Nothing can steal you away; not plagues, nor famine, nor talk of war or peace. You are mine. Let the truth sink in. You are mine, a child of the Most High God, daughter of Israel, son of the King. You are mine.

Go forth in that security and in My authority; speak to those situations. Speak in faith and mountains will move. Stop the double-minded manner, the highs and lows; speak like you mean it. Say it like you would tell your kids to do something. When you know you are the parent, you speak like it. Now speak like you are a child of the King, bearing My ring upon your finger. Speak from the authority you have been given and watch the angels set to flight. Watch mountains tremble and enemies fear; mountains will move in the Name of the One True God.

Let boldness rise within you. You are My child. Act like it. Walk like it, hold your head high. Talk like it; be who I call you to be.

September 26, 2012

LIGHT IN THE DARK

The Lord your God has spoken volumes in these past months; Rhema words. Are you heeding the messages, the words of My heart through My servants who have ears to hear and eyes to see? They see what is on the horizon. They have been given a glimpse into the time to come and the ramifications of disobedience to My Word.

This is not a competition of one party or another; this is a clash of ideals, of moral compass, of light against dark, and the stakes are high. Can you hear what the Spirit of the Lord is speaking? Are you still in slumber or are you awake, ready in armor and sword to confront the battles that lie ahead? The "ites" in the land have risen against the One true God, the God of your fathers, the God of this nation.

What will you do with me? What will you do when it is not popular to speak My Name? How about when you are threatened in My Name? What will you do with the Lord your God? Will I still be your God, the God of your today and your tomorrow? Will you trust Me? Can you have faith in Me when all around you looks like anything, but life as you know it? Will that shake you, or are you ready to face the world ahead which is rapidly changing and will one day be unrecognizable to you?

Your God lives. Your God loves. Will you love? When all is bleak and dark, will you know that My love shines brighter in you, in the dark, than in the light. Will you know My light is a beacon of hope to the hopeless, for only in Me is their hope. This slogan has been borrowed and abused but I am hope, I am the love that cannot be extinguished, the love in the night, to bring you safely home.

Your God lives. The Lord your God is with you. I will not leave you nor forsake you, but I call upon you this day to rise. You cannot afford to be silent or minimized. Chose this day who you will serve...whose mouthpiece will you be...Mine, or the enemy? Whose agenda will be your agenda?

Will you speak truth when it is not popular? Will you be the living truth of My Word and deed, or will compromise mark your time on earth? What will your name be when it is all said and done, good and faithful servant, or wicked one?

Would you recognize Me if I was standing right in front of you, or would you be filled with doubts and fears because you are living a lie, giving Me lip service in order to look good to those around you while your heart is far from Me? Do I know you? Choose this day who you will serve.

September 28, 2012

SOVEREIGN

I am the Lord God, the sovereign God, Maker of the Heavens and Earth. All gold and silver is Mine. I have laid up treasures taken from the evil one for your good, to do the work of the Lord. The time is coming when there will be a massive shift in the Spirit.

Set your hearts upon Me, My kingdom, My Word; obey Me. Walk the narrow way without compromise and watch Me move in your midst. Narrow is the road that leads to Me, but broad is the road that leads to death. Many are on it, following the pied piper; lulled by the sweet words, music, and promises that will be broken.

My promises are yes, and amen to My children, for what concerns you, concerns Me. Therefore, let what concerns Me, concern you. Raise your voice in prayer and praise to the One true God. Humble of heart, stand before Me. I can move in humility; I exalt the humble and resist the proud. The sovereign God is still sovereign and I change not.

Let Me be God; strip your selves of all human expectations and plans and trust in faith that the One, true God, knows what is best and knows the way. The ways of man lead to death and destruction; every evil pervades the hearts and minds of men.

However My child, a child after My own heart has not been given a spirit of fear, but the mind of Christ. Let My words and thoughts, be words of faith that proceed from your mouth. Activate your faith into being; turn those plans into reality. The angels and demons wait to see what comes out of your mouth. You will have what you say, for good or evil. Make your words expressions of faith.

September 30, 2011

You Are My Child

You are My child, and I am the Lord your God. I do not make mistakes. I made you. I formed you. I guided you for such a time as this. Do not let man, or the things man does, tell you any differently.

My child, you are loved by the King Himself, the Lord God Almighty. How can it get any better than that? Stand strong, stand in faith. Believe in Me as I believe in YOU, My child. You are My creation and, like My Son, when you are in Him, I am well pleased.

Keep walking My child, keep going. Place one foot in front of the other. I know you have little strength, but you have been faithful to My Word. I have set before you an open door. This is a time of cleansing, use it wisely. What you do in this time will hinder, or allow you to move forward through the open door to the next season.

This is not a time of New Year's resolutions, but a time of forgiveness and cleansing; a time of removing the dead things in your life and replacing them with thoughts that are alive in Me. You are building MY kingdom, one stone at a time, and if everyone works on the wall in front of their own house, the walls will be built in record time.

You have the Holy Spirit. You have the skills. Look to Me for the knowledge to accomplish your unique task. My kingdom reigns. The enemy has been defeated. What it looks like does not matter. Look up, My child, for the day of your redemption draws nigh, closer than when you first believed.

September 30, 2012

No Less Sovereign

I am sovereign. I draw you by My Spirit, says the Lord to Me. Everything that rises to touch you passes through My hands. As with Job, Satan needed permission, but the difference is that I orchestrate the storms of your life to make you strong, to make you a mighty warrior for your Lord God and King.

Every day you make decisions to follow Me, to move closer or step away, but I am no less sovereign. I see the end from the beginning. Yes, you will suffer consequences for the decisions you make when you turn away from Me. The entire Word of God is a record of decisions made by man and the directions those decisions took him; obedience or disobedience, blessings or cursing, but I will not be mocked. What a man sows, he shall reap. I am no less sovereign.

Sovereign: Supreme ruler. A person who has sovereign power, or authority, a group, or body of persons, or a state having sovereign authority. Belonging to or characteristic of a sovereign or sovereignty; royal. Having supreme rank, power, or authority. Supreme; preeminent; indisputable: A sovereign right. Greatest in degree; utmost or extreme. Being above all others in character, importance, excellence, etc. (*Dictionary.com*)

October 1, 2012

THE KING HAS NO CLOTHES

The King has no clothes. The king is bewildered and does not know what to do to fix this mess that he has created. Truth be told, he has no intentions of fixing it. You can see by his ranting and raving and blaming.

He brought the destruction and stands idly by, more enamored with himself and his hobnobbing with celebrities on the campaign trail. He knows Me not. He is not listening to the One true God, but he is listening none-the-less. He listens to the one bent on the destruction of this great nation.

The time is not yet, but My people failed to stem the tide of evil. Lazy in prayers and apathetic in deeds, they have become powerless and careless. Like the sons of Skevia, the demons taunt, "I know Jesus, I know Paul, but who are you," and they overrun a people without power, without understanding, without exercising the authority in My Name. Having a form of godliness but denying My true power, while embracing all kinds of evil and chasing after false signs and wonders which were brought to mesmerize and intrigue, to pique curiosity but not lead to Me. They lead to a form of godliness, a form of religion, a worship of sorts, but not Me, the One true God. This God is not a God of compromise.

I am a God who expects honor and integrity from those who call themselves My own. Honor and integrity ~ both words whose meanings have been lost in the pages of time. The Lord, your God, never changes. Do not say that was just for yesterday or days gone by, for not one word will fall to the ground, not one word I have spoken will be lost. I will not be mocked. My Word will not return void, though the pages of time have yellowed and dog-eared the edges.

I am a God of power. That power resides in you, yet you act like it does not and you live in fear. Do you not know your words contain power? You know, for I have been speaking this through the teachers and the prophets, yet you ignore My teachers and prefer to speak as the world speaks. Even the enemy believes in the power of positive speaking and dreams of the future.

Where are My people? Where are the ones of My namesake? I see the remnant crying out to Me, but I am addressing those half-hearted ones who are straddling the fence. You know who you are, running with the world. Your compromise has found you out, exposed the heart within your chest that does not belong to Me, though you speak My name.

Turn your heart to Me in word and deed. Turn your heart over unconditionally to your God, Maker of Heaven and earth. I am life, I am truth, and those who recognize Me know Me in Spirit and in truth. You cannot worship with something you do not have, but it is yours for the asking.

It comes with a price. Death to self and life in Me. My yoke is easy and My burden is light. You have a cross to bear, for a servant is not greater than his master, and what they did to Me, rest assured they will do to you. Do not consider it strange these trials you are going through, for what they did to Me, they will do to you.

I say again, My hand is upon My children and they will be kept safe, guarded under the shadow of My wings. Angels standing watch over these I call My own to take you by the hand in danger and lead you to safety as they did with Lot. Do not look back, for the days of old are gone. There is a new order in the land and it is rapidly gaining ground.

As My people sleep and compromise, the hordes of Hell have gained power. They are emboldened to promote their agenda in the land, for it starts at the top. It starts at the head and trickles down to the people, calling good evil and every kind of evil good; a backwards world, blind to the foolishness of their wisdom.

God help us, you say? God have mercy, you say? I am looking at you! What will you do to stem the tide? What will you do to change the land? I have told you the only way out. It is through the Old Testament. Repent and obey the Lord your God. Turn from your wicked ways and I will heal the land. Not one man alone can reverse the tide of evil unleashed, it is only the Lord your God, who is Jehovah - salvation and Jehovah Rapha (healer).

Original Word

October 2012

Measuring Line Is In His Hand

Part 2 Addendum

To follow is the *original* word The Measuring Line In His Hand, Part 2, published in book one along with the 2012 addendum.

BEFORE the Lord gave me the message yesterday about the Measuring Line In His Hand, BEFORE I heard the terrible things our President said about Israel, the Lord had a word.

I had no idea at the time I was writing this word that President Obama called for the division of Israel back to the 1967 borders. I stand with Israel and I am proud to do so, not because I am Jewish and my family is from the tribes of Judah and Napthali, but because Israel/Jerusalem is God's heart, and for nothing more than it is the RIGHT thing to do. I am deeply grieved over the recent events of this president refusing to meet with Netanyahu, lying about not having the time to meet with him, and the cover up of the events of the death of our Libyan ambassador and the attacks on our Libyan embassy.

I am ashamed and embarrassed for our President and his arrogance. He is not speaking for the people of this nation. I have been grieved and crying out to the Lord for Israel and for mercy on this nation, as much of its "new" agendas are a far cry from the values most of us hold dear. I have asked God to forgive him and to forgive the people who were blinded to vote for "change" that has been leading us on the road to destruction.

The Lord showed me a vision of Belshazzar on his throne, drunk, and the people partying as he called for the sacred challis and items from the temple and they drank and partied on. Disrespectful, treating the holy as common while the enemy is standing at the gates, ready to attack. This administration, in its mindboggling arrogance, has disrespected the precious apple of God's eye. The leaders He placed in power have been treated as common and disposable. Can you see God's handwriting on the wall?

Daniel 25: *23 For you have proudly defied the Lord of Heaven and have had these cups from his Temple brought before you. You and your nobles and your wives and concubines have been drinking wine from them while praising gods of silver, gold, bronze, iron, wood, and stone—gods that neither see nor hear nor know anything at all. But you have not honored the God who gives you the breath of life and controls your destiny! 24 So God has sent this hand to write this message. 25 "This is the message that was written: MENE, MENE, TEKEL, and PARSIN. 26 This is what these words mean: Mene means 'numbered'—God has numbered the days of your reign and has brought it to an end. 27 Tekel means 'weighed'—you have been weighed on the balances and have not measured up.28 Parsin means 'divided'—your kingdom has been divided and given to the Medes and Persians."*

The word yesterday, discussed the division in the nation and the division in the church. Now it speaks of the division of Israel, all three of which had been blessed and held position as the apple of God's eye. The nation and the church have turned against God, going their own way, as the nation of Israel did so many times in the past, but God still loves them, and He still loves His church. Just as in days past, God ALWAYS has a remnant. The remnant has been crying out to him as Abraham did, asking if He would destroy the city for 10 righteous...There are more than 10 who love You, Lord!

As the scriptures yesterday from **Zechariah 2:1** said, *"Then I looked up, and there before me was a man with a measuring line in his hand."* *2 I asked, "Where are you going?" He answered me, "To measure Jerusalem, to find out how wide and how long it is."*

God has measured Jerusalem. He knows exactly how long and how wide Israel is; it is NOT what man says the borders are, it is what God says the borders are in the original covenant!

Zechariah 2: *3 While the angel who was speaking to me was leaving, another angel came to meet him 4 and said to him: "Run, tell that young man, 'Jerusalem will be a city without walls because of the great number of people and animals in it. 5 And I myself will be a wall of fire around it,' declares the LORD, 'and I will be its glory within.' 6 "Come! Come! Flee from the land of the north,"* declares the LORD, *"for I have scattered you to the four winds of Heaven," declares the LORD. 7 "Come, Zion! Escape, you who live in Daughter Babylon!" 8 For this is what the LORD Almighty says: "After the Glorious One has sent me against the nations that have plundered you—for whoever touches you touches the apple of his eye— 9 I will surely raise my hand against them so that their slaves will plunder them. Then you will know that the LORD Almighty has sent me.*

10 "Shout and be glad, Daughter Zion. For I am coming, and I will live among you," declares the LORD. 11 "Many nations will be joined with the LORD in that day and will become my people. I will live among you and you will know that the LORD Almighty has sent me to you. 12 The LORD will inherit Judah as his portion in the holy land and will again choose Jerusalem. 13 Be still before the LORD, all mankind, because he has roused himself from his holy dwelling."

God is the God of Israel, even if most of the population is secular and have not believed. God scattered the people, but He has been calling them home from the four winds to *Aliyah* (return) to the Jewish homeland. He is the God of fire. He is the wall that surrounds the land and as in **Zechariah 2**: *8 For this is what the LORD Almighty says: "After the Glorious One has sent me against the nations that have plundered you—for whoever touches you* *touches the apple of his eye— 9 I will surely raise my hand against them so that their slaves will plunder them. Then you will know that the LORD Almighty has sent me. God established Israel, and if God establishes a thing who is man to dare come against them...?*

God will raise His hand against this nation as He raised his hand against nations past who "Poke Him in the eye." He is a jealous Father. Just as with our kids, they may do wrong and that upsets us, but we still love them. We still want to protect them and bless them. God does the same.

Addendum 2012

One thing I have learned clearly over the years is that when the Lord gives a word there can be many layers and meanings that unfold over days, weeks, months, years and even decades. The Lord gave a word for the nation and the church. Today He has given an addendum.

We cannot be deceived. God is no respecter of persons or nations. We have been taunting and taunting like bullies, shaking our fists and pointing our fingers in HIS face in all our arrogance, but there comes a point where the one who has quietly and patiently taken the abuse will stand up and confront the bully. If this nation and the church do not change our ways, the disasters, economic collapse, and attacks of the enemy, the oppression of the powers at be will continue. God will get our attention. He will bring us to our knees to get us to look up.

However, I fear it is fast becoming too late, as I preached in the message for September 7, 2012 (on Youtube.com – search bearwitnessmin). If we-elect more of the same, judgment will fall upon this nation like we never dreamed. More of the same will lead those who claim to be believers into greater captivity.

God help us. God forgive us. Your remnant is crying out to You, Lord. The heart of your remnant aches along with Yours, crying God have mercy. I have said many times in the past, the next election will mark a dramatic turning point in this nation. In

273

spite of the hardships we have faced, we are still in a time of grace. God granted the choices of the people to see if this is the direction we really wanted for this nation, or if we will see the error of our ways and turn back before it is too late.

If you have eyes to see and ears to hear what the Spirit is saying, rise up and pray! Rise up and speak. Rise up and stand firm for what is right. Rise up and be the salt and the light to the church, to this nation, and to the world.

October 2, 2012

A God Of The Suddenly

I am the Lord your God, and today I send a greeting and a blessing for My children. The Lord your God loves you. The Lord your God sees you struggling. The Lord your God reminds you to rest in Me.

Stop your striving. Stop trying to "make" things happen, for as long as you are trying to force the issue in your flesh you will not find the success you desire. The results always disappoint you.

I am not a God who rushes, I am a God who lines up the pieces to produce a "suddenly" in your life. I am a God of the "suddenly." What seems like a "suddenly" has been years in the making. Go in peace, My child. REST in Me.

October 3, 2012

CHEERLEADERS

Today is the day I renew a spirit of hope within you, for many of My children are weary in well doing. They clearly see what is on the horizon if the body of Christ does not rise up, and become the true body. They see hope and change that have turned to change and despair.

This is not the change they bargained for, but that is what happens when eyes come off God and on to man.; a man elevated to the status of MY Son and worshipped. You now see how easy it is for the blind and deaf masses of people to follow the anti-Christ. His promises are full of vile lies and poison, designed to steal, kill, and destroy.

I have allowed you to witness how the latter events will unfold. People willingly following the son of perdition. They will run after him as if he is rock star; they will idolize a man. His smooth talk will calm their fears and override My Spirit screaming into their hearts and minds, alerting them of DANGER.

I have allowed a glimpse into the future events. This man has sold you out as a people and a nation. Prideful and arrogant in all his ways, thinking he knows better than the Lord your God the way this nation should go. A cunning fox disguised, a wolf in sheep clothing, eaten up with every kind of perversion, sorcery and cunning; I have said I would expose the wolf, and I have.

I have risen up men and women with the boldness, wisdom and expertise to do the job, but people are deaf and blind, not listening. Even the media whose job it is to expose are asleep at the wheel, and have become puppets of the highest office in the land; cheerleaders blindly following, repeating lies as if they were truth and the world marches on to disaster.

My children see the dangers ahead, the watchmen are warning but the people choose blind ignorance; not to see, fingers in their ears, "la, la, la, don't talk to me. Do not tell me the truth. I do not want to see it," their choice will put them in prison, in bondage they will be. They have become an unruly mob for change. Change at the sake of mercy. Change at the sake of tolerance. Change at the sake of love. Change at the sake of truth. You cannot say you have not been warned.

No one will be able to stand before Me and claim they did not know. I have made it plain, but you refuse to see. A hard hearted, lot, you refuse to hear. You refuse to speak and act. Your silence will be your prison and your words; your food for the next four years.

October 12, 2012

DISTRACTIONS

I am the Lord your God, King of all, Master of the Universe, and I hold all in My hand. Nothing happens of which I am unaware. I know the end from the beginning, and in Me, you move and breathe and have your being. My righteous right hand upholds you, My child. Nothing can pluck you from My hand. I have chosen you, handpicked from the nations, to be My hands, My feet and My voice to multitudes. I have chosen you. Each one of you, My children, for such a time as this.

Though the nations and people faint with fear for what is to befall upon the earth, you have no need to fear. Tune up your listening skills to hear My voice, and follow what the Spirit of the Lord says. Follow His directions, in small and large, and He will guide you safely home.

Do not get distracted, for the distractions are many. They are loud and they will only become louder, vying for your attention. Every kind of evil thing, anything and everything to lead you astray, to distract, to cause you to miss My instructions.

Calm your Spirit before Me, to hear Me Spirit to Spirit. I speak. I am the still small voice, though I can also be the thunder. Listen; learn to listen and obey, for your future is dependent on this. I will be the voice of hope in the night. Respond in faith. I will be the light in the dark night that shines through you. You will be the voice of reason. My voice will speak through the confusion that invades.

Speak truth, never stop. Be the truth. Live the truth, for it is by that example many will come to Me, snatched from the fires of Hell. A mighty witness for My name, each life transforming the next, creating an army to invade the darkness. Speak the Name of Jesus. There is power in My Name and that power manifesting in your life will increase the more you speak Jesus...use the authority you have been given.

October 15, 2012

BE SILENT

This is a follow up to the word from yesterday called "distractions."

Be silent. Be still before the Lord your God, for My kingdom reigns. Strategies from Heaven come down to meet your needs; be silent before Me and hear Me call to your heart. Hear My instructions just for you which steer you in the direction you should go. My thoughts should be your thoughts, and your actions, My actions. How can you tune in to Me, My frequency, if you are too busy?

Settle yourself to hear fresh revelation and fresh strategy; receive Rhema words like rain. Nations rise and fall, but I am still on the throne and those who have ears, let them hear what the Spirit of the Lord is speaking to you as an individual today. Today I want to talk to My children. Listen to your Father.

Where I have been silent, I shall speak. You shall hear when you incline your ear. Your ability to hear and obey will be critical in the times to come. Can you hear what the Spirit of the Lord is speaking to your heart?

Be silent before Me. I repeat, find time to be silent before your God of Mercy. Critical times are here; anguish of nations not knowing the way out, but that is not for you. Those who have ears to hear, whose hearts are soft before Me, be silent before Me. I want to speak to you and the distractions are vying for your attention, louder and louder they become until you can no longer hear Me without interference. There is static on the line and confusion. Be silent and hear from Heaven.

October 19, 2012

RIVER RUNS

The Lord your God is still God of this nation. My signature still rests on the land and the hearts of My remnant children who I will not leave nor forsake. There is a river of My Spirit that still runs through it, and the wells are percolating with the prayers of My children. Wells of living water will spring forth into the darkness of the land.

A mighty move of My Spirit will come forth in the land, the Land of your forefathers, the land of a praying people who sacrificed much to come to settle this nation. You are not forgotten, though the enemy has gained tremendous ground in these last years.

The time is not yet; too many souls hang in the balance, too many are going to hear, "I knew you not."

They will say, "Did we not prophesy in your name and perform many miracles?" The works of thy hand, but hearts who knew Me not.

Rise up children of the living God, for My Sprit resides within you to guide you in all truth. Pray that My will be done. Pray to expose, to shine My light on the enemy agenda, for in the light, the plans of darkness are exposed. A tremendous fraud has been perpetrated on this nation and I have exposed, but blind eyes and ears refuse to hear.

I the Lord your God, know the hearts of men. I can turn hearts any way I desire, and I desire a return to Me. I desire the wells of living water to spring forth in this land. I desire the anointing to flow with ease into a yielded vessel to fulfill My plans and purposes, unashamed, and unafraid to be who I called you to be, a carrier of My power and glory within you, to have the sick healed and the dead raised. I desire for the gifts to operate in the workplace and the field. I want people to see Me in you, to set the captives free from the lies that contain and enslave them.

October 22, 2012

RAIN

I am the Lord your God, the Lord who provides for all your needs. My hand is upon you, My child, for better or for worse. I will never leave you nor forsake you. The world is Mine and the contents, therein. I rain on the just and the unjust. The rain of My Spirit, the rain of My abundance, My power and glory is reserved for the just.

Hope springs eternal, for without hope, without vision, My people perish. I, the Lord your God, is with you. My child, through all the circumstances of life, I love you.

October 23, 2012

CORRUPTION IN THE AIR

PRAY PEOPLE, PRAY FOR THE LORD TO EXPOSE THE PLOTS
AND THWART THE PLANS OF THE ENEMY!

The train is on the track. This nation travels toward a day of reckoning! There is corruption in the air, a sense of urgency. Arrogance won't choose to change the direction this nation is headed.

There has been a change in the air of late, a mighty army rising up to change the tide, but the powers at be are displeased, plotting and planning how to stop the momentum taking hold and spreading across the land.

Pray for the evil to be exposed. Pray for the change to be change in Me, and not changes of man. In all his wisdom, he cannot find his way out of this mess he has created.

October 24, 2012

YOUR ASSIGNMENT

I am the Lord your God and no one, but no one, supersedes Me. The nation's rock and rumble under My feet. All that is, was, and is to be, rests in My hand. Do not tell the Lord your God, this is the time or that is the time, for no one knows the exact time but Me. Watch the seasons change, the signs of the times, but do not convince yourself in pride that it will be one way or another, for My ways are not your ways.

Why is My church bickering about the end times and the day of My coming when souls hang in the balance? Souls are lost every day. You have a job to do. I laid it out clearly. Heal the sick, raise the dead, cleanse the lepers, cast out demons, reach nations, love your neighbor, love the Lord your God. I said signs and wonders would follow you, for the Jew seeks a sign and the Greeks seek wisdom. That is your assignment. Get back to it; all the rest is just a byproduct of your main assignment.

Do not be ignorant of the signs of My coming, but do not lose focus of My will for you to reach nations and your neighbor, for as darkness increases, many are and will continue to be, in fear. It helps them not to know and fear the coming events, when knowing Me intimately will quench the fear and free them to fulfill their unique assignment. I have an assignment for each and every one.

How will they know if you do not speak? How will they see if you do not believe I live in you, and you in Me, to perform the same signs and wonders the early church did? Why do you choose what you will believe when I guided and directed the writing of My Word and its compilation?

The Acts of the Apostles were a sign of My presence with them and it is a promise of My presence with you. Think big, bigger, let the resistance leave. Surrender once and for all your doubts and disbelief. Choose to trust Me that it is for you, and it is for today.

Repent for your wrong thinking, wrong words, and fear of man. They refused to believe and did not see. They refused to believe because they did not see. Faith comes by hearing, and hearing by the Word of God. My words are there as a witness of My power and glory that wants to work through you to change hearts and minds. They are a mighty witness of My presence within you and My presence in the land of your fathers.

Claim the victory in Me and move ahead. Cast off those old garments of disbelief and doubts. Remove them from your midst. Put on the garments of praise and seek the face of your Father in Heaven. Surrender.

Bare back the breastbone and let Me extract the tares. I will remove the tares from your heart and mind that have taken up residence there. I will set you free. Emptied of wrong mindsets, I will fill you to overflowing with My Spirit. Rivers of living water will flow unheeded; all will know you are My child and I am your God. I am God of mercy and grace, coming to bring grace to the humble, deliverance to the bound and strength to the weak.

October 26, 2012

JUST ONE KIND WORD

I am the Lord your God. The Lord your God is One God, King of Heaven and Earth. All therein is mine; from the firmament to the molten core ~ all belongs to the Lord your God. I am speaking from Heaven to My children to look up, for your redemption draws nigh. Look to the God of Heaven and Earth, for I am your salvation. I am your hope that springs eternal, for no man knows the day or the hour except the Lord, your God, who planned you before the foundation of time.

Return to Me, all you who are heavy laden and I will give you rest from the troubles that are common to this life. Return to Me, those who have one foot in and one foot out of the kingdom, for one foot in does not make you a kingdom dweller. Do not be as the foolish virgins who did not have enough Holy Spirit to keep themselves burning with My love until My coming.

The Lord your God sees all that is going through your heart and mind; your focus is broken as the enemy throws his darts at you. Learn to focus; the arrows will come fast and furious as the darkness increases.

There will be a season of relative calm; take care and do not go back to living like the world during this period, of time. Do not let your guard down. This is a time of preparation for the times to come. Distractions can appear good or bad, but they are distractions, nonetheless.

Keep your eyes on the prize, the hope of My coming. Do not forsake your assignment (see previous word called Assignment). Many souls hang in the balance. The enemy of your soul is roaring and roaming. He has placed fear in the hearts of man; anguish not knowing the way out.

For many the enemy has even removed their last glimmer of hope; they are removing themselves from this life, having rejected Me, seeing no hope. They have taken it upon themselves to go off into eternity instead of trusting the author of all hope; that hope that springs eternal. They have chosen to follow the enemy of their souls, unable to hang on until tomorrow when the sun would shine on their circumstances of life. They have been fooled.

Show Me to those who are in despair. Never miss an opportunity to speak life, to support those struggling and in need. Just one kind word, one touch of your time and heart invested into the life of a hurting soul can save and change a life.

RE-DIG THE WELLS

I am the Lord your God, and today I make all things new. As a seed planted in fertile soil, new life will spring up from the water of My Word planted in your heart. Watch for new life; that tiny sprout breaking through the darkness. The roots must form first to make you strong so you can withstand the wiles of the enemy. The roots will go deep before there is ever a sign of life in the natural. Nonetheless, you are given new life.

Those hopes and dreams you thought were dead are not, they have just been given time for the roots to grow deep, for your character to change, for your relationship with Me to grow. Behold, I make all things new. Springtime in winter, the dormant seeds will come to life in a season when you expect it not. This makes no sense to man, but it makes perfect God sense, for I never do things the way you expect. My ways are not your ways.

Still waters run deep and the river has not dried up, it is here for you. It is for today. Rivers of living water will spring up from old wells. Wells that you abandoned, wells the enemy contended for, wells that were filled-in, by the enemy with the circumstances of life and the days in which you are living. Contend for the wells; watch fresh water spring forth.

October 31, 2012

SET THE ANGELS TO FLIGHT

I am the Lord your God. Kingdoms will rise and fall, but My kingdom is everlasting. Choose this day who you will serve. Some have not made that decision, while others only think they have.

I interfere in the affairs of man; judgment has come upon the land for disobedience. Arrogance, pride, and deceit have run wild. Priorities are out of order and eyes are not on Me. Lip service does not make it, but a heart completely mine will change the tide of a nation.

Seek Me and repent on behalf of yourselves and this nation. It is not too late, for I am a God of mercy and I give grace to the humble. I incline My ear to hear. I hear a mighty army rising.

Bless your enemy and watch Me move. Stop the division and strife; pray for your enemy. Truly, you do not wrestle against flesh and blood. More division has risen among you, but division is a good thing for it exposes which side of the fence you are on and what you need to do. As I continue to reveal hearts, motives become more obvious.

Bless your enemies; heap coals of fire on their head. They have taken a position against Me while claiming to serve Me. Can you stand for the things and values I hold dear? Can you stand on My Word and have faith enough to put Me first? Can you be a voice for the unborn and speak against the worship of Moloch? Can you be a voice opposed to sinning against the flesh, and stand for marriage? Can you stand when others fall? Can you be a reflection of Me on the earth? Can you reach one heart at a time with My love, My grace, and My mercy? Will you stand when others put their selfish desires ahead of My Word and desires, ignoring My sacrifice? Can you stand for the Lord your God and that which I hold dear?

When others choose self-worship and fleshly desires over Me, will you continue to speak? When you face a life or death situation will you choose Me, the Lord your God, or fear of man?

The time is coming when you will have to choose, but I say to you, choose this day whom you will serve, for the stakes are high, and you are not guaranteed a tomorrow.

The sins of this generation have risen up like a foul stench before Me. I desire to breathe new life into you; new life, new purpose in Me. I desire to revive the embers within your soul into a roaring flame within you, that you would be bold for Me, speak without fear, and know that all things are possible for those who believe and trust in Me.

The Lord your God knows your heart. Deceitfully wicked are the hearts of man, but I see the hearts of My children. They are transformed by the power of My Spirit and molded like clay by My hands. Hold your tongue. Speak My Word into your situations, into this nation, into others who cross your path. Help them to see who they are in Me. They are not, and I remind you My child that you are not, who others say they/you are.

In Me, My precious child, you are transformed by the power of My Word. My Spirit residing within you does mighty works in the earth that have eternal value to transform lives, cities, and nations. The evil has risen to new heights, but it has always been present. Generation after generation has had to deal with these same decisions that face you this day.

Whom will you serve? Whom will you trust with your future? You know it is only My hand that can change this nation. The choice is yours. Put out the sinner from among the camp; a little leaven spoils the whole lump.

Compromise is a deadly thing, opening the door for every kind of evil. It is difficult to close the door and stem the tide that floods in after it has been opened. Let us close some doors that never should have been opened, for where you rise to do My will, My angels are there to fight the battles. Set them to flight at the sound of your words spoken in faith.

Deuteronomy 28

Blessings for Obedience

¹If you fully obey the Lord your God and carefully follow all his commands I give you today, the Lord your God will set you high above all the nations on earth. ² All these blessings will come on you and accompany you if you obey the Lord your God:

³ You will be blessed in the city and blessed in the country.

⁴ The fruit of your womb will be blessed, and the crops of your land and the young of your livestock—the calves of your herds and the lambs of your flocks.

⁵ Your basket and your kneading trough will be blessed.

⁶ You will be blessed when you come in and blessed when you go out.

⁷ The Lord will grant that the enemies who rise up against you will be defeated before you. They will come at you from one direction but flee from you in seven.

⁸ The Lord will send a blessing on your barns and on everything you put your hand to. The Lord your God will bless you in the land he is giving you.

⁹ *The Lord will establish you as his holy people, as he promised you on oath, if you keep the commands of the Lord your God and walk in obedience to him.* ¹⁰ *Then all the peoples on earth will see that you are called by the name of the Lord, and they will fear you.* ¹¹ *The Lord will grant you abundant prosperity—in the fruit of your womb, the young of your livestock and the crops of your ground—in the land he swore to your ancestors to give you.*

¹² *The Lord will open the Heavens, the storehouse of his bounty, to send rain on your land in season and to bless all the work of your hands. You will lend to many nations but will borrow from none.* ¹³ *The Lord will make you the head, not the tail. If you pay attention to the commands of the Lord your God that I give you this day and carefully follow them, you will always be at the top, never at the bottom.* ¹⁴ *Do not turn aside from any of the commands I give you today, to the right or to the left, following other gods and serving them.*

Curses for Disobedience

¹⁵ *However, if you do not obey the Lord your God and do not carefully follow all his commands and decrees I am giving you today, all these curses will come on you and overtake you:*

¹⁶ *You will be cursed in the city and cursed in the country.*

¹⁷ *Your basket and your kneading trough will be cursed.*

¹⁸ *The fruit of your womb will be cursed, and the crops of your land, and the calves of your herds and the lambs of your flocks.*

¹⁹ *You will be cursed when you come in and cursed when you go out.*

²⁰ *The Lord will send on you curses, confusion and rebuke in everything you put your hand to, until you are destroyed and come to sudden ruin because of the evil you have done in forsaking him.* ²¹ *The Lord will plague you with diseases until he has destroyed you*

from the land you are entering to possess. ²² *The Lord will strike you with wasting disease, with fever and inflammation, with scorching heat and drought, with blight and mildew, which will plague you until you perish.* ²³ *The sky over your head will be bronze, the ground beneath you iron.* ²⁴ *The Lord will turn the rain of your country into dust and powder; it will come down from the skies until you are destroyed.*

²⁵ *The Lord will cause you to be defeated before your enemies. You will come at them from one direction but flee from them in seven, and you will become a thing of horror to all the kingdoms on earth.* ²⁶ *Your carcasses will be food for all the birds and the wild animals, and there will be no one to frighten them away.* ²⁷ *The Lord will afflict you with the boils of Egypt and with tumors, festering sores and the itch, from which you cannot be cured.* ²⁸ *The Lord will afflict you with madness, blindness and confusion of mind.* ²⁹ *At midday you will grope about like a blind person in the dark. You will be unsuccessful in everything you do; day after day you will be oppressed and robbed, with no one to rescue you.*

³⁰ *You will be pledged to be married to a woman, but another will take her and rape her. You will build a house, but you will not live in it. You will plant a vineyard, but you will not even begin to enjoy its fruit.* ³¹ *Your ox will be slaughtered before your eyes, but you will eat none of it. Your donkey will be forcibly taken from you and will not be returned. Your sheep will be given to your enemies, and no one will rescue them.* ³² *Your sons and daughters will be given to another nation, and you will wear out your eyes watching for them day after day, powerless to lift a hand.* ³³ *A people that you do not know will eat what your land and labor produce, and you will have nothing but cruel oppression all your days.* ³⁴ *The sights you see will drive you mad.* ³⁵ *The Lord will afflict your knees and legs with painful boils that cannot be cured, spreading from the soles of your feet to the top of your head.*

36 The Lord will drive you and the king you set over you to a nation unknown to you or your ancestors. There you will worship other gods, gods of wood and stone. 37 You will become a thing of horror, a byword and an object of ridicule among all the peoples where the Lord will drive you.

38 You will sow much seed in the field but you will harvest little, because locusts will devour it. 39 You will plant vineyards and cultivate them but you will not drink the wine or gather the grapes, because worms will eat them. 40 You will have olive trees throughout your country but you will not use the oil, because the olives will drop off. 41 You will have sons and daughters but you will not keep them, because they will go into captivity. 42 Swarms of locusts will take over all your trees and the crops of your land.

43 The foreigners who reside among you will rise above you higher and higher, but you will sink lower and lower. 44 They will lend to you, but you will not lend to them. They will be the head, but you will be the tail.

45 All these curses will come on you. They will pursue you and overtake you until you are destroyed, because you did not obey the Lord your God and observe the commands and decrees he gave you. 46 They will be a sign and a wonder to you and your descendants forever. 47 Because you did not serve the Lord your God joyfully and gladly in the time of prosperity, 48 therefore in hunger and thirst, in nakedness and dire poverty, you will serve the enemies the Lord sends against you. He will put an iron yoke on your neck until he has destroyed you.

November 1, 2012

DIVINE APPOINTMENTS

Today is the day I set apart My people and empower them for new purpose in Me. It is not really a new purpose, but an old purpose; something buried in the sands of time. The enemy of your soul has sought to rid the world of the fullness of Me. People say that it is not necessary, it is not for today, it was just for a few people who lived ages ago, but that is not the case. I never change. My perfect will has not changed and I desire you walk in the fullness of Me. New things that are really old things of Me; true power, not counterfeit lying signs and wonders from days of old for a new generation to see.

Be careful, for many of you will be entertaining angels unaware. You will have divine appointments, so do not be too busy, do not miss the blessing I place in front of you. You never know who I will choose to use to bless you. As is often the case, they will not look like you expect, or even act like you think, but look closer to see if I am in it. They will lead you. They will guide you with a look, a word, a deed. Keep your eyes fixed on Me, your thoughts on Me, and you will not miss your moment.

Your anointing, your gifts, in use for a new generation; one who seeks after power, one who seeks to make sense of the world that makes no sense. They are looking for power in the wrong places to fill the void deep within their soul. My words, My power, My touch will flow through you to reach nations and My angels will protect and sustain you (I saw a vision of an angel with cake) through the trials and tribulations for you do not fight alone.

The battle belongs to Me, but you have a part to play. Stand and obey, pray and believe. Just like Gehazi (**2 Kings 6: 16-17**), your eyes will be open to see what is surrounding you from the

Heavenly realms, and your enemy will see them too, for every battle is a spiritual battle that spills over into the natural.

You do not wrestle with flesh and blood, though that is what it feels like. The enemy has a dwelling place living in a walking, breathing person that takes your focus. Look beyond their words, and lies, their deceit and anger. They are hurting and miserable, vulnerable to the actions of the enemy of their soul. In reality, their battle is not with you, it is with the Me; Holy Spirit within you. They want what you have, they just will not admit it.

They want your peace. They want your faith to believe, but they are unwilling to surrender to the unknown God. They have erected gods in their life and bow to gods that can be seen and touched. This is no different than the Jews, Greeks, and Romans leaving Me for gods of sticks and stones. The gods have changed size and shape over the years, but remain gods just the same. These false gods draw focus and attention from the true Lord, your God. I will be making appointments for you in the Heavenly realm. Awake o' sleeper and keep awake. You may be entertaining angels unaware.

November 7, 2012

GLORY OF THE LORD

Behold I come quickly, like a thief in the night. The bridegroom is ready, the table is set, yet the world spins on and people are oblivious as the midnight hour approaches. They are lost in their own worlds. They can neither see nor hear truth, deaf to the Spirit and ignoring the Word of God. Disobedient to My Word, even the ones who call Me their own, living like the days of Noah, oblivious to the danger about to befall them. They are a stubborn and prideful lot.

I did this (election). I allowed it. The time is not yet, there are things that need to come to pass. Exposures that need to be made in the hearts and the minds of the people. Again, out of My mercy and grace, people will choose whom they will serve.

When facing and confronting the facts of whom they have empowered, they will have an Isaiah moment. They will exclaim, "Woe is me, I have seen the Lord" and will have to choose. They will see the error of their ways and the deception they have been living under. They will either continue on, or see Me and repent.

The Lord has mercy. I give ample opportunity for grace and mercy; no one can claim they did not know. It will be a delineated point in time where the final decision will be made to serve Me or not. No man can argue, for in that day they will see the evil of their hearts and desires in the face of a Holy God. No man can speak, for they will know in their heart of hearts their true condition; unworthy of eternity with a Holy God.

They had every chance to know Me. I was with them in every step of their lives, but they refused to see or hear from Me. They will be reminded of every time I intervened in their life and every fork in the road where they turned away from Me, rejecting the Lord God.

I am a God of mercy, but no man comes to the Father except through the Son. Blood bought, blood washed children will stand before Me. I will welcome them into My rest. Eyes have not seen and ears have not heard, nor can hearts imagine, the things I have in store for My faithful children.

Come to Me, all who are weary and heavy-laden, and I will give you rest. I will hide you in the shadow of My wings. Treacherous times are here to reveal the glory of the Lord, your God. Whom shall you fear? Fear the Lord, not man, for thy eyes have seen the glory of the living God.

Then I heard singing:

Oh, be swift, My soul, to answer Him! Be jubilant, My feet!

Our God is marching on.

(Chorus)

Glory, glory, hallelujah!

Glory, glory, hallelujah!

Glory, glory, hallelujah!

Our God is marching on.

In the beauty of the lilies Christ was born across the sea,

With a glory in His bosom that transfigures you and me:

As He died to make men holy, let us die to make men free,

While God is marching on.

(Chorus)

Glory, glory, hallelujah!

Glory, glory, hallelujah!

Glory, glory, hallelujah!

While God is marching on.

He is coming like the glory of the morning on the wave,

He is Wisdom to the mighty, He is Succour to the brave,

So the world shall be His footstool, and the soul of Time His slave,

Our God is marching on.

(Chorus)

Glory, glory, hallelujah!

Glory, glory, hallelujah!

Glory, glory, hallelujah!

Our God is marching on.

All My troubles will be over,

When I lay My burden down.

All My troubles will be over,

When I lay My burden down.

Lord, I'm feeling so much better,

Since I laid My burden down.

Lord, I'm feeling so much better,

Since I laid My burden down.

The Battle Hymn Of The Republic. *Lyrics: Julia Ward-Howe.*
Music: William Steffe 1861

What is God saying he wants us to do now that the election is over? FIRST, AND FOREMOST, Pray. He wants *the body of Christ to BE THE BODY OF CHRIST*, TO DO THINGS HIS WAY. He wants us to bless and to honor others, in Him.

November 10, 2012

HORDES OF HELL 2

The "Hordes of Hell," have been released against you and your family, and against many others. They were released because you stood and spoke truth. The enemy is not pleased. Those across the land have been given eyes to see and ears to hear the enemy's agenda in the land.

Rise up My sweet ones. Put on your armor. Draw your sword and fight with My Word. Get on your knees. The hordes are stirred up and empowered by their agenda, wanting it to go forth unheeded, but My children stand in the way of their plans and purposes.

Life as you know it has changed. The innocence of the past is long gone. You, My chosen ones of a chosen generation, I call you out of Babylon. Come out of her, for the influences are everywhere. There is no time for compromise. The time has accelerated. I cry out to you My children, hear My voice and obey.

Forsake all others, their agendas and distractions, and move forward in Me. Move into your destiny, for in the midst of judgment, miracles will abound. Be true and faithful to My Word.

You are safe. The angel of death will pass over if you anoint your hearts, minds, and doors. Judgment is coming, it is here, but miracles will abound. Strengthen one another. Let your conversation be uplifting and worthy of blessing. Let no cursing proceed from your mouth. Speak My words over your situations, and over the people you meet. I will have freedom to move in your life unhindered and you will fulfill My end time assignment in the land of your inheritance.

November 14, 2012

ORACLE

Faithful you are; faithful are few to My Word and deed. The world is changing and there is knocking on many doors to see which one you will open; a door to distraction, division, and strife, or a door of peace and faith in Me to provide for your needs.

My children, love Me for Me, not for what I can give you, just as the Lord your God loves you without condition, striving or strife. The Lord your God is One God, a jealous God. I want your heart. I want your life. In Me, I will give life, life more abundant. I will give you a new heart, one that understands Me and the things of Me. I will give you a new perspective and divine discernment.

Shout to the Lord, all you who lack wisdom, you who are heavy laden, and I will give you rest. The wicked strive in their own strength. Evil empowers them, but you My children. My faithful remnant are works of My hand, directed by the Spirit within you. Do the works of your Father in Heaven.

Stop. Stop the distractions and the striving. Cancel the agenda of the enemy of your souls and focus upon Me. Seek My will, My Word, My guidance for the directing of your life. You have been, entrusted for such a time as this. My eyes, My ears, My spokesmen are not to be echoes or parrots, but to be oracles of the Lord your God, speaking for Me. When the words are of Me, they will bear witness in your spirit; in the spirit of one who has ears to hear with a heart receptive and true.

The end time agenda has been released in the land. Truly you are living in these times. The birth pangs have begun and the frequency of the contractions have escalated, as has the force of the contraction and duration. You are birthing the kingdom of God. You can feel the heat turned up in the furnace, but I am with you in your midst, in the fire and the pains.

Proverbs 16:10: *A king's speech is like an oracle; in a judgment, one can't go against his words. (CEB)*

Proverbs 16:10: *Rulers speak with authority and are never wrong. (CEV)*

Oracle: A person who delivers authoritative, wise, or highly regarded and influential pronouncements, a divine communication, or revelation.

November 18, 2012

HORDES IN THE NIGHT 3

My mercies are fresh and new. My Word burns like fire from your lips, for there is a fire burning in your heart for My Word, for more of Me. The enemy has done his best to steal, kill, and destroy in this past season which has been full of distractions. All the while you have experienced a season of over-analyzing, second-guessing what the Lord your God is doing and allowing in your midst.

I said I was shaking all that can be shook, so only what is founded on Me will survive the shaking. At the same time, I have given the world over to lusts, perversions, and wrongful desires. The world loves sin, calling every kind of good, evil, and every kind of evil, good. Many continue to call evil, good, in My Name.

I can see the hearts and the minds of men; wicked and perverse, growing more wicked by the day. Calling evil good, as if convinced in their own minds that truth is a lie, and lies are truth. How will this nation survive pure evil unleashed as hordes in the night?

The righteous stand tall and proud; stand and await your deliverance from the hand of evil. I tell you the truth, you are living the birth pangs. Though these things have always been, you can see the escalation; an acceleration in the spirit, for it seems as if evil took over quickly, and it did. An acceleration has occurred and these events will happen rapidly compared to years gone by. They will occur in rapid succession, for the end time agenda is in the earth.

Trust Me, My child, trust Me. Put your heart in My hands and let Me lead the way through the madness. Your Father loves you and praises you for your faith to stand and believe when others have wavered and fallen, walking away from Me, angry that things did not go their way or work out like they planned. They wanted plans of man, plans of self, not plans of Mine, says the Lord God. The only safety is in Me. The only plan to be desired is My perfect will for your life, for I know your hearts desires; I gave them to you.

November 19, 2012

PRECIOUS

It is time that you understand how precious you are to Me, My children. You are ones after My own heart, My called out ones. You ARE precious to Me. You have been walking around dejected and defeated, but why? I am still God. I am still on the throne. It is I who holds your future in My hands. It is I who is the author and finisher of your faith.

It is not over. You are living the birth pangs, but in the midst of great loss, shaking, and tragedy, there will come great blessing, hope, and a move of My Spirit. It is not over. It has only just begun. Do not lose hope. Do not take your eyes off of Me. Allow Me to guide, mold, and direct your path. I know the plans I have for you. Go in peace, My child, knowing your Father's great love for you. You are My precious child.

November 20, 2012

THE LORD LOVES YOU

The Lord your God loves you. The Lord your God reigns on high. High above the earth, the Heavens expand ad infinitum. The maker of Heaven and Earth resides above the fray where I can see clearly the wiles of man, yet I am within you as personal and close as one can possibly be.

I hold your heart in My hand. My resting place where I dwell is within you. All that I have and all that I am, I desire to share with My children who love Me. You cannot imagine the wonders I have in store for you. I prepared them with My very own hand; wonders unceasing, allowing you to experience what I intended before the disobedience and fall of man. I am the God of wonders unceasing, without stress or strife. When the peace of God descends upon you and never lifts again, that peace that surpasses all understanding, that peace which is unending; when this peace resides in your heart and mind, you will know My wonder.

Wonders unceasing, beauty you cannot fathom, all of nature alive and praising Me. My name is praised in all the earth. I so love to see the faces of My children when they come face to face with Me for the first time, looking into My eyes, drinking in the love I have for them. It is a love so deep, so wide and so grand, that it cannot be described; only experienced. I am love that fulfills all the hurts and pain, a love that will never end.

I hug you now. Can you feel me hug you? Can you feel My love surround you? Perfect love casts out fear and fulfills your every desire. My love fills every hole in your heart and life.

Your God loves you, My child. Hold on to Me and all will be well. I tell you the truth. I cannot lie, cease the striving and abide in Me. I long, to spend time with you. Do not rush, just sit with Me, and let Me tell you about the Mysteries of life. Do not worry about what is going on around you. The world is a dangerous place.

Treacherous times are here, but I am with you My child and when you abide in Me, no weapon formed against you shall prosper; it can't, because when they form the weapon at you, they form it against Me. When they say all manner of evil against you and reject you, they are rejecting Me. They reject the Me, in you.

Do not think these things strange, these challenges are not different than any other generation had to face, in greater or lesser degrees. The Lord your God is one God and I have one people, and the divide is wide, and the road is narrow and difficult is the path, but I am here to lead the way. I am here to guide you home. I am here to turn everything meant for evil, into good for My glory in the earth.

Your enemies are My enemies of the cross and one day they will look upon who they pierced, and the earth will be My foot stool, with every enemy under My feet. He bruised My heel, but I will crush his head, and fire will consume the dross. The Lord your God will wipe every tear from your eyes, and My peace will never leave you. It will sustain you. Wonders unceasing you will partake. Wonders unceasing, love eternal, is what I offer you.

Do you love Me My child? Do you really love Me? The wonder is not, in how much you love Me. As a mere human, you cannot comprehend the depth of My love for you. The wonder, is in the depth of My love for you, love eternal, and out of that love springs a future and hope to sustain you through these difficult times. Nothing can pluck you from My hand, My child.

No matter what is said or what you see, do not believe the lies of the enemy. Do not become discouraged or defeated. Do not become weary in well doing. Do not fall away from your faith in Me, as many have. They believed those lies, and when they reach the end of their days, the enemy laughs; you fool, I fooled you. Stand firm, stand tall. Stand on My Word, on My love for you, for you are the disciple that I love. Do not stop seeking My face until we are standing face to face.

December 8, 2012

I AM THE GOD WHO LOVES YOU

I am the God who loves you. I am excited, anticipating the day you see Me face to face, the day you will feel My love surround you and its depth overwhelm you. There is no love like Mine on earth. Most of My children have never known true love. A form of love exists on earth, but it cannot compare. Even the love you feel for Me and from Me is nothing but a shadow, a reflection dimly seen.

My love is so complete. In it, you lack nothing. It is unconditional; you do not have to earn it. My love is overwhelming; you cannot contain it. It overflows deeper than the deepest oceans, higher than the highest heavens, wider than one can measure.

Love is a funny little word with all sorts of meanings. Mostly it is not understood because it is rarely experienced. It is talked about a lot, and for the most part, its meaning is lost. Seems you love a lot of things these days, and you judge My love by the misunderstanding you have about love. You judge My love, by man's conditional love, but I do not love like that. I love you for you; for whom you are, and who I created you to be. You cannot earn My love, nor can you lose it. You cannot manipulate it. It just is, just as I am. I am love.

December 24, 2012

FOOLISH THINGS

I am the Lord your God. All of nature sings My praise. The oceans roar and the birds sing. All of nature sings My praise, for I, the Lord your God, have come to save. I came to give life and life more abundant. I came to save you from the fiery pits of Hell.

I know the plans I have for you, to bring you a future and a hope. That has always been My plan for you. Many refuse to hear. So many refuse to believe I exist, but I do exist. I am One without beginning or end; I am. I am the God who loves you, the God who came to serve. It is better to serve than be served. I am full of contradictions, many would say, but this is not truth; I chose the foolish things of the world to confound the wise. I am the Lord your God who loves you.

December 25, 2012

OPPORTUNITY

I asked the Lord if he had anything to tell us for this coming year and he said one word, "OPPORTUNITY."

Those things you thought were dead and buried in the sands of time will resurrect; dry bones to life. Those dreams you thought were dead were just sleeping. Why do you weep? Set aside all unbelief and doubt; believe the dead will rise again in Me. No plan, no desire of your heart, will go unfulfilled when you stand in faith in Me. I am a faithful God. I gave you these desires. My hand is upon you, My child, and I will see your God dreams come to life when your heart is fixed on Me.

Life is a journey of putting one foot in front of another, obeying one instruction after another, even when it makes no sense. You see through the glass dimly, but I see the whole picture. I have an aerial view that knows the beginning from the end, and I know all the bumps along the way.

Do you trust the Lord your God? Do you really trust Me? Do not answer lightly or with flip response. I pose that question to the heart of your being. Do you trust that I can see it come to pass? Do you trust that I am the God of the resurrection and the harvest? Do you trust that I am is I am?

Am I the God of your heart, or the god of today? Do you have an eternal purpose, or a focus on today and what you can obtain? Are you seeking My hand or My face? Are you seeking My heart in the midst of turmoil that surrounds you? I am the God who brings you through. No one can snatch you from My hand. Try as they might to assault and insult, try as they might to tear you down rather than build you up, know and be comforted that the world hated Me first. I cover you. I will not let you fall.

The God who created everything, higher than the highest mountain, grander than grandest sea, I came to serve. I came to save. I came as nothing to make you something; My child, My heir, My love, My sons and daughters.

You are worth My all; every hurt, every pain, every nail, and every insult. You were on My mind as I submitted to the cross. I saw you, I saw your face as I hung, pain searing through My flesh. I saw you; I knew you before you knew Me. Before you came to Me, I saw your face and I saw your life. I saw YOU. I knew you; every intimate detail. I would choose to do it all over again, for you are that important to Me.

No life wasted. No life useless. Each is filled with purpose; a plan to effect eternity. You make a difference in an eternal plan and purpose. Never say, "It is just me." You minimize your worth and your purpose in Me. Everyone who did something great for Me minimized their self and their worth, unworthy they felt. Do you not know that it is the Me, in and through you, that gives you power to effect changes, to preach My Word, and to stand when others would faint in fear?

Do not lose heart. Stand, for I stand with you. Speak, for I speak through you. Love as I love, give a drink to the thirsty, food to the hungry. Do it for the least of these, for when you do it for the least of these, you do it for Me. Believe and watch for opportunity to bless others. Tell Me, what do you see? Can those dead bones rise to life?

December 26, 2012

INVENTORY

I am the Lord your God, and I rain down mercies in the midst of judgment. Judgment has come and birth pangs are growing more frequent. Many are hurting, living in fear. In the midst of all, I am still God. I am still on the throne. I am still *for* My children, not against them. I am still the author and finisher of their faith. I am still their future and hope.

I know all things. They rest in the palm of My hand. I have no plans to harm. To the contrary, it is I, who comes in the midst of turmoil to reach down and grab your hand, pulling you from the miry clay and setting your feet upon the rock. It is I, in the midst of your fiery furnace. It is I who lives in you, who goes through all things with you; your constant companion. You are never alone.

People may come and go, their fickleness ever changing. I change not. I am the great I am, I am the same yesterday, today and forever. I am God of your today and tomorrow. I am God of your yesterdays. I saw you through all, and you are stronger for it, stronger in Me; a light for the world to see. You stood when others refused to stand and you refused to compromise My Word and My will.

You have stored up treasures in Heaven where moths and rust cannot consume. You have taken My Word seriously. I will never leave you nor forsake you. You have fought the good fight and stood upon the truth of My Word and the blood of My Son. I have noticed; but so has the enemy of your soul.

My hand of protection is upon you, My child. I am not through with you yet. You still have an open door, so bloom where you are planted. The steps of a good man/woman, are ordered by the Lord and what looks like a setback is a set up. What looks dead will come to life in My time and season, which I have set aside in order to fulfill My plan.

You cry out, "Lord, have mercy," and I do. He who has begun a good work in you will surely finish it. I am not a hater; I am just and holy and cannot tolerate sin in My midst. For that very reason, out of My undying love for My creation, I sent My son, My One and only Son, to suffer and die for you.

Do you know what it is like to send your only child away, knowing they will suffer many things for your decision? Do you know what it is like, separated from your child, and the heartache that ensues? Do you know what it is like to watch your very own child, flesh of your flesh, suffer and die? I do. I know. Some of you do know, as you, have been given a glimpse into the very heart of the Father, and you suffered as I suffered.

I do as a good parent does and put the greater need above My own firstborn of creation. He was sacrificed for the remainder of My creation, to reconcile and restore My family to Myself.

I am the Father who loves you. Every good gift comes from My hand. Take inventory of your gifts. I have abundantly blessed you, yet often all you do is complain that it is not enough. It is more than enough; it is your definition of blessing that is wrong. The focus is wrong. The expected manifestation is wrong. You have been led astray by false teachers, so you get upset and disappointed. You are always looking for more, blaming Me that it is not enough. You would feel blessed if you would just stop and take inventory with a biblical perspective instead of a false belief. Blessing is not what others claim it to be.

Many prosperity teachers are rich. It is not because I have blessed them, but because people give them their money and have made them rich, believing they too, will become rich, by doing so. The result is that the rich get richer. The reward you expect is flesh-based, not spirit-based. You did not give to Me from your heart of worship; you gave to get what they got.

Did you stop and think that is not how I operate? Who are you serving, the Creator, or the created? Who is being served? How do you know it is I, who is blessing? How do you know it is not man pouring out the financial blessing on his own accord upon these teachers, out of the desires and greed of his flesh?

Take inventory. Have you been blessed? When and where have you chosen to sow? When given in ignorance, I will command the blessing if your heart is in the right place, but repeatedly giving to get is making a deal with the devil.

Lord, have mercy, you cry. And I do. Listen, do not be led astray. Wolves are everywhere, sent to lead you astray. Stop and take inventory of the blessings that come from My hand. Repent for misguided giving. Repent for tolerating and repeating wrong teachings.

The Lord your God is a loving God, but I am also holy and true. I cannot tolerate sin in My midst. Serve Me on My terms, not your own. Know My Word is truth and refuse to compromise. Do not tolerate houses in My name, preaching and perpetuating lies. Do not make excuses for the distortions of My Word or for compromise. Do not remain in their midst; flee.

Is the focus upon My Word? Is the focus upon Me and My ways, or is the focus upon power, signs, and wonders instead of Me? The enemy of your soul is subtle and conniving. He speaks in half-truths which sound quite good. They feel good, too, so you are lulled into death based on feelings rather than truth, seeing through veiled eyes, rather than clarity of spiritual vision. I tell you the truth, do not be deceived, for many have gone amongst you who look good, and talk smooth, but are disguised as angels of light. Do not be deceived, for the enemy is cunning. So many lies accepted as truth. Compromise and distortion of My Word is prevalent, and many accept and perpetuate these lies; parrots echoing the teachings.

The Lord your God has spoken. Yet again, I sound the warning. I desire none be lost and all come to full repentance. My Watchmen speak by the Spirit and are minimized and ridiculed. They continue to speak, prompted by the Spirit to sound the warning from My heart; so many have strayed from the true unadulterated faith. Listen, for I am calling each one back to basics. Leave your idols, the Jesus you have created, and return to the true vine, the source of all truth. The Lord your God has spoken.

I urge you to listen, My child, and take a hard look at your life and those things you have placed your trust in. Renounce all that is not of Me. Evaluate everything to make sure, it is founded on Me and not man. Use My Word as your guide and compass; truth, that points to Me, the Lord your God.

Do not reject Holy Spirit. Reexamine yourself with His help. Examine what you believe and open your heart to His light. Lay it all down at My feet, in the light of My presence and allow Holy Spirit to walk you through everything you have depended upon and accepted as truth, that you may determine if it actually is truth. Keep the truth and those things founded on that rock. Renounce and flee from all which is not.

December 31, 2012

OPPORTUNITY KNOCKS

Opportunity knocks. Opportunity is knocking on the door of your heart, for in great darkness and despair, opportunities abound to demonstrate the love of your Father in Heaven. Many hearts are hurting and in fear, not knowing the way. The way out is clear to you. The way out is Me, the Lord your God, the rock of your salvation, the author and finisher of your faith. I have come to set the captives free and to proclaim My Name and love to the nations.

Great evil has gone into the world, the likes of which, has not been seen until this day. The hearts of many have grown cold. They do not know Me; they only speak My name in vain.

Justice is served upon mankind in My name and mercy, but I am also severe in My judgment. My name is Love. Love comes with a cost; the price is high to be My disciple. Like a fine wine, it is getting higher every day. Gloom and doom sit on the horizon according to the talking heads, but I am the author and finisher of your faith. In My great mercy, you will abide in the shadow of My wings. My protection and favor surround you like a shield, and the work of the Lord will go forth in the night seasons to accomplish all that My Word set in motion. My Word will not return void.

The Lord has mercy, but He also has anger upon the unrighteous, hence the two-edge sword. I am love, but I cannot tolerate sin. I am mercy, but I am also judgment. I am grace, but will not allow the unrighteousness to enter My kingdom. My Son and His sacrifice are available to all, the mercy of the Father poured out as a drink offering. It pleased Me to bruise Him in order that He might save you, My child. Choose this day whom you will serve, as the days are short and the nights are long. Choose life in Me.

THE MESSAGE SATAN DOES NOT WANT YOU TO HEAR
Preached During Praising in the Park;

Summer 2012

For those who prefer to watch a sermon, rather than read, this sermon can be viewed on my You tube channel, Bear Witness Ministries. The video is titled; *"The Revised Message Satan Does Not Want You To Hear."* The exact url is:

http://www.youtube.com/watch?v=EO82mNxPlpI&list=UUa1Y Uw_pXuSF1D--8q-5Xg&index=13

THE MESSAGE SATAN DOES NOT WANT YOU TO HEAR
Sermon Transcript

Ezekiel 33 - ⁷ "So you, son of man: I have made you a watchman for the house of Israel; therefore you shall hear a word from My mouth and warn them for Me. ⁸ When I say to the wicked, 'O wicked *man,* you shall surely die!' and you do not speak to warn the wicked from his way, that wicked *man* shall die in his iniquity; but his blood I will require at your hand. ⁹ Nevertheless if you warn the wicked to turn from his way, and he does not turn from his way, he shall die in his iniquity; but you have delivered your soul.

As with everything the Lord gives me to preach, tonight's word is something that he gives first to me and then to others. I do not pick and choose what I will speak -- without fail the Lord gives me a message and the bulk of it is dictated to me and tonight is no exception. God has a serious word of warning to those who claim to be a member of the body of Christ. First and foremost I lived this word.

I was raised Jewish. We went to Temple, my family, and most people I knew did not know God. No would dare speak the name Jesus unless it were a cuss word. I always believed in God. I always believed every word of the old testament was true. I prayed every day. When I was 19, I came to believe in Jesus, but in 1981, God led me to a book that showed all the Old Testament prophecies pointing to Jesus and where they were fulfilled in the New Testament. At that point, I was convinced Jesus was who he said he was. I never prayed the sinners prayer. I knew nothing about that. There was no internet back then. I did not know anyone who was a true believer in Christ. I prayed all the time, I read the bible, I was church hopping looking for answers, I was not finding.

Yet I knew there was something missing and I was not seeing what was missing in the lives of people who claimed to be Christian. I was not seeing it in the churches. 13 years ago - I broke. This so called Christian walk was not enough. If God was God - then there HAD to be more. I realized I was not seeing the signs and wonders and the miracles that we read about in the Bible. I was not feeling or hearing from God and I believed the Bible said I would. I repented before the Lord for trying to hold back this part of my life or that part of my life and not fully trusting him. I told him I wanted him to come out of the box I kept him in. I was sick and tired of hearing from people who claim to be Christians what he would and would not do, what he could and could not do. That the gifts were not for today. I wanted to know the heart of God. I begged him to take away the head knowledge and give me heart knowledge of him. I wanted to serve the huge God of the Bible, the one who parted the Red Sea, the one who healed the sick and raised people from the dead and I would serve him on his terms, not my own. That day I really got saved. Three years later, I was baptized by Holy Spirit. I was flooded with revelation and I could see more truth than I ever imagined. I could discern the lies that I had been taught my entire life and in the church. I began to prophesy and speak in tongues. I can tell you looking back there was a huge price to pay, but I would not change a thing.

But the story doesn't end there, because for the first 24 years of my marriage, my husband claimed to know God, claimed Jesus was his Savior but he was full of demons and would not know God if he danced a jig in front of him. I heard the pride and arrogance and claims of being a godly man. He would tell all who listened he was saved at seven years old. The fact he sang in church for his childhood and teenage years and was baptized was proof of that salvation. But in spite of those words, he lived like the world, he acted like the world. He was a mouthpiece of the enemy seeking to destroy all those around him. There were no fruits of the spirit, no change of heart, no renewing of the mind. He desired the things of the world. He trusted more in money, himself and his being in control of his life and in that prayer he recited at seven years old more, than he trusted in Jesus himself.

I contended for his soul. I prayed and begged God to change him, to let him see the truth, to do what he did for me. But he has free will and he could choose to listen, and receive and act on the truth or not. For all those years, I knew he was not saved. I prayed he would have what I call an "Isaiah woe is me I have seen the Lord moment." It took 13 years but he finally had that God encounter. The blinders were removed and he saw his true condition in the presence of a Holy God. He is now saved, baptized by Holy spirit and speaks in tongues. He now sees the truth from the lies. He will be the first to tell you he was full of demons and blinded by the enemy. He was so SURE he was saved but he was on the fast track to hell.

Can you say Praise the Lord? So when I say this message is personal...it is. My husband and I lived it.

According to an ABC poll, 83% of Americans claim to be Christians. If this were true, our world would be a very different place, amen? How can the statistics be true? God wants me to share truth about this. You may have never heard it before, and some may not want to hear. We are going to videotape this word and post it to YouTube, because so many sitting in and out of the church today are blind to their true condition. They are told, and therefore believe, that words can save them. Thousands go forward to repeat a prayer at mass evangelism events or in churches across this county. They are lulled into a false sense of security, believing this prayer gives them salvation.

Statistics demonstrate that only a fraction of those who come forward at mass evangelism events and church services, or even those who feel compelled to say the sinner's prayer, go on to become committed Christ followers. The majority put their faith in the prayer, rather than in Jesus Christ; this is why we have such a huge disconnect between true and false salvation.

In the church today, people will tell you that if a prophetic word is not encouraging, it is not of God. God *is* love. However, He is also truth. When He confronts us and gives us a word of correction it is always given in love, but given nonetheless. God loves us and desires no one to be lost. He is ALWAYS about bringing restoration. Amen?

It seems that God keeps pushing me along the narrow road. He gives me a difficult word to release, and then tells me, *"As it was with Jeremiah, so shall it be with you."* I would venture to say that a majority of pastors would not preach this message; it is not popular today to share something that isn't warm and fuzzy. This message does not condone sin, in fact it flies in the face of the view of God many have today. But, it is truth. Prayerfully, each and every one of us will hear this word of the Lord, heed the warning, and examine ourselves in light of scripture. Let's seek the face of God before it's too late.

Father, I thank You for the words You have for us. They speak a hard truth; a truth we may not want to hear, but we need to hear. This truth cuts through the lies that surround us; lies that we hear preached in churches or on television, as well as half-truths we have come to believe which leave us vulnerable to the enemy's deceptions. The old saying "Truth hurts" applies to the words You have for us here. We thank You for preparing our hearts, and minds to receive Your truth. May the blinders be removed; may we, just like Isaiah, get a glimpse of our true condition in the presence of You, Our Holy God.

We ask God, that You would give us the glimpse; that we would see our real condition, our desperate need for You ~ for a Savior. May we know in our heart of hearts our true standing before You.

Lord, do not allow our pride to prevent us from total surrender to You, Your ways, and Your Word. May we understand what Your grace and mercy really mean. May we approach You on Your terms, allowing ourselves to be drawn in by Your love. Holy Spirit, minister to us. Prepare our hearts and minds to hear the truth. Help us truly be reconciled to You, our God.

Ezekiel 33:7-8 ⁷ *"So you, son of man: I have made you a watchman for the house of Israel; therefore you shall hear a word from My mouth and warn them for Me. ⁸ When I say to the wicked, 'O wicked man, you shall surely die!' and you do not speak to warn the wicked from his way, that wicked man shall die in his iniquity; but his blood I will require at your hand. ⁹ Nevertheless if you warn the wicked to turn from his way, and he does not turn from his way, he shall die in his iniquity; but you have delivered your soul.*

As with everything the Lord gives me to preach, this teaching is something that He first used in my life, which I learned and have been called to pass on to others. I do not determine what I will share with you. Without fail, the Lord gives me a message. This word is no exception. God has a serious warning for those of us who claim to be members of the Christ's body. This word may sound harsh to some, but too many people are walking around with a false security that they truly follow Christ, yet they are in deception. First and foremost, I want you to know that I have lived this word.

I was raised Jewish. We went to Temple. My family and most people I knew did not know God. No one dared to speak the name Jesus unless it was used as a cuss word. I always believed in God, and also believed that every word in the Old Testament was true. I prayed every day. In 1979, I was introduced to Jehovah Witnesses. Since I didn't know any better, and there was no one in my life to explain to me that this was a cult, I followed from a distance. I never fit in. Somehow, deep inside, I had understanding that something was not quite right. I did not believe all of their teaching. Actually, most went in one ear and out the other and they were angry at my constant questioning.

When I was 19, I came to believe in Jesus. God led me to a book that was given me by the Jehovah Witnesses. It showed all the Old Testament prophecies pointing to Jesus and where they were fulfilled in the New Testament. God can truly use anything to reach us! At that point, I was convinced Jesus was who He said He was. I never prayed the sinner's prayer. I didn't even know what that was. There was no internet back then, and I did not know anyone who was a true believer. I prayed all the time and read the Bible. I was church hopping, looking for answers, but not finding any.

I was convinced that something was missing from my faith walk; something that I was not seeing in the lives of people who claimed to be Christian, nor was I seeing it in the churches. I lived in a desert for decades. Finally, thirteen years ago, I broke. The so-called Christian walk I had learned was not enough. If God was God, and His Word was true, then I realized that there HAD to be more. I realized I was not seeing the signs, wonders, or miracles about which I had read about in the Bible. I was not feeling God's presence, nor hearing from Him. I believed the Bible when it told me I would hear His voice and experience Him, yet this was not happening in my life, or so I thought. In retrospect, God was right there.

I repented before the Lord for trying to hold back parts of my life and not fully trusting Him. I wanted Him to break out of the box I kept Him in. I was sick and tired of hearing from people who claimed to be Christians about what He would and would not do, or what He could and could not do. They believed spiritual gifts were not for today but I didn't. I wanted to know the *heart* of God. I begged Him to take away my head knowledge and give me heart knowledge of Him. I wanted to serve the huge God of the

Bible; the one who parted the Red Sea, healed the sick, and raised people from the dead. I desired to serve Him on His terms, not my own. As I cried these things out to Him from the depths of my soul, it was then when I truly became "saved." Three years later, I was baptized by Holy Spirit. I was flooded with revelation and could see more truth than I had ever imagined. I could discern the lies which I had come to believe from teachings I had received. I began to prophesy and speak in tongues. Looking back, I can see that from that point forward, there was a huge price to pay. However, I wouldn't change a thing. When I say this message is personal, it is! I have lived it. Praise the LORD that He is faithful!

Father, I come before you now, in the Name of Jesus...You know everyone reading this book. You brought them to it. You know those who are posers and those who are truly Your children. You know every heart. You know those whose hearts belong to You, and those reading this sermon who are deceived; so sure they are saved, but actually on the road to destruction and damnation. From Your Word, we know You alone have the power to save. We also know that You do not desire any of us to perish. I pray that You receive great glory as You produce life from our hearts of stone. I pray that You give each of us, including me, an Isaiah moment, and instill in us the fear of the Lord. May Christ's will become precious and consuming to us. Father, You commissioned this word to be used to resurrect the dead in the pews, through the power of Your Spirit. I pray that Your will be done, in Jesus name, Amen.

Preaching is a dangerous thing. If what I tell you today is not true, I am in big trouble according to Ezekiel 33 However, if what I tell you is true, it is God's truths being spoken through me, and your challenge with it will not be with me, the messenger, it will be between you and God. As this word goes forth, each person must determine for him or herself if what I am telling you is the truth or a lie. I stand in faith, believing that you will know in your hearts that these words are not from me. If you decide these words are truth, then you have a responsibility to receive them and embrace God's word.

One of the biggest dangers on Christian TV, and in many pulpits across the nation these days, is the teaching and preaching of psychobabble, biblical half-truths, and even blatant lies. For those who take what is preached at face value, not investigating the Word of God for themselves, a half a truth is a dangerous thing. Half-truths always leave us with a blind side that misses the mark. We quote scripture all the time, but often when we do, we take the encouraging half of the verse and ignore the rest, or we just quote the verses that we like.

God IS Love. HOWEVER, He also *hates* sin and wickedness. There are many things we choose to do each day that God hates, yet He still loves us. We are called to renew our minds in His so that we will have the mind of Christ. He tells us we are to love the things He loves, and hate the things He hates...but do we? God is love, grace, and mercy. He is also justice and judgment. He tells us repeatedly we are not to be like the world; we are not to be like the majority of those who claim to be Christians. The ways of the world are backward from the ways of God. God does not want us to dress, speak, or behave the way the world imparts.

God does not want us loving sin, wickedness and rebellion; He desires us totally surrendered to Him. He does not want us to pick and choose what parts of His Word we will believe or which parts of our lives we will allow Him to access, yet this is what we do. We think certain passages of scripture do not really apply to us, or we point toward those around us who are walking in ways that are out of agreement with Truth in order to justify our own behavior. When we compare our lives with the lives of others who claim to be Christians, we think we are okay in God's eyes *because we are not as bad as they are.* But, our standard is not how we compare to others. The Bible tells us to examine ourselves in the light of scripture. In **2 Corinthians 13:5**, Paul exhorts us, *"Examine yourselves, whether you are in the faith; prove yourselves,"* yet we rarely compare our lives with the Word of God because it is often convicting. We feel so much better about our choices when we compare ourselves to others. We think to ourselves, "I may be sinning, but at least I am not sinning the way so and so is,"...or, "I may not be doing what I am supposed to be doing" and we point our fingers and say; "but *at least I am not as bad as they are.*" We get a false sense of security in this. Our standard needs to be God's Word, *not* comparison with the world.

While I was in college, some of the professors graded on a bell curve. There were two of us who made others mad after every test because our results threw off the curve. We achieved A's, which meant the vast majority pulled off C's or lower. God does not work this same way; His standard is holiness. He does not "grade" on a bell curve. We do not fully understand holiness, and we have no idea what it means when God is pronounced a *Holy* God. We try to make ourselves feel better by thinking God's grace covers our willful sin; that He grades on a bell, rather than an individual basis.

We may rationalize that we are safe because we said the sinner's prayer, but often we choose to continue our journey on the broad way that leads to destruction, never making a transition to the narrow road. Poll after poll finds little difference between the viewpoints and behaviors of those who claim to be Christians and those who do not. Abortion and divorce statistics, for instance, are the same both inside and out of the church. Statistics tell us up to 92% of people in this nation claim to believe in God, and 83% claim to be Christians, yet only 5% subscribe to a biblical world view.

Why is there disconnect? Let me ask you, how do you know you are really saved? Is it because someone told you that you were, or do you feel confident because you said a prayer? Maybe you believe you are saved because you were baptized as an infant. The modern American church has reduced salvation to a magic formula; just answer yes to a series of questions, recite a simple prayer, and be "saved." People clap and churches brag about how many came to salvation...but it's often nothing more than a than a lie which promotes a false sense of security.

What we do not understand is that we truly have to repent meaningfully; we must have a heart change, be "born again," evidenced by a change in lifestyle that displays fruit of the Spirit. We can deny the Holy Spirit as an inconvenient God. We can deny His gifts and His role in our Christian walk. We can choose to just say a prayer, believing this means we have been born again, but this is deception.

I watched a video of Pastor Paul Washer, who stated that faith, for many, is nothing more than a creed. A creed is defined in the online dictionary (*Dictionary.com*) as 1. Any system, doctrine, or formula of religious belief, as of a denomination. 2. Any system or codification of belief or opinion. People who have put faith in a doctrine, denomination, opinion, formula of religious beliefs, or recitation of prayer, are going to Hell every day. Churches want to be "seeker friendly," and the emergent church is presenting a diluted gospel. Occult and New Age have invaded the churches, which are afraid to offend the populace. Churches today desire to keep us engaged and entertained rather than focused on deepening our walk with the Lord. Their plan is to tolerate and legitimate everything by slapping the Name of Jesus on it. However, that is not loving. In an effort to keep it simple, encouraging, and entertaining, churches have perverted grace. They have removed the true power of God's transforming fire, all in the name of love. Tolerance is not love. Jesus never tolerated sin. He urges us to go freely, but *sin no more,* once we have encountered Him.

We promote clichés, half-truths, and even blatant lies, rather than telling the whole truth. Pastors are communicating to people that they are saved just by reciting a prayer. We should fear for those who tell people they are saved by saying a prayer...believing there is nothing more to salvation. The Word tells us repentance is required, yet I often hear pastors preach that we do not have to repent. God alone assures people of their salvation. His Spirit will bear witness with our spirit. God is the only One who sees the hearts of men.

Jesus told us in **Matthew 7:13**, *Enter by the narrow gate; for wide is the gate and broad is the way that leads to destruction, and there are many who go in by it.* We hear the first part of the verse quoted all the time; it sounds simple enough. We like this part, even though we really do not understand the full impact of the statement. However, we do not like the last half, so we don't often share that scripture which states, *Because narrow is the gate and difficult is the way which leads to life, and there are few who find it.* We do not want to talk about the inconvenient fact that Jesus said the way is narrow, difficult, and few find it. Those words do not make us feel good; especially if we assume that because we said a prayer of relinquishment, we are automatically translated from the broad to the narrow road without further challenge to our hearts and minds.

The gate, of course, is Jesus. We speak often, both inside and outside the church, about *coming to Jesus,* or *coming to the cross.* We know many do just that. Many come to the gate; they come to Jesus. Most know of Him, claim to serve Him, and claim He is Lord of their lives. However, there is one glaring problem, just responding to Jesus' call does not save us. The rich young ruler came, but he refused to follow. Obviously, there must be more than just coming to Jesus. This choice to respond marks only the beginning of our journey.

We promote clichés, half-truths, and even blatant lies. Jesus taught that after we go through His gate, the *way* is narrow. Way is defined by the Merriam Webster Dictionary as: *a method, plan or means for attaining a goal, a direction or vicinity*. This suggests that we have to do something more than come to the gate and gaze upon the narrow road. I have preached about a vision the Lord gave me of people stuck; fixated on the cross, but never moving beyond it. We must actually move along the narrow way, beyond the cross, to attain the prize in Christ Jesus.

Jesus declared that the way is difficult. The Bible warns us repeatedly that a servant is not greater than his master. When we read of the hardships Jesus endured, and we look at the lives of the Apostles and their persecution, we must expect that our walk will be difficult, too. They were jailed, beaten, and martyred. The disciples who followed Jesus were persecuted and murdered in the coliseum in Rome. Some were dipped alive in tar and lit on fire in the gardens of Nero. Back then, it was obvious that the way was difficult; for many around the world, the dangers are real even now. I have a friend, Davide, who lives in Gambisara. They regularly try to kill him for bringing Muslims to Jesus. In this country, we have some stressors, but other than an isolated incident like Columbine High School in Colorado, where kids were killed for their faith, our lives usually are not in danger...at least not yet. Persecution for faith will be coming to the United States. Knowing what you know about your own faith journey right now, will you be able to stand when persecution assails you?

Jesus said the way is difficult, and because it is difficult he said *few* would find it. If we have been a believer for any length of time, we know that even fewer still are willing to walk that difficult road. Many bail when the going gets tough. **Matthew 13** attests, Then he told them many things in parables, saying: *"A farmer went out to sow his seed. ⁴ As he was scattering the seed, some fell along the path, and the birds came and ate it up. ⁵ Some fell on rocky places, where it did not have much soil. It sprang up quickly, because the soil was shallow. ⁶ But when the sun came up, the plants were scorched, and they withered because they had no root. ⁷ Other seed fell among thorns, which grew up and choked the plants. ⁸ Still other seed fell on good soil, where it produced a crop—a hundred, sixty or thirty times what was sown. ⁹ Whoever has ears, let them hear."*

Few are willing to obey God's voice. They are worried that they will be embarrassed or people will make fun of them. This may happen. Many claim to be Christian, but being a true Christian comes with a cost. Few are willing to pay the price that comes with standing up for God and His Word. To take a stand for truth, the price is high. Many have been bullied into silence or political correctness; deceived by the enemy and mistaking tolerance for love. Nearly every kind of sin is tolerated within our churches, in the name of love. We do not want to offend anyone, but apparently we are okay with offending the God we claim to serve. We need to be sure we are clearly demarking between loving the person and hating the sin...not just accepting the sin because the person is struggling and desires to be a Christian.

When we confront sin, we are quickly accused of judging. However, God's love is not about tolerance. Jesus never tolerated sin. He confronted it. He showed mercy for sin, but repeatedly told us to sin no more. The apostles spoke blunt truth; they never tolerated sin in their midst from ones who claimed to be followers of Jesus. All were held to God's standard. How can we forget Annanias and Sapphira, who, in the book of Acts, dropped dead for lying?

Grace was never an excuse or license to live or sin as one pleased. Paul told us in **1 Corinthians 5:12**, *What business is it of mine to* *judge those outside the church? Are you not to judge those inside? 13 God will judge those outside. "Expel the wicked person from among you."* He said we are not to judge outsiders...those outside the church, the ones we tend to think it is okay to judge. However, the ones we think we should not judge, those who claim to be our brothers and sisters, we are called to judge. The very same chapter in which we are called to "judge not," we learn about the narrow way and hear that we will know those who are truly of God by their fruit.

When we look inside churches today, and at the lifestyle of so many who claim to be followers of Jesus, we see the opposite of what we would expect. Many are on the broad road. Fruit is bruised, moldy, and rotten. People are living like the world; talking and acting like those in the world. They are carnal Christians. Carnal, as it is used by the American church, is a term that promotes an excuse for sin. We hear people state that the person walking in overt sin is a carnal Christian. I am here to tell you there is no such thing as a carnal *Christian*; at least not as it is used today. That is a lie from the enemy. One cannot live in sin, display no evidence of fruit of the Spirit, and be a Christian. In **Romans, Chapter 7**, Paul pronounces that he is carnal, stating *14 For we know that the law is spiritual, but I am carnal, sold under sin. 15 For what I am doing, I do not understand. For what I will to do, that I do not practice; but what I hate, that I do.* **Romans 8:7 follows**, *Because the **carnal** mind is enmity against God; for it is not subject to the law of God, nor indeed can it be.*

Carnality is a lie that leads us to believe that we are still on the path to life in Christ. I am not sure who defined the term as it is used today, but I am confident it has become America's churches' way to explain, or make excuse for, the condition of the people in the pews. It has become a way to make sin more palatable and more tolerable in the church. This is a self-defeating lie which avoids the responsibility of confronting sin in our churches.

Every so called *carnal Christian* is on the fast track to Hell, yet nobody has the nerve, let alone the love of God, to speak truth and rebuke the lies of the enemy, snatching this person up from the fires of Hell.

People are saved by believing, trusting and faith in Jesus Christ. Mere words or prayers cannot save us. Nor are we saved because we answered yes to a series of questions at some point in our lives. If we are not walking in Biblical truth and assurance, we are not assured of salvation. Recitation of a sinner's prayer is not found in the history of the church, but it is how we have done evangelism since the 1950's. This is one reason many people believe they are saved, who are not.

The majority, both outside and inside the church, will tell you they have trusted in Jesus. However, when you look at their lives, they have the same desires of the world; there is no evidence of Christ's Spirit working within them, bringing them to conviction and repentance. It is not in their dreams, goals, or passion. Nor is it evidenced in their talk, or desires and wants. The only visible difference between these people and the world at large is that they attend church regularly on Sunday. When you ask a person of this caliber about their faith, they will express to you that it is none of your business, or they will demand that you stop judging them. Often they will assert that they prayed the sinner's prayer. When you ask about the confidence of their decision for Christ, it will be seen to be superficial. They are trusting in a rote prayer, not Jesus.

There are others who believe they have been saved, as they attend church and seem to bear fruit for a while...but then step off the path and go back to living like the world. As we witness these behaviors, we ask ourselves what happened. We wonder if they are backsliding or perhaps have lost their salvation. It is more likely that their understanding never went deep enough to penetrate their hearts. Scripture talks about seed that falls on rock, withering away because it lacks moisture after sprouting. It also refers to seed that fell among thorns, and the thorns sprang up and choked out the plant. More than likely, these people were never saved in the first place. They knew of Christ, but they never really *knew* Christ; their faith was imitated from the start, never penetrating.

Some people we see every week live relatively moral lives, remain in church, and have a bit of religion but no passion for God. They are stagnant, never growing in the things of the Lord. There is rarely conviction for their sins and change of direction. They can be religious yet not weep or have remorse for things in their lives that do not line up with God. They feel no need to repent over their sins. People in this position are often more concerned with the man or woman behind the pulpit then the actual Word of God. We hear them sharing, "My pastor says this, my pastor says that," idolizing men and ministries versus God, or focused on looking good and spiritual, but unconcerned for the things of God. They are what God calls *the dead in the pews*, and our churches today are full of them. We cannot rely on saying a sinner's prayer without a true encounter with Jesus which moves our hearts and minds.

Some might say I am judging. Others may feel themselves becoming angry. How do I know these people are not saved, you question? I do not have to prove they are saved or not, because they can do that all by themselves. Although they claim to have walked through the gate onto the narrow road, they are still on the broad way. Their lifestyle never changes, there is no heart change, and there is no renewal in their mind. Fruit of the Spirit is not visible in their lives, and they continue to live as they always have done. It will be their own words and lifestyle choices that will condemn them when they reach judgment day.

How many people tell you they know that they are saved because they believe in Jesus? It is not enough to just believe; the word tells us that even demons believe and tremble. Truth be told, demons are more spiritual then many who claim to be Christians today. Many express belief, but do not tremble at the majesty of God. There is no fear of the Lord; God is not precious to them. They are not able to glimpse, as Isaiah did, their true state of being face-to-face with a Holy God. God becomes their good luck charm or BFF (best friend forever), but He is not *Lord* of their lives. There is no evidence they have passed through the gate and are living in the narrow way. They may be convinced that their recitation of a prayer acknowledging sin has saved them...even to the point they will argue that they are just fine, yet they may be far from justified, sanctified and blood bought.

Matthew's Chapter 7 warns us to beware of false prophets. That applies not just to pastors, teachers and prophets, but also to any one influencing our Christian life. A true friend is one who tells you the truth even at risk of making you angry. I have nothing to gain making you angry. If I were seeking money, fame, crowds and security, I would not speak hard words. I would adjust my sermon to share the parts that would speak to you of everything your heart desires, but I am not a "tickle your ears" preacher. I love souls. I cry out for souls. My heart breaks for the state of our "church" and our nation.

I've come to preach a word from God, as a voice crying in the wilderness; a watchman on the wall. We know from many past words the Lord has been speaking through me and others that judgment is coming to the churches. It is a judgment upon false doctrines, bad fruit, and those who preach half-truths and lies. It stands against those who speak only what people want to hear. We have created a god in our own image; one who tolerates, condones and makes excuses for sin.

Many of you are angry right now. You are thinking I am crazy and overreacting. You are mulling over the scriptural truths of *Judge not lest you be judged*. However, as I stated already, the same chapter that says this also talks about the narrow way to Life in Christ being difficult, and few finding it. This chapter also expresses that we will know who are Christian by their fruit. We will know who is saved *by the way they live,* not by what they say! How can we assert that we know what is in someone's heart? Only God can see the heart, but we do not have to see, we can judge through scripture which reminds us...*out of the abundance of the heart the mouth speaks* (**Luke 6:35, Matthew 12:34**). God's Word also shares that we will be *judged for every empty or careless word* (**Matthew 12:36**) on judgment day.

Some say you can't judge a book by the cover, but Jesus asserted that we could. He explained in **Matthew 7:16-18**, '16 *You will know them by their fruits. Do men gather grapes from thorn bushes or figs from thistles?* 17 *Even so, every good tree bears good fruit, but a bad tree bears bad fruit.* 18 *A good tree cannot bear bad fruit, nor can a bad tree bear good fruit.* Our behaviors may not reflect the intentions of our hearts, yet our hearts represent who we are and overflow into how we speak. When Jesus enters our heart, He changes our entire being. When we believe we love Jesus and are surrendered to Him, it only makes sense that His love and power will affect every part of our life. If we are driving a car that gets hit by a truck, there will be evidence of that encounter; how can we have an encounter with a Holy God, the God of the universe, an omnipotent, omniscient, omnipresent God and have no evidence of that encounter? He said we will know believers by their fruits. A true God encounter will produce evidence; there will be fruit of the Spirit, renewing of the mind, true repentance and a transferring from the broad road to the narrow road in life.

Sadly, in many there is never a heart change; there is no renewing of the mind, no true surrender, and no real relationship with God. These people are trusting in false security and are not saved. They have not experienced an encounter with the Holy

One. They continue living the broad way, no different from the world, without transformation or power. They talk and act just like the world, except that they are religious and go to church. The Lord showed me that these "believers" are deceived by a lying and religious spirits which have convinced them that their empty religion and ritual has saved them. They believe in performance ~ external appearances and saying the right things. They do not understand the Truth.

Jesus and the apostles were brutal. They were blunt with their words. The Jesus I read in God's Word, was pretty darn bold and people got insulted. Paul, James and Peter were the same; they spoke harshly, saying such things as *brood of vipers, get behind me Satan, Hypocrites!* Jesus even made a whip and used it to drive moneychangers out of the temple. He did not do and say this to the world, He was this way with the church of the day. All who followed Jesus closely spoke the hard truth, with compassion, to everyone they met. That, my friends, is real love!

Real love is not lies, compromise, or distortion of truth in order to keep peace. We do not condone sin, thereby loving people into Hell. To the contrary, we speak truth and love people to life. No one accused Jesus, or the apostles, of not being loving. What if they came and said some of those very same things in our churches today as they said in the Word? I am convinced if Jesus or the apostles showed up in our churches today, declaring many of the same things recorded in the bible, they would not be recognized, nor would they be accepted. They would be accused of judging or not walking in love, because the church has a wrong definition of love. Paul said in 1 Corinthians that we are to judge those inside the church, the ones who claim to be members of the body of Christ. However, we judge outsiders and turn a blind eye within the church, making excuses for people's sins. These are the wolves among the sheep, tares among the wheat, and they make the church look bad. Their behavior, when accepted, leads thousands down the broad road that ends in the fires of Hell.

Jesus said, *"Why do you call me Lord, and do not do what I say?"* (**Luke 6:46**), We need to be doers of the word and more. Going back to **Matthew, Chapter 7**, it also stated, *Jesus said that many will say in that day "Lord, Lord, have we not prophesied and cast out demons in Your name, and done many wonders in Your name?" 23 And then I (Jesus) will declare to them, "I never knew you; depart from Me, you who practice lawlessness!"* Many have heard me share these words dozens of times; I have not been able to shake them for past few years. His words of condemnation make me cry. Too many will hear them and be astounded.

These people were sincere in their service to the Lord. They were doing powerful things in His name, but they were sincerely wrong. All of their sincerity will not get them into Heaven. Everything they have done in the name of Jesus will do nothing but land them in Hell. There is no way to make changes, nor are there restarts at that point in time; it will be too late.

It is true, everyone who believes in Christ is saved by this faith, but how do we know we truly believe unto salvation? We can walk around any park, and even any city, and many of the people will tell us they are saved and going to Heaven. Yes, it is true; if we are truly born again, the power that saves us is the power that keeps us, but how do we know we truly have experienced true belief?

The scripture teaches the only way for a man to be saved is to pass through the small gate, which is Jesus. To trust Him in faith, that there is no other means of salvation, no multiple choice, no "all roads lead to God." The evidence that we truly passed through this narrow gate is that we are remaining on the narrow path of life. Our belief in Jesus has tangible evidence in the form of transformed life which is being conformed to the will of God. We are obedient to His Word. We are repentant and have

341

experienced a change of heart. We have gotten a glimpse of our need for a Savior, and fallen to our knees in gratitude that He is welcoming us to His Lordship.

Isaiah 6:5 reflects. "*Woe is me, for I am undone! Because I am a man of unclean lips, And I dwell in the midst of a people of unclean lips; For my eyes have seen the King, the Lord of hosts.*"

Isaiah got a glimpse of his true self, in the presence of a Holy God, and he trembled. He broke. The question to me is not whether you know God. The question should be *does God know you?* As we as wind down, I would like us to listen, *really* listen, to the word the Lord dictated to me;

"There are a lot of people going their own way, trying to achieve salvation by the works of their hands. They sit in church, they may even call upon My name, but they know Me not. They may say or do the right things, but I know them not, and the number of people who claim to know Me is staggering compared to the number of people I know. The remnant, the true followers, are but a fraction of the number who claim to be My children. Many are on the road to Hell and do not even know it. Lying spirits, pride, and arrogance have blinded them to their true condition. They refuse to surrender, preferring to live like the world with a little bit of Jesus thrown in. This is why My church is impotent. This is why signs and wonders do not follow. This is why they know Me not, and I certainly, in that day, will tell them, "*Depart from Me, I never knew you.*" On the slippery slope to Hell, they care not, but they will care one day. For many it will be too late; doomed for eternity. My voices are crying out in the wilderness, sharing truth that will set them free, but they are deaf to the call; unable to discern truth from lies, thinking they know best.

You can tell them nothing, and the world spins into the future. Time is short, but you love the world and the things of the world more than you love Me. Pretenses are there. Pharisees act of piety and religion, but I do not look at outward appearances. I look at the heart. I know each man's heart, and hearts are far from Me. I hold your heart in my hand; I control your next breath. The universe fits in the palm of My hand, yet you fear Me not.

You are not taught about My holiness. There is no fear of the Lord in teachings today. I am a rabbit's foot to bring you luck; a blessing. You take Me out when it is convenient; you rub my foot and make requests. It is a game called life, and most do not see the gravity of their situation. I am a holy God. I will not tolerate sin in My presence. In that day, many will cry out *"Lord, Lord did we not do this in your name?"*

I will tell them the truth, *"I never knew you."* Words and actions are cheap; man can be fooled by outward appearances, but I cannot be fooled, and your heart needs more of Me, less of man's wisdom. It needs more of My presence.

Surrender to Me, this day; you know who you are. I am convicting you right now. Stop the games. Stop pretending and surrender to Me. Stop holding back and making areas of your life off limits to Me. Bring down the walls. If you say you can trust Me with your salvation, then why can't you completely surrender to Me? I am waiting. I desire none to be lost. I am opening your eyes to expose the false sense of security that has come over the body who claims to be in Christ.

The Bible makes it clear that those who are genuinely saved are righteous and holy. They still sin, but with decreasing frequency. A true believer hates his sin **(Romans 7:15-25)** and repents of it. He hungers and thirsts for what is right, and will please his Lord, for it is his reasonable service. He is obedient to God, yields to the leading of Holy Spirit, hates evil in the world, and loves his brother and sister. How can we be a Christian and continue living the way we did before he knew Christ? Making a decision as a child, or being baptized as an infant; saying the sinner's prayer, walking down an aisle, kneeling at the altar, and reading a tract, are not biblical criterion for salvation. We should be daily dedicating and reaffirming our relationship with the Lord. Repentance is not a one-time thing. It, too, is a continual process. What is our life like right now? If sin characterizes our life, there is a great possibility that we are not a Christian at all.

There must be evidence in our lives that we are on the narrow way. When we ask you about the confidence of your salvation, instead of saying "I prayed a prayer," you should be able to express from the depth of your being, "I am surrendered and trusting Jesus. I can see and feel Him working the changes He has made in my life. I sin less and desire the things of the world less. He replaced my heart of stone with a heart of flesh, tender for the things of Him. His heart beats in my chest and His breath flows through me. I have come face to face with my sin and wept. I see my need for my Savior. He disciplines me as His child. I have struggles, but there is progressive victory over sin. There is evidence of fruit in my life, and I am making progress." If we step off the narrow way, Our loving Father disciplines us and brings us back, **Matthew 7:19** says, *"Every tree that does not bear good fruit will be cut down and put in the fire."* Yes, God disciplines those He loves. He disciplines His children like every good Father. **Hebrews 12:6** explains, *"For the Lord disciplines those he loves, and he punishes each one he accepts as his child."* This is reiterated in **John 15:2**, *"He cuts off every branch of mine that doesn't produce fruit, and he prunes the branches that do bear fruit so they will produce even more."* It is not just the enemy who comes after us to edit the call of God on our life, it is also God who disciplines and prunes us. He puts us on the potter's wheel, then molds and shapes us into the image of Christ. This is part and parcel of being a Christian. We should be grateful God takes us through this process. However, we should be worried if we are *not* going through this process, as it is part and parcel in our walk with God along the narrow way. This is what God does to his children, He disciplines. If you are not going through struggles, then maybe you are not his child. The other side of the coin is that maybe you are not a threat to the kingdom of darkness, either.

We do not want to hear these things. We prefer not to know that God disciplines His children. We would rather focus upon God's grace that allows us to live as we prefer ~ the "warm fuzzies," in our lives...living our best life now and learning how we can be blessed, prosper, and not worry about accountability. We do not want to hear we must make a sacrifice to serve Jesus, or that there is a high price to pay to be His child. The price could be our very life which we hold dear.

Maybe while reading these words and you have realize you aren't where you need to be. Perhaps you are playing games with God. You may have been running with the world, believing what the world says is truth, and perpetuating the lies. Maybe you have created a god in your own image, who never challenges you and only speaks warm and fuzzy things to your soul? Perhaps you have imagined a god who condones and makes excuses for your sins and gives you a false sense of security that because you prayed a sinner's prayer, you are saved by grace even though you continue to run with and love the world's ways. If so, you are on the broad road, and this is a dangerous place to be. If 83% of people polled will look you in the eye and say they are a Christian, are you one who walks in the truth of what that means?

There is only one way to Heaven, and that is through Jesus Christ. The narrow road is difficult, and few find it. True repentance comes when we get a glimpse of our wretchedness, our sinfulness, and our helplessness in the face of a Holy God. We have fear of the Lord, recognizing our need for a Savior and our need for the blood of Jesus to take away our sins, the moment we break and humble ourselves before God. Anything less than an authentically experienced change of heart is not genuine salvation. Even the sinner's prayer, so popular in churches today, is nothing more than words, and empty words cannot save you. Without the heart exchange, without our hearts of stone being replaced by God's heart and Spirit, there is no salvation.

My desire today is not for you to report that you know God~ **but for you to recognize whether or not God knows *you*.** Maybe I should not say this, but after the Lord dictated much of the previous message to me, He continued, stating, "*I want you to preach this word. Most will not receive this message, thinking they are just fine, blinded by their true condition, but preach it anyway, that way they will never be able to say they did not know.*"

MY SINCERE PRAYER IS THAT YOU WILL EXAMINE YOUR LIFE IN LIGHT OF SCRIPTURE, THAT YOU WILL CRY OUT TO HIM, RIGHT NOW, COMPLETELY SURRENDERING YOUR LIFE TO THE LORD. PLACE UPON THIS SURRENDER NO LIMITS OR CONDITIONS. COME TO HIM ON *HIS* TERMS, NOT YOUR OWN, NOR THE WAY YOU HAVE BEEN TAUGHT THROUGH TELEVISION EVANGELISTS OR CHURCHGOING MEN. REPENT FOR TRYING TO CREATE A GOD IN YOUR OWN IMAGE; FALL TO YOUR KNEES BEFORE THE ONE TRUE GOD WHO LOVES YOU.

A special thank you to Paul Washer for your word and giving me the boldness to speak what I have been thinking for years.

Rapture?

Too many are living as if they will be caught in a rapture before the hard times come. They believe that God will take care of everything, so they do not have to prepare for the tribulation to come. The pre-tribulation rapture teaching is accepted as fact in many United States churches, but is not taught in most of the rest of the world. The truth is, no one knows exactly how these end-time events will actually play out, but the Father.

I would like to share with you what I believe the Lord shared with me several years ago concerning the rapture and the great apostasy (the great falling way). I pray, just like all of you, that it is a pre-tribulation rapture. I do not want tribulation any more than anyone else, of course. The pre-tribulation teaching is prevalent throughout the body of Christ. I always had a check in my spirit when I heard or read these teachings, but I accepted it as truth for a long time, thinking it *had* to be true because most everyone has been teaching it.

Please do not write me back with all the scriptures that seem to support a pre-tribulation rapture. I am aware of them, but truth be told, many seem to require too much reading between the lines to support the hypothesis.

I believe the Lord showed me something, which I would like to share with you. The truth is, as I said, no one knows how the end time events will be fulfilled. We must keep our eyes on the Lord and He will lead us through and safely home.

The pre-tribulation rapture has been used as an excuse, consciously or subconsciously, by the body of Christ to neglect many things God expects us to do. It has made us lazy and apathetic. It has made us silent and complacent, thinking along the lines of *what does it matter, we are going to be out of here anyway?* Therefore being used as a tactic of the enemy.

As for the United States, we have had it very good, for a very long time. God's hand of blessing truly has been on this nation until now. We as individuals are not used to hard times or persecutions here, let alone tribulation and martyrdom as many have endured throughout the centuries.

Many have walked away from God over the past few years due to the difficult circumstances we find ourselves in both economically, and as a nation in general. I believe the Lord showed me that the Great Apostasy, or falling away, referred to in His word will be due to people leaving the faith when the going gets tough and persecution escalates, as they discover there has not been a pre-tribulation rapture.

We will have to endure tribulation and people will blame God. This is not as far-fetched as one may think. Over the years that I have led Praising in the Park ministry, many have commented that if there is not a pre-tribulation rapture, they will walk away from God because He cannot be trusted.

My response is always the same. It is not God, who cannot be trusted, He is not a man that He should lie. It is man and his teachings that cannot be trusted. In my experience with the Lord, He never does anything the way I expect Him; not how I expect, through whom I expect, or when I expect. Yet it is always perfect. This suggests to me that we just need be ready for whatever comes!

God could remove us before there is any tribulation, which would be nice. He could remove us after the first three and half years, just before he pours out his wrath which would be a blessing, too, or we may be here as the Israelites were, through all the "plagues."

We must not allow the enemy to deceive us. It is a huge mistake based out of pride we convince ourselves that it has to be one specific way. God's ways are not our ways. The Sadducees and the Pharisees *thought* they knew how Messiah would come, and what He would do. They KNEW scripture, but Jesus did not seem to fit their understanding. However, He *did* fit scripture from a retrospective view! The Sadducees and the Pharisees failed! They looked Jesus in the eye. They marveled at His teachings and the miracles, but they did not recognize the God they claimed to serve. They missed their life defining moment.

The truth is, the end time events will not look like we think. It is unlikely even though we know scripture, the events look like we think or have been taught by man, but they will fit scripture from a retrospective view. Although I have had self-proclaimed prophecy experts tell me they know exactly how things will play out, in my humble opinion is pride to think that we are any more knowledgeable than the Pharisee's were. It was not the "religious," the scribes and scholars who recognized Jesus, it was the regular folk.

My prayer as you read these words from the heart of the Father, is that you will keep an open mind to hear from Him on this issue, and others.

Bear Witness Ministries

CONTACT INFORMATION

www.bearwitnessministries.org

www.praisinginthepark.com

www.remnantamerica.com

www.forapeopleandanation.com

www.propheticwords.org

Book Store: www.bearwitnessbooks.com

youtube.com channel: bearwitnessmin or search Bear Witness Ministries

Facebook link for Kerrie/Bear Witness Ministries https://www.facebook.com/#!/bearwitnessministries

Facebook link for Prophetic Words Book:
https://www.facebook.com/PropheticWordsFromTheHeartOf The Father

About The Author

Kerrie Bradshaw is a bondservant of the Lord, Jesus Christ, and fellow laborer with the saints, who lives in Yucaipa, CA. Kerrie became a registered nurse in 1979, having completed her Bachelor of Science in Nursing (BSN). In 1988, she launched *Medically Speaking*, a successful medical legal consulting business. Additionally, together with her husband, Bill, she Pastors Bear Witness Ministries and Praising in the Park. Praising in the Park is a weekly summer gathering that brings praise, worship and a Rhema/prophetic word to a public setting.

Born Jewish, and believing in God all her life, Kerrie received Jesus as Lord and Savior when she was 19 years old. The Lord moved in her life in a dramatic and powerful way in 2001, and has personally taught her the ins and outs of His Word, His Spirit, and His Truth through dreams, visions and prophetic gifts. He has endowed her with an amazing sensitivity to His voice. Many of the words contained in this book were dictated from Holy Spirit; He has given her a heart that parallels God's in its crying out for people to hear Him and know His truth that they might be saved from eternal death.

In addition to her daily work, Kerrie has raised 14 children (four of her own, and 10 she and her husband took in). She has also led a community youth group, ministering to disadvantaged teens. It is one of her prayers that proceeds from the sale of her books will help her realize the dream of building a Teen Center/Youth Church in her hometown.

BOOK ONE REVIEWS:

★★★★★
A must read.
Sep 24, 2013 by Carol Cook

This book is so wonderful. The content includes incredible WORDS FROM GOD that Kerrie hears so clearly and shares so truthfully. It is definitely a must read! The book is well written and very relevant. Kerrie is transparent and shares so much of herself in this book. She is easy to relate to and everyone who reads it will be both touched and blessed by this her first book.

★★★★★
Helpful Insight and Guidance for End Times
Aug 1, 2013 by angellake

I highly recommend this collection of prophetic words from the Father. They are very helpful and give much insight for a time such as this. I believe Kerrie to be a genuine modern day prophet. Thank-you, Kerrie, for your faithfulness to the call on your life!

★★★★★
Thoughts From My Heart
Aug 28, 2013 by jimzlaw

I'm not much for reading, but I must say it was difficult to put the book down.
Page after page produced deep spiritual thought; causing me to re-examine who I am and what I should be doing with my life.
This book has pointed me in the right direction so that I may draw closer to God.
Thank you Kerrie Bradshaw. Your book came to me at the right time.

★★★★★
Profound Messages
Jul 26, 2013 by Blessings

Tears came to my eyes as I read this book. I like how Kerrie starts by telling us she is a new Christian, under spiritual attack, and doesn't know what to do about it. In her silence she learns to hear from God. It's an amazing story and like her many of us wouldn't feel worthy of such a calling, but God knows a persons heart, and God needs a voice in such a time as this. Not all Chrisitans will embrace the words in this book but for those who walk close to Jesus, who read and know His word, it will speak to their hearts like it did mine.

www.ingramcontent.com/pod-product-compliance
Lightning Source LLC
Chambersburg PA
CBHW051813090426
42736CB00011B/1460